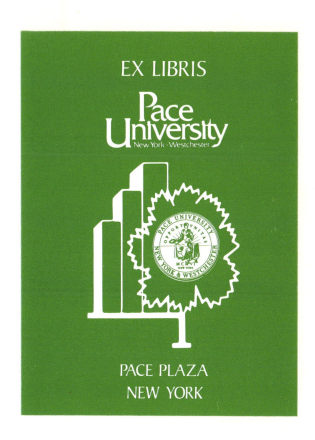

THE
WORKERS'
UNION

BY

RICHARD HYMAN

CLARENDON PRESS · OXFORD

1971

Oxford University Press, Ely House, London W.1

GLASGOW NEW YORK TORONTO MELBOURNE WELLINGTON
CAPE TOWN SALISBURY IBADAN NAIROBI DAR ES SALAAM LUSAKA ADDIS ABABA
BOMBAY CALCUTTA MADRAS KARACHI LAHORE DACCA
KUALA LUMPUR SINGAPORE HONG KONG TOKYO

PRINTED IN GREAT BRITAIN
BY WILLIAM CLOWES AND SONS, LIMITED
LONDON, BECCLES AND COLCHESTER

THIS BOOK IS DEDICATED

TO THE PIONEERS
OF THE LABOUR MOVEMENT

THAT WE MAY LEARN BOTH FROM THEIR ACHIEVEMENTS
AND FROM THEIR FAILURES

PREFACE

THIS book derives principally from the thesis which I submitted in 1968 for the degree of Doctor of Philosophy at Oxford. In the interests of brevity, a large part of the detail of the original (which was over twice the length of the present volume) has been omitted. In the course of editing the text I have added a concluding chapter which owes much to the views I have developed while teaching industrial relations and industrial sociology at Warwick.

Acknowledgements are due, first, to Nuffield College, Oxford, where I spent three years as a research student, and in particular to Philip Williams and Allan Flanders who provided valuable assistance as successive College Supervisors. I owe special thanks to Hugh Clegg for his guidance throughout the evolution of the present work, first as University Supervisor, then as my Professor at Warwick. Bill McCarthy gave helpful comments on the revised text, while George Bain offered incisive criticisms of a draft of the final chapter. Whatever deficiencies of fact or judgement may remain are, of course, my responsibility alone.

My research was made possible by the willing assistance of the Transport and General Workers' Union, in which my father was for thirty years an official (and, before that, on the staff of the Workers' Union itself). Jack Jones and Norman Willis bore the brunt of my repeated queries and requests for help, but I benefited also from the co-operation of many other officers at national, regional, district, and branch level.

Many former members and officials of the Workers' Union devoted time and energy unstintingly, through correspondence and personal interview, in detailing their experience of the union and its activities; in addition, many provided valuable documentary material (and so also did Mr. J. C. Beard, son of the union's President). While I cannot mention all by name, the enthusiasm of those whose knowledge of the Workers' Union was direct and personal proved a vital stimulus to me in my work.

Any protracted piece of research can become at times a burden. For this reason, I owe a special debt of gratitude to Judy. My long preoccupation with the Workers' Union made me boring—and often non-existent—company, but I received constant encouragement to continue with my task. I hope this volume makes it all worth while.

University of Warwick, Coventry   R. H.
January 1970

CONTENTS

LIST OF ABBREVIATIONS

AEU	Amalgamated Engineering Union
ALU	National Agricultural Labourers' and Rural Workers' Union
ASE	Amalgamated Society of Engineers
BSA	Birmingham Small Arms Company
DC	District Committee
EC	Executive Committee (or Council)
EEF	Engineering Employers' Federation
GEC	General Executive Committee (or Council)
GFTU	General Federation of Trade Unions
GLNC	General Labourers' National Council
ILP	Independent Labour Party
LRC	Labour Representation Committee
MEA	Municipal Employees' Association
MEF	Midland Employers' Federation
NAUL	National Amalgamated Union of Labour
NAWU	National Amalgamated Workers' Union
NFGW	National Federation of General Workers
NFWW	National Federation of Women Workers
NUAW	National Union of Agricultural Workers
NUGMW	National Union of General and Municipal Workers
NUGW	National Union of General Workers
TGWU	Transport and General Workers' Union
TUC	Trades Union Congress
WU	Workers' Union

INTRODUCTION

THE WORKERS' UNION has been ill served by historians. Founded at the turn of the century, it struggled for a dozen painful years as an insignificant appendage to the labour movement, then rose in one spectacular decade to the position of Britain's largest integrated trade union. Thanks to their merger in 1929, the present Transport and General Workers' Union holds the same leading place today, with a firm stake in the nation's expanding sectors of employment. Though the Workers' Union as such no longer exists, the structure of British trade unionism still bears the indelible imprint of its achievement.

Thus the record of the Workers' Union might seem of considerable significance for the student of labour history or industrial relations. Yet it demands some diligence of such a student to learn even of its name, let alone the barest outline of its works. To date, most general histories of British unionism make no reference whatever to its existence; few of the remainder permit more than the isolated grudging footnote. The Workers' Union committed the cardinal sin, in the light of history, of ultimate failure. Its losses in the bitter depression years of the 1920s cost the union its independent identity—though it remained to the end an organization of no small importance, and its achievements live on through the resulting amalgamation. It was born too late to gain a pedestal in the pantheon of the pioneer organizations of general labour. It died too soon for its memory to affect the recent course of labour historiography. Moreover, its leaders lacked the colour of the more flamboyant characters who have caught the attention of trade union biographers.

The principal aim of this book is therefore to redress the balance. What is offered is first and foremost a straightforward narrative covering the union's origins, its growth and decline, and its merger with the Transport and General Workers' Union. The approach, inevitably, is sympathetic to the activities and objectives of the Workers' Union; though this has not prevented critical scrutiny of both policies and actions. It would be invidious to offer here an impartial evaluation of the union's significance within the development of the broader movement; but if the account provided allows future students to make their own informed assessment of this question, this book will have justified its aim.

This is not, however, the only purpose of the book. The 'history' and 'theory' of the labour movement, it has been wisely said, can have little meaning in isolation.[1] The story of the Workers' Union raises many problems of analysis and evaluation which are of far wider relevance. Why do workers join trade unions? Are trends in membership primarily explicable in terms of the motivation of recruits, the characteristics of the union and its leaders, or of external structural influences? What are the necessary objectives of trade unionism? How far are the goals and activities of trade unions shaped by their own institutional characteristics? Is democratic control possible within a large modern union? And what indeed in meant by democracy in the trade union context? What are the typical patterns of interaction between unions and the wider social environment?

Such questions of 'trade union sociology' inevitably arise in the course of the following narrative. An attempt is therefore made, in the final chapter, to relate the experience of the Workers' Union to the body of theoretical analysis which has accumulated as previous writers have confronted these problems. Though it would be rash to generalize too far from the experience of a single organization which was in many ways untypical of the movement as a whole, such a case can still offer a valid basis for theoretical discussion. It is for this reason that this book attempts to provide, not only a contribution to labour history, but a contribution also to the sociology of trade unionism.

[1] J. T. Dunlop, 'The Development of Labour Organization: a Theoretical Framework', in R. A. Lester and J. Shister (eds.), *Insights into Labor Issues*, 1948, p. 163.

I

INCEPTION

On May Day 1898 a new trade union began its existence. Its aims were ambitious: the recruitment of all unorganized workers, skilled or unskilled, regardless of occupation. It was committed to a militant policy, scorning normal friendly benefits and offering only those that were essential for a fighting organization. Orthodox industrial activities would be supplemented by political action: initially, the union would intervene in elections to influence legislation in the interests of labour; its final aim was nothing less than a socialist society. Its name was at once simple and all-embracing: the Workers' Union.

The birth of the Workers' Union must be seen in its historical context. For over a decade the structure and objectives of the British labour movement had been subject to searching criticism from within its own ranks. With only three-quarters of a million workers organized out of a labour force of some twelve millions, trade unionism was very much a minority movement among the working class of the 1880s.[1] It was a movement, moreover, which was traditionally dominated by the exclusive societies of skilled craftsmen—the 'aristocrats of labour'. Relying on their organized monopoly of key sections of scarce labour, these could maintain comparatively favourable wages and conditions, offered extensive financial benefits to their members, and showed little concern for the mass of their less fortunate fellows. By now the craft societies probably contained only a minority of organized workers—for major 'open' unions had become established in such industries as coal, iron and steel, and cotton—but they remained typical of the spirit of trade unionism as a whole.

The 1880s saw the emergence in Britain of socialist organiza-

[1] See H. A. Clegg, A. Fox, and A. F. Thompson, *History of British Trade Unionism*, vol. 1, 1964, pp. 1, 466. Even among adult male manual workers, only one in ten was organized.

tions, committed to the creation of a mass working-class movement, and thus naturally opposed to the complacent exclusiveness which they saw as characteristic of trade unionism. Their
criticisms found some response within the craft societies themselves; for craftsmen had experienced the long lean years of the
'Great Depression', and were now faced with radical changes in
technology; many were beginning to doubt their ability to
protect their conditions by their exclusive industrial strength.
At the end of the decade the growth of these critical ideas
gained an explosive impetus, with the rise of the 'new unionism'
—an event symbolized in our historical consciousness by the
London Dock Strike of 1889.

The new unions which burst upon the labour scene had many
of the features which the Workers' Union was to adopt a
decade later. They were often 'general' unions whose membership was not limited by industrial boundaries; though this may
often have been more by accident than design. While invariably
regarded merely as labourers' unions, in many industries they
organized all categories of workers regardless of skill. Usually
they offered only the most limited of financial benefits; this was
inevitable given their need to charge low contributions, but
was often proudly acclaimed as a sign of militancy. Finally,
many of the new bodies emphasized the need for independent
political action by labour, and they were at times closely associated with socialist ideas and activities.

The new unions reached the peak of their membership in
1890; then economic conditions worsened, and employers
fought back to weaken the unions' hold. In two years they were
reduced to half their former size and this decline continued,
more slowly, for most of the decade. At the same time, under the
exigencies of day-to-day union activity, the new movement
became in structure and policy 'uncomfortably like the "old
unionism" it had once fought'.[2] But important differences
remained, and formed the basis for intense controversy throughout the 1890s. In the turbulent debates at the Trades Union
Congress, the arguments in the union branches, and the
discussions in labour and socialist journals, two issues stand out:
the demands for a federation of trade unions to bring closer

[2] E. J. Hobsbawm, 'General Labour Unions in Britain, 1889–1914', *Economic
History Review*, 1949, p. 135.

unity and more militant industrial action, and for a political organization to win the independent representation of labour interests in Parliament.

The trend of industrial relations in the 1890s added weight to the pressure for change. The counter-attack which so drastically weakened the new unions had wider repercussions. With growing foreign competition, employers became increasingly critical of the status and practices of the traditional unions. Changing attitudes were reflected not only in the strike figures for these years but also in a series of judicial decisions which appeared to undermine the legality of trade unions' industrial activities. In addition, a firmly established Conservative government showed little willingness to heed the wishes of the unions in the sphere of legislation.

Of all these threats to union security, the most dramatic was the national engineering dispute. Against a background of increasing friction in their industry, London engineers struck in July 1897 in support of their demand for an 8-hour day.[3] The newly-formed Employers' Federation retaliated by declaring a national lock-out. The impact of this protracted dispute on the entire labour movement can scarcely be exaggerated. The ruthless efficiency with which the Federation enforced its lock-out showed how well employers had learned the lesson of combination; and the views freely expressed by some of its members suggested the possible application of this new-found strength. Thus it was widely believed that the Federation would apply the brutal union-smashing tactics of the American trusts and combines, and that this example would be quickly followed by employers generally.[4] The reaction of the world of labour was seen at the TUC in September 1897: the demand for trades' federation, rejected only two years previously, was now endorsed with only one dissentient.[5] This swing in opinion also

[3] Several unions were involved in the dispute, but the Amalgamated Society of Engineers (ASE) was by far the largest and most prominent.

[4] Even the Fabian Society, not normally the most alarmist of bodies, produced a pamphlet arguing that 'the Engineers' dispute . . . stands revealed as a gigantic conspiracy of organised capital. . . . The employers make no secret of their resolution to sweep away industrial democracy and replace it by the absolute despotism of capital.'

[5] The outcome was the General Federation of Trade Unions—a body which was soon to disappoint the advocates of federation. For an account of the federation movement, see my original thesis.

laid the basis for the unions' conversion to the principle of independent political action, culminating in the creation of the Labour Party. But there was a third product of the change in consciousness which the engineers' dispute precipitated: the Workers' Union.

The call for a new trade union appeared, somewhat surprisingly, in the columns of the *Weekly Times and Echo*—'one of the pioneers of the penny weekly press, distinguished for nearly forty years for its fearless and advanced Liberalism'.[6] Its leading article of 26 December 1897 discussed the breakdown of attempts to reach a compromise in the engineering dispute, predicted the unions' defeat, and speculated that this would herald a general attack on the labour movement. There was little hope, it argued, that the existing sectional organizations could withstand such an onslaught:

The Trades Unionism of the highly-skilled minority of workers *must*, in our opinion, expand itself or give place to some more elastic organisation of the whole of the workers, which shall cover the whole ground threatened by the Federated employers, and be able to take up the fight all along the line instead of leaving it to the masters to pick out the weak places for attack. Has not the time come for the formation of one great all-embracing Labour Union, which shall unite every worker, federate the existing weak Unions, stretch out its hands on the one side to the political and social organisations, and on the other to the Co-operative and Friendly Societies, and, with the lowest possible subscription that can be fixed, accumulate funds that shall guarantee a minimum strike pay to all, sufficient to keep body and soul together during any Labour dispute?

On a practical note, the article concluded that 'the first requisite is character on the part of the leaders. Are there men who have had sufficient experience in Trade Unionism and who are yet dissatisfied with the slow progress made in the past, and ready to trust this "larger hope"?... Where is the genius that shall gather in the unorganised millions and lead them to victory?'

This appeal obtained a speedy, and notable, response. The January Report Sheet of the International Federation of Ship, Dock, and River Workers, deploring the lack of solidarity which

---

[6] *Labour Annual*, 1897, p. 53.

had left the engineers on the verge of defeat, went on to announce that 'we are glad to learn that considerable discussion is taking place now as to the necessity of a national organisation that shall be both a Trade Union and a Political Organisation for advancing the true interests of labour.' The statement then described in detail the proposed aims and constitution of the new body, and declared its whole-hearted approval. 'We say "Good luck to the new idea", as we see that if it be largely adopted brighter days are in store for the labour movement, and the engineers' experience will not have been in vain.' The statement was then issued as a manifesto; its author was the President of the International Federation, Tom Mann.[7]

The new venture could not have found a more illustrious sponsor. Mann's energy and enthusiasm had made him without question the most prominent of the left-wing militants within the trade union movement of his day. As a skilled engineer he had long been associated with the struggle to change the cautious and exclusive policies of the ASE, coming within a thousand votes of being elected its General Secretary in 1893. He achieved fame in 1889 as one of the leaders of the London Dock Strike, having already written what was perhaps the first manifesto of the 'new unionism'.[8] Mann was still President of the Dockers' Union, and had been a leading official of the International Federation since its formation in 1896. Politically, he had been a leading member of the Social-Democratic Federation in the 1880s, while since 1894 he had been Secretary of the Independent Labour Party.[9]

As a figure of such stature in the movement, Mann succeeded by his intervention in focusing widespread attention on the proposal for a new labour organization. And inevitably, though almost certainly mistakenly, the original idea was identified as his.[10] In any event, he threw himself into the work

[7] The text was cited in *Justice*, 8 Jan. 1898, and *Weekly Times and Echo*, 9 Jan. 1898.
[8] This was the pamphlet *What a Compulsory Eight-Hour Working Day Means to the Workers*, produced in 1886.
[9] The SDF had existed as a Marxist organization since 1884; its history had been marked by rigid sectarianism and internal dissension. Its failings were a contributory cause of the formation of the ILP in 1893; despite its more moderate approach the latter achieved no greater popular success than its older rival.
[10] The evidence suggests that Mann was not aware in advance of the proposal in the *Weekly Times and Echo*; though the paper's editor, E. J. Kibblewhite, was a

of creating the new body with characteristic vigour. He
became its chief spokesman in the press and leading advocate
on the platform; chaired its meetings and played the major part
in drafting its rules and constitution; canvassed support from
his wealth of personal contacts throughout the country; and
provided its first funds out of his own savings. To free himself
for this important work he resigned his official position in the
ILP at the earliest convenient moment, so as 'to give up the
whole of his time . . . to advancing the cause of Trade Unionism
among the unorganized workers'.[11] Thus in an important sense
the new union became Mann's own creation.

It was the prospect of the engineers' defeat which inspired
the new venture; within a month the prospect had become
reality. With the ASE's acceptance of Terms of Settlement
which constituted a humiliating surrender, the previous
criticisms of union structure and policies were forcibly under-
lined. Discussion of the proposed new 'Labour League'[12]
filled the editorial and correspondence columns of the *Weekly
Times and Echo*, and spilled out into the wider labour and
socialist press. The most detailed case for the new organization
was made by Mann within a week of the engineers' defeat.
First, the trade union movement could withstand the employers'
policy of combination only if it increased its strength by
organizing the unorganized. To achieve this, it was essential to
build a truly *general* union. 'Hundreds of thousands of men are
compelled by economic pressure to change their occupation a
dozen times or more in as many years. It is only a portion of the
working community that is called upon to keep to one occupation for life. . . . *If* men were wise, no doubt with every change
of occupation they would connect themselves with a Union
representing their particular occupation; but that's more than
can be expected, in any case it don't come off.' Only a general
union, open to all, could overcome this problem. But secondly,
this must be a *fighting* union. 'Threepence per week, the sum

socialist and friend of Mann, and may well have had the latter in mind when he
wrote. Mann's memoirs, published in 1923, throw no light on this question.

[11] *I.L.P. News*, Apr. 1898. Mann's resignation may have been partly motivated
by his own declining influence within the Party's leadership, and dissatisfaction at
its lack of electoral success.

[12] This title, first used in a *Weekly Times and Echo* leader on 16 Jan., was intended
to stress both the industrial and political nature of the proposed body.

now paid by the docker to his existing Union, would provide for dispute pay. . . . Another threepence per week for those able and willing to pay it would provide out of work pay. This would be all that need be attempted by the proposed British Labour Union.' Finally, it would have to be a *political* union, with a specific programme, intervening in elections, and ready 'to show an utter disregard of Liberal and Tory and go purely for Labour.'

Mann concluded on an optimistic note: '. . . if there should be any general willingness on the part of those who are anxious to see something done, and to be in at the doing of it, such an organisation might be launched in a few weeks as would soon enable the Labour world to avenge the Engineers' defeat, and would inspire those who have rightly been lamenting our hitherto feeble line of action'.[13]

This preparatory work indeed progressed rapidly. At the beginning of February a preliminary conference was held at Mann's office in Blackfriars; at this 'gathering of leading trade unionists and others', Mann as Chairman submitted a manifesto which repeated his previous arguments. This was unanimously accepted, as was the following 'brief statement of the basis of organization':

NAME: 'The Labour League' or 'The Workers' Union'.
OBJECTS: The organization of all Sections of the Community on an Industrial and Political Basis for the purpose of raising the standard of Social life of the workers, and the ultimate realization of an Industrial Commonwealth. The raising of funds to provide, first, dispute pay in case of strike or lock-out; out of work pay; legal assistance in the case of accident.

The support of Labour candidates at all Parliamentary, Municipal, School Board, and other elections. No entrance fees on first joining. Two classes of members; one class paying threepence a week, the other sixpence, the latter receiving Unemployment benefit. The Union to be managed by Branches, Local Executives, a General Executive, and an Annual Delegate Meeting.[14]

This was the first occasion on which 'The Workers' Union' appeared as a possible title for the new organization. Mann

[13] *Weekly Times and Echo*, 30 Jan. 1898. These arguments were for the most part ones that Mann had often used in previous years.
[14] Ibid., 6 Feb. 1898.

himself evidently favoured the new alternative, which from this date he used exclusively. 'The name,' he wrote later, 'was important. The idea was to have a short name yet genuinely comprehensive. "The Workers' Union" was decided upon, and it proved to be exactly the right name. It barred none; it welcomed all. It was wide, yet definite. . . .'[15] The conference went on to adopt a programme of political demands. Finally a Committee was appointed to supervise the preliminary work of the organization, and to draft rules to be submitted to a further conference.

The Provisional Committee functioned as intended. By the end of February, the first circular of the Workers' Union had been issued. It was decided that the union should be officially launched on May Day, allowing ample time for propaganda and preliminary organization, and the Committee kept well within this schedule. By the beginning of March the rules had been drafted and circulated, and at a meeting on 9 March various amendments were received and adopted. At the same meeting it was announced that the response to the first efforts was most encouraging: branches were already in the course of formation, and it was hoped that they would 'start in May with a membership of at least 150,000'.[16] An appeal for 'fairly representative and earnest persons willing to help in the formation of branches in their respective districts'[17] had resulted in a number of applications which were considered also. Within another three weeks, over two dozen of these applicants had been appointed unpaid local organizers, and a second circular was issued instructing other supporters in the correct procedure for forming a branch. Branch books and rules had by now been printed, and by early April a number of branches were operating: in Manchester, Oldham, Halifax, Bradford, Leeds, Middlesbrough, and London, where seven branches had been formed.

At the end of March Mann had resigned his ILP Secretaryship, and his energies were now concentrated on addressing meetings in London and provincial towns, explaining the new union's purpose and method of working. By now, the Workers' Union possessed a General Secretary: Tom Chambers, an ILP

[15] *Tom Mann's Memoirs*, p. 151.
[16] *Weekly Times and Echo*, 13 Mar. 1898.   [17] Ibid.

pioneer who was Secretary of the International Federation of which Mann was President. It was left to Chambers to supervise the central organization while Mann was fully occupied with propaganda activities. Finally, expecting 'to enrol and maintain many thousands who have hitherto stood aloof from the Trade Union Movement',[18] the Executive Committee decided to receive the first returns from the branches on 8 May.

It was soon apparent that all extravagant expectations would have to be abandoned. 'The Executive met. The result was less than expected—much less—less than thirty branches were registered, and many of those were very small branches. The total membership was about eight hundred. . . .'[19] There had already been ample indication that the optimism of the union's founders was misplaced. There, had, it is true, been a welcome for the venture, and pledges of support, from many parts of the country. But Mann had also noted that 'some of my warmest friends showed a noticeable coolness in connection with my advocacy of the new union, as if it were an interloper.'[20]

The industrial and political roles intended for the new body both aroused opposition in areas not originally anticipated by the union's founders. The political aspect of its objectives was ill received, not only by 'old unionists' who insisted that trade unionism should be kept out of politics, but also by the existing socialist bodies. The reaction of the Social-Democratic Federation was perhaps predictable: '. . . the mere participation of trade unionists in politics, without any definite principles or objects, means nothing, and will land them nowhere. A mere "labour party" may be Conservative, Liberal, Radical, Socialist, anti-Socialist, or nondescript, particularly the latter.'[21] Criticism from the Independent Labour Party, though slower to materialize, followed on similar lines. After an initial display of benevolence[22] the Party's weekly paper, the *Labour Leader*, attacked the political programme of the Workers' Union: 'nine times out of ten the Liberal candidate would swallow the programme, and if returned would add one more to

[18] Ibid., 24 Apr. 1898.
[19] J. Beard, 'The Early Struggles of the Union', *Record*, May 1919.
[20] *Memoirs*, p. 151.   [21] *Justice*, 8 Jan. 1898.
[22] *Labour Leader*, 5 Feb. 1898.

the crowd already in the House of Commons crammed full with unredeemed election pledges.'[23]

It is doubtful if this was the main cause of the ILP's hostility— since the Party was itself not unwilling to risk a dilution of its socialist principles in the pursuit of tactical advantage. There would seem to have been a fear, hinted at in its monthly organ,[24] that the ILP might be eclipsed if the Workers' Union were to achieve success. Perhaps most important, the new body threatened to cut across the plans of Hardie and other ILP leaders to win the support of *existing* unions for a Labour Party. Finally, the advocates of the new union tended to justify its proposed political role by pointing to the tiny membership and electoral failures of existing socialist bodies; yet this was an approach calculated to attract resentment rather than support.

In the industrial sphere, again, criticism of the Workers' Union could be anticipated from 'old unionists' opposed to militancy and committed to the maintenance of rigid craft distinctions. But more ominous were the adverse comments of many socialist trade unionists whose support was hoped for. There were frequent misgivings that friction would be caused with existing unions—fears that were increased when Mann announced that 'we do not propose to refuse to enrol those who present themselves simply because another Union exists willing to enrol them, as in some instances existing Unions have not organised more than 5 per cent of those in the trade.'[25] 'Wouldn't it be a more sensible plan to help the unions to organise the other 95 per cent?' was one rejoinder.[26] Even in trades where no union could claim an exclusive right to organize, it was suggested that a new union was superfluous. This was indeed the argument of the General Secretaries of the two largest general unions: Dipper of the National Amalgamated Union of Labour urged that the lower-skilled would be best served by having 'one union only';[27] Will Thorne of the Gasworkers pointed out that his own organization already

---

[23] Ibid., 26 Feb. 1898. Keir Hardie elaborated on this criticism on 21 May 1898.
[24] *I.L.P. News*, March 1898.
[25] *Weekly Times and Echo*, 24 Apr. 1898.
[26] Ben Turner, *Yorkshire Factory Times*, 6 May 1898.
[27] *Weekly Times and Echo*, 13 Feb. 1898.

performed both the industrial *and* the political functions proposed for the new body.[28]

Again, the only justification for establishing a new union was the failure of those already in the field. 'Have the existing Trade Union organisations,' asked Chambers, 'shown any real desire to bring the large number of unorganised into line with the others? Have they really attempted the work of organisation in a scientific manner? . . . No! Well then, let someone else have a try.'[29] Such criticism clearly rankled; here too, efforts to win support all too easily resulted in alienating potential sympathizers.

Given the existence of such widespread suspicion and resentment, the refusal of many of Mann's 'warmest friends' to be associated with the Workers Union is understandable. It is perhaps arguable that the ambitious objectives of the union's founders were absurdly unrealistic; certainly the absence of widespread support from Mann's fellow socialists made inevitable the abject failure of all hopes of creating a mass organization. The heroic aspirations were of necessity abandoned, to be replaced by a more limited objective: sheer endurance. Twelve testing years were ahead for all British trade unions. For the Workers' Union, the resolution of members and officials was to be tested to the full.

[28] Ibid., 6 Mar. 1898. [29] Ibid., 20 Feb. 1898.

ENDURANCE 1898–1910

IN its early years, the union's fortunes followed closely the pattern of national economic activity. Founded during a short period of trade expansion, it reached a peak of membership at the end of 1899. As industrial activity slackened and unemployment mounted it suffered severely, and in 1903 and 1904 was barely a quarter of its former size. Trade revival brought a new period of growth, which while checked by the short depression of 1908–9, was again evident by the beginning of 1910.

The Workers' Union commenced in May 1898 with three national officials. Charles Duncan, a young skilled engineer from Middlesbrough, was full-time President and General Organizer; an active socialist, he had aided Mann in his earlier struggles in the ASE and was happy to co-operate in the new venture. Mann himself, who now held the title of Vice-President, worked vigorously as an unpaid organizer, addressing recruiting meetings in all parts of the country. Meanwhile Chambers—who retained his previous post in the dock-workers' International Federation—concentrated on administrative duties as General Secretary.

Further full-time organizers were subsequently appointed: one, covering London, during 1898, four others in the following year. But the exertions of these officials—supplemented by the enthusiastic assistance of rank-and-file supporters wherever branches existed—produced painfully small results. By the end of 1898 the union could boast two thousand members; a year later there were 4,172 on the books, contained in sixty branches. This slow progress was due in part to the heavy turnover which beset the new union: in its first year and a half over three thousand members lapsed, and nearly forty branches closed. As Chambers commented ruefully:

Some of these . . . can hardly be said to have had a real existence.

One week's contributions paid and then not heard of again; others going on well for a time, then the members falling off gradually until the branch had to be closed. Good branches have left the Union in a body and gone over to various sectional organisations. . . . Several sections which received special attention and seemed like going well have turned out altogether hopeless.

Even so, the union's Secretary could review its early progress optimistically:

Although we have gone through a hard struggle for our existence, things are now looking very bright. We are now settling down to steady work, all the useless members and branches seem to have been weeded out, and if the officials and members pull together the success of the Union is assured.[1]

Such hopes were quickly dashed: as economic conditions changed the union's very survival was soon in question. In four years membership slumped to little more than a thousand; not until 1906 was there any significant recovery. With fewer members paying subscriptions, drastic economies became necessary. Since organizers' wages and expenses had by 1901 come to account for over half the union's expenditure, this was inevitably where the main savings were made: of the five district officials currently employed, three were dismissed and one was reduced to a part-time basis.

Changes also occurred at the top. Towards the end of 1900 Chambers was compelled to leave the Workers' Union in order to devote his full time to the Dockworkers' Federation. Duncan was elected Secretary in his place, and was succeeded as President by Robert Morley—the union's Halifax branch secretary, a skilled iron-moulder, and an active member of the ILP. A year later Mann left the country—as it transpired, for a decade—and the union thus lost the services of its Vice-President.[2] For the next dozen years it was the partnership of Duncan and Morley which guided the union's policies and administration.

[1] *First Report*, 1898–9.

[2] Mann retained the title of Vice-President (apparently a purely honorary position, never mentioned in the rulebook); but after his return to Britain in 1910 he played no part in the conduct of the union's affairs, though for many years a welcome speaker on its platform. He continued to be listed as Vice-President until the 1920s, when his Communist activities clearly estranged him from the union's leaders.

Following the drastic organizational economies the threat of bankruptcy was averted, thanks largely to Duncan's painstaking work as Secretary. The financial basis of the union's early activities was scarcely satisfactory: it had been launched by loans of over £100 (including £53 from Mann and £40 from Chambers); there was no bank account; and after two years liabilities still exceeded assets. Duncan was determined to regularize the situation. He started by opening a bank account, and thereafter the level of its balance was his central preoccupation (far more important, to judge from his Annual Reports, than the size of the union's membership). To cut expenses he closed the office, sacked the office boy, and ran the union from his own home; the expenses of the surviving organizers were controlled with similar rigour. 'If it had not been for him it is difficult to see how the union could have lived', one of these argued later. 'The same rigid economy he enforced on others, he applied as rigidly to himself—and it was this grim characteristic that won.'[3]

It was possibly a sign of Duncan's administrative ability that the situation recorded by Chambers in 1900—'an average contribution of 1s. 5d. per member per quarter, with arrears of 1s. 10d.'[4]—was greatly eased; arrears were gradually reduced to half this level. For this reason, the union's income did not fall as rapidly as its membership. Duncan's election as Secretary also brought a transformation in policy in relation to friendly benefits. As already described, the militants of the 1890s despised the old craft societies as 'coffin clubs', so concerned to protect their benefit funds that they shrank from aggressive industrial action. The Workers' Union was accordingly established as a 'fighting union', free from such encumbrances. It did indeed provide an optional out-of-work scheme—a remarkable innovation for a general union—but this was intended as a direct complement to the union's industrial activities, supporting unemployed members who might otherwise be tempted to undercut established wage rates.

In 1901 there was a radical shift from these new unionist principles: a change of rule introduced funeral benefits for

[3] Beard, Triennial Conference, June 1916.
[4] *First Report*, 1898–9.

members and their wives, and an optional sickness scheme.[5] These changes, clearly designed to stabilize the union's dwindling membership, were a striking reflection of the change in leadership. From the union's inception, when Mann and other spokesmen had emphasized the absence of friendly benefits in the new organization, Duncan had chosen to stress the out-of-work benefit which *was* offered.[6] His years as a Poor Law Guardian in Middlesbrough, and lengthy personal experience of unemployment, had convinced him of the value of financial benefits at times of crisis in the working-class household; while as an ardent member of the ASE he was proud of the range of benefits which that Society offered.

Duncan's philosophy was expounded fervently in the pages of the union's *Annual Reports*. Membership turnover was a major problem for all general unions, but a member with a financial stake in a benefit fund would be less liable to lapse: 'each Benefit operates like an anchor and holds the membership more firmly and staunchly to the Union.'[7] Stronger in numbers and finance, the union would be better placed to win improved wages and conditions. These would in turn more than compensate the members for their union contributions; they would thus, Duncan argued, 'obtain the various Friendly benefits purely as a gift'.[8] This had been the formula of success for the societies of skilled craftsmen; the Workers' Union had only to 'imitate and emulate' and it might 'surpass any or all of the Skilled Unions, both in membership and finance'.[9] While the optional nature of the union's benefit funds meant that its basic contribution (3*d.* weekly) remained within the reach of the low-paid labourer, Duncan's constantly repeated aspiration was that the bulk of members should contribute to at least one of the

[5] In 1900 the union had also introduced minor benefit payments for industrial injuries; these were a natural complement to its legal assistance for injured members, described below. Several of the earlier new unions had introduced funeral benefits on or soon after their foundation. Because of the working-class dread that poverty might prevent a 'proper' funeral, this could be an important factor in attracting and retaining members. At the same time it had important advantages for the union: each member would qualify once only, at an actuarially predictable rate, and for the most part in the distant future.

[6] *Cotton Factory Times*, 10 July 1898.

[7] *Annual Report*, 1906. Duncan's arguments may have derived in part from the Webbs' analysis in their *Industrial Democracy*.

[8] Ibid.

[9] *Annual Report*, 1905 and 1906.

optional funds. In this he was only partially successful; on average about one-quarter of the membership contributed to each optional fund; since some contributed to both, the majority of members could have paid only the minimum union dues. While it is unclear how far these funds did help stabilize the union's membership, they clearly aided its finances: the sick fund showed a steady annual surplus, amounting to £900 by the end of the decade, while over the same period the out-of-work scheme proved self-supporting.[10]

Though membership continued to decline after 1901, under Duncan's guidance the union's financial position was secured. After four years there was a balance of £350 in the bank, and the Workers' Union was well placed to take advantage of the ensuing improvement in economic conditions. In 1906 and 1907 new organizers were appointed, and the geographical area of recruitment was extended. With rapid recruitment, membership rose above 5,000 for the first time in the union's history, while the balance of funds passed £1,000. Though a sudden economic slump in the following year raised unemployment to its highest level for twenty years, it proved possible to absorb the consequent losses in membership and finances. The crisis was fortunately short-lived, there was no resort to the drastic economies of 1901, and by the end of the decade the trend was once more upwards.

DISTRICT ORGANIZATION: PATTERNS OF INSTABILITY

The history of the union's activities at local level shows how volatile was the basis of its organization throughout this period. The most striking example of this instability may be seen in the rise and decline of the London branches.

Much of the support which led to the creation of the Workers' Union was based on the capital. Half of the union's first dozen branches were formed here, by the end of 1898 the number had doubled, and a year later no less than twenty-six London branches had been opened. While this reflects the concentration

---

[10] The published accounts of the benefit funds did not include the costs of their administration; even so, the funds must have made a significant positive contribution to the union's finances.

locally of active socialists willing to work for the new union, it also indicates the pressing need for such organization in the metropolis. A contemporary study estimated that there were 70,000 'general labourers' in London; 13 per cent earned less than 20s. a week, and a further 30 per cent less than 25s.[11] It was towards this section of workers, whose conditions were the most wretched and deplorable, that the union's efforts were directed.

A pattern soon emerged which was depressing in its implications. A recruitment campaign, with leaflets and public meetings would attract sufficient response for a branch to be opened; more workers would be encouraged to join; then their employers, alarmed at this threat to their authority, would act to smash the infant organization. Intimidation often caused the new recruits to abandon the union as speedily as they had joined; while the odds were stacked heavily against those who chose to resist. The predicament of the 'unattached labourer' had been aptly described two decades earlier: '. . . his strikes . . . are seldom important, or of long duration. Living from hand to mouth when in work, he has nothing to fall back upon, and is soon starved into capitulation. Or, failing that, it is comparatively easy to replace him by others.'[12]

The first serious struggle was at the Army and Navy Stores in Pimlico, allegedly 'a sweating machine for the purpose of grinding unjust and unfair profits'.[13] The workers involved— packers, porters, clerks, and assistant countermen—had long had to endure low wages, long hours, bullying foremen, and insecure employment. Their grievances were brought to a head in the summer of 1898 when management announced that employees would lose all benefits in the firm's Provident Fund (financed by compulsory deductions from wages) if they instituted claims against the Stores under the new Workmen's Compensation Act. So great was the resulting unrest that the employees responded enthusiastically to a series of recruiting meetings arranged jointly by the Workers' Union and the Shop

[11] C. Booth, *Life and Labour of the People in London*, vol. 7, 1896, p. 473. Booth subsequently estimated (vol. 9, p. 426) that 24s. a week was the 'poverty line' for a moderate family; since his wage statistics were derived from a survey of employers they may well have understated the poverty problem in London.

[12] 'A Working Man', *Working Men and Women*, 1879, p. 114.

[13] Frank Smith, speech quoted in *Reynolds Newspaper*, 16 Oct. 1898.

Assistants' Union; within two months the union's Westminster branch, drawing its membership exclusively from the Stores, was its third largest in the country.

The scale of recruitment led the union to appoint its first full-time district organizer: Will Banham, 'a forceful and impetuous character, possessed of unflagging energy',[14] who was chairman of the Clerkenwell branch and had been one of the union's earliest supporters. With his help a programme of demands was submitted for the members at the Stores; a minimum wage of 30s., overtime pay, control over the Provident Fund, and other concessions; proceedings were also commenced to test the legality of management's arbitrary attack on the rights of employees.

The firm now reacted forcibly. Known union members were dismissed, a private detective was hired to follow Banham, and threats of personal violence were made.[15] With only partial organization at the Stores, the union was in no position to fight back. Despite this weakness, its members proved remarkably loyal: well over a hundred remained at the end of the year.[16] But gradually their enthusiasm waned; it became clear that the union could achieve no concrete concessions, while the risk of victimization remained acute. Inevitably their numbers finally dwindled, and the once promising branch was closed.

Efforts were next concentrated on the immigrant Jewish workers of the East End. The difficulties were immense: the workers were mainly occupied in seasonal trades such as tailoring, conducted by numerous small employers. Language differences created problems of communication (for one meeting the Whitechapel branch advertised 'speakers in Russian, English, Yiddish, Polish, German, etc.'). The union was also handicapped by a growing mood of racialism, and by occasional police violence.[17] Even so, several branches were opened, and recruitment was subsequently extended to Jewish tailors in the Soho area. But while a membership of some two hundred was maintained for a year or so, this too collapsed entirely.

[14] T. H. Smith, *The National League of the Blind*, 1949, p. 8.
[15] *Labour Leader*, 17 Sept. 1898.
[16] Ibid., 26 Nov. 1898.
[17] *Weekly Times and Echo*, 13 Nov. 1898.

Success was similarly short-lived among London's window-cleaners, some of whom were said to earn as little as 2*s*. a day. Organization began early in 1899 in the heart of the City and spread to all districts where the union had branches. Again, the union was unable to enforce the demands which it formulated; it could promise only that 'when all had joined, they would demand a minimum living wage or else strike'.[18] With rapid recruitment, such an objective seemed for a time attainable; but as elsewhere, the membership quickly collapsed in the face of victimization by employers.

The most notable of the London struggles began in June 1899. Sir Thomas Lipton enjoyed public fame as a philanthropist; but the conditions of the 1,300 employees at his City Road warehouses were allegedly the worst in the trade. While other employers paid an hourly minimum of 6*d*., wages here were in some cases as low as 13*s*. for a 55-hour week. Women's earnings were lower still; for some, under 1½*d*. an hour. Girls worked a 10-hour day with only one half-hour break, carrying heavy loads in unhealthy conditions; often they fainted, and the time lost was then deducted from their wages. They were subject to bullying foremen, and those who complained were frequently dismissed on trivial pretexts.

Banham's attempts to organize these workers met a ready response. A meeting held to form a Workers' Union branch was packed to capacity, and over a hundred Lipton employees joined on the spot. The union's leaders were clearly encouraged; a second London organizer was appointed to assist with the work of recruitment, and an approach was made to the Lipton management to discuss wages and conditions. But as in previous cases, the union's overtures were ignored; instead the firm resorted to a policy of victimization. At first this failed to crush the workers' urge to organize—in October it was still reported that girls were joining at the rate of 160 a week[19]—but the management merely intensified the scale of repression. Inevitably, this policy was eventually successful; in the following January it was announced that 'Sir Thomas J. Lipton . . . has carefully refrained from redressing any of the grievances of his workpeople, but has succeeded in dismissing so many leaders of

[18] Banham, speech quoted in *Weekly Times and Echo*, 9 Apr. 1899.
[19] *Reynolds Newspaper*, 8 Oct. 1899.

both sexes, that the remainder have again been cowed into submission.'[20]

After this defeat, organizing activity soon waned. Will Banham, the energetic chief London organizer, resigned early in 1900. In the previous year he had helped form a national trade union for blind workers,[21] and he now became its full-time Secretary. The other local organizer, J. Wade, fell victim to the financial stringencies and was dismissed a year later. Duncan himself, in addition to his work at Head Office, was far more involved than Chambers in provincial visits and had correspondingly less time to devote to the London membership. Few of the branches formed during the period of intense activity proved able to survive when deprived of the close attention they had previously enjoyed. By the end of 1902 only four remained; of these, two closed during 1904 and another in 1906. As for the sole survivor, 'owing to the fall in membership it became necessary to economise in rent, and the branch moved its meeting place to a coal shed in a back street'.[22] Though its headquarters remained in London, the union's membership became almost wholly provincial.

In several districts the union's organization was even more unstable. The Middlesbrough branch, with Duncan as its secretary, quickly established itself as the union's largest. Membership was drawn mainly from among Corporation employees, who formulated a demand for a minimum wage of 21s. At the municipal elections of October 1898 the union was able to press candidates for their support; and with Duncan already a councillor, the campaign proved successful. Local progress was so satisfactory that a second organizer was appointed during 1899: John Mahoney, like Duncan an ILP member and a fellow-activist for many years in the local labour movement.

But disaster soon followed. In 1900 the fifty-six members employed by the Corporation staged an unofficial strike against two non-unionists; all were dismissed. Soon after this the branch lost both organizers: Duncan moved to London as General Secretary, and Mahoney left at about the same time. They

---

[20] *Labour Leader*, 20 Jan. 1900.
[21] The National League of the Blind, a union which is still in existence.
[22] *Record*, Jan. 1921.

were replaced by the assistant secretary of the union's Halifax branch, Harry Barrett, but he was among the organizers dismissed in 1901. Numbers then fell rapidly, and the branch closed early in 1902.

Attempts to organize Corporation employees were also made in Coventry. Here the Secretary of the Trades Council, George Newcombe—a skilled engineer and an active socialist—took charge of the union's efforts. By early 1899 about half the Corporation's manual employees had enrolled, and Newcombe became a full-time official. But here a demand for an hourly minimum of 6d. met with no success, and attempts to attract public support at the autumn elections failed miserably. The union also attempted to attract the unorganized cycle workers of the city. The local skilled unions were worried at the influx to this expanding trade of workers with no engineering experience. Moreover, the cycle workers suffered alternately from long periods of short time and bursts of frenetic activity to meet the fluctuations in seasonal demand; while over recent years the piece rates had been considerably reduced in the face of a recession in the trade. Though many members of the local labour movement co-operated in the attempt to bring union organization and conditions to the industry, the task proved hopeless. In 1900 Newcombe ceased to be organizer, and the branch closed soon afterwards.

Elsewhere the union's early organization was more successful. The major achievement was in the Yorkshire West Riding, where despite strong organization in the textile trades and considerable membership in the Gasworkers' Union there remained a mass of unorganized labour, enduring 'low wages, long hours, and generally obnoxious conditions'.[23] From its inception the Workers' Union could count on a number of supporters in the area, and Mann and Duncan both gave considerable attention to establishing local branches. The most active was in Halifax, where the branch secretary—Bob Morley, a local stalwart of the ILP—had helped Mann fight a by-election in the previous year. Towards the end of 1898 Morley began recruiting labourers at the Corporation gasworks, where a major grievance was smouldering: some workers employed on maintenance earned only 5½d. an hour, whereas a minimum of 6d. applied

[23] Mann, speech quoted in *Yorkshire Factory Times*, 27 May 1898.

in the local building trade and was therefore enforced by the Corporation, under a Fair Wages Clause, on private contractors employed in the gasworks.

In January 1899 the members of the branch submitted a formal application for the 6d. minimum for all gasworkers, together with various improvements in conditions. After a lengthy delay the Council's Gasworks Committee replied in June that 'the remuneration of their workmen and conditions of labour were equal to the best and superior to many. . . . The Committee therefore declined to make a new departure that would involve a third party'.[24] To add insult to injury, the Committee recommended a salary increase of £100 for the Gas Manager. A campaign of protest was immediately launched, under the auspices of the Trades Council. Morley alleged that the Council's refusal to negotiate heralded an attempt to smash the union: moves had already been made to victimize their leading member in the Gasworks. 'They were going to put in more work at the Gasworks', he promised, 'and would make such members in the next few weeks that the Gas Committee would have to eat their letter.'[25]

Morley was as good as his word: in September the demands were again presented, signed by 219 of the 228 workers to whom they applied, and there was talk of strike action if the grievances were not soon remedied. The Gasworks Committee now decided to hold a ballot of all gasworkers to establish whether they wished to be represented by the Workers' Union. This was seen merely as a delaying tactic, and the result was emphatic: 427 voted in favour, only 45 against. By now the fight had been taken into the political sphere: Morley stood in the autumn Council elections, and accused the Gasworks Committee of 'inhuman conduct to the men, and with working conditions being unbearable'.[26] He won his contest, the only Labour candidate elected, and obtained a seat on the Gasworks Committee itself. It was then agreed that the Committee should meet representatives of the union; and a deputation led by Duncan presented figures supporting their demands. After further charges of delaying tactics, a settlement was finally reached: the average rates of nine Yorkshire towns should form

[24] *Halifax Guardian*, 20 May 1899.   [25] Ibid.
[26] *Halifax Guardian*, 11 Nov. 1899.

the minimum for Halifax gasworkers engaged on the same type
of work under similar conditions. In February 1900 the new
rates took effect: the 6*d.* minimum for labourers, advances of
2*d.* to 4*d.* a shift for other workers, improved holiday payments
and other concessions. This victory was justifiably regarded as
the union's major achievement of the period in the field of
collective bargaining.

This success, together with Morley's vigorous defence of
working-class interests on the Town Council, proved a valuable
advertisement for the Workers' Union. Recruitment continued
apace among other municipal employees, and in the local
foundries and engineering shops—where there were many
black spots for trade unionism. By the middle of 1900 the
Halifax branch was 600 strong—easily the union's largest—and
it soon surpassed in size all other unions in the town. Morley's
election as President at the end of the year was a natural
reflection of this achievement.

After its early success the branch suffered—though on a less
severe scale—from the decline which the union experienced
nationally. Corporation employees proved unstable members,
and even the gasworkers fell away. Heavy unemployment in
the engineering and foundry trades aggravated the situation,
and by 1903 membership had fallen below 300. Thereafter
numbers fluctuated around this level to the end of the decade.

The President was by rule 'responsible for the organisation
and extension of the union'. Morley followed in the tradition
already established by Duncan, acting as a roving national
organizer. Naturally he was able to concentrate most attention
on districts within easy reach of Halifax. Of these the most
important was Manchester, where a branch had been formed
at the union's inception. For a brief period the district had had
its own full-time official, but activity had soon declined. In
1902 Morley succeeded in reviving the flagging organization;
subsequently several new branches were opened, and by the
end of 1907 there were 300 members in the district. It was then
decided once more to appoint a local organizer. The man
chosen was George Titt, a former President of the Saddlers'
Union and a full-time official of the ILP in the Midlands
(where he had previously helped the Workers' Union in its
activities). Titt at first achieved great success, doubling local

membership in a few months. But Manchester suffered from exceptionally high unemployment in the last two years of the decade, and numbers fell once more to well below 300.

Further north, in Preston, Morley opened a branch in 1904. With the assistance of local craft societies a solid membership was achieved among engineering labourers; in three years numbers rose to 300, and good improvements in wages were obtained. Losses in the subsequent depression were partly offset by a new source of recruitment: in 1908 a strike occurred in the bobbin manufacturing trade of Preston and Blackburn, and the union organized the unskilled men. After twelve months Morley was able to negotiate acceptable terms, thus stimulating further organization in the trade.

A dramatic opportunity for geographical expansion occurred in 1903, with a major dispute in the welded boiler industry. Halifax was the centre of the trade, and a few workers from this strenuous occupation were members of the union's local branch. In April 1903 one of the three principal firms, Hartley and Sugden, announced reductions of up to 50 per cent in piece rates, and its sixty-eight boilermakers and ninety labourers came out on strike. Though most strikers were unorganized the union decided to give financial support, and a special levy was agreed by members in the trade. Morley visited or contacted several other centres of the industry to appeal for financial and moral support; as a result not one blackleg 'troubled the shop for work' during the long dispute,[27] and over £200 was collected. After fifteen weeks a settlement was finally reached allowing a 5 per cent reduction in prices; in view of the depressed state of the trade, and the firm's original demands, this was rightly hailed as a signal victory. Soon the Halifax branch had organized 90 per cent of the trade locally, while branches were opened in Rotherham, Derby, and as far afield as Glasgow. Two years later a similar dispute in Derby gave a new fillip to organization. On neither occasion was the original enthusiasm sustained for long; but in several districts—notably South Yorkshire—the branches which were opened provided the basis for recruitment in other occupations.

Significant organization was achieved in two other areas in the union's earliest years. One was the Merthyr Tydfil district

[27] *Yorkshire Factory Times*, 14 Aug. 1903.

of South Wales, home of the famous iron and steel combines of Guest and Crawshay at Dowlais and Cyfarthfa. Though the industry was in general well organized, these two great employers were notorious opponents of trade unionism; and the union discovered that their employees were 'working for 1s. 11d. per day, without the courage to call their souls their own, and receiving no compensation for the accidents which are of almost daily occurrence'.[28] In August 1898 Mann addressed a mass meeting which set up a joint committee of men from the two works. Soon afterwards Duncan visited the district and opened several branches. Membership rose steadily; by the end of 1899 there were ten branches and numbers had reached 1,300. The union was fortunate that its advent coincided with a boom in the iron and steel trade, causing an acute shortage of labour—soon accentuated by the call-up of reservists to fight in the Boer War. So great was the scarcity of workers that 300 vacancies were advertised in Cork, and skilled men were obtained from Spain. In this situation workers could enrol in the union with little fear of dismissal, and were sufficiently confident 'to openly avow their membership'.[29] Soon even the Spaniards had joined.

In January 1900 a local organizer was appointed: Joe Cauhlin, an Irishman who was Vice-President of the local Trades and Labour Council and an active member of the ILP. The union was still too weak to attempt to bargain collectively with the companies; but a sliding-scale agreement had been accepted by the men while still unorganized, and an attempt was made to secure the election of members to the sliding-scale committee—'knowing that only Union men will dare to give vent to the opinions of the workers when in conference with the employers'.[30] This was apparently a long-term objective; but there was one area in which the union could benefit its members directly. The Workmen's Compensation Act, 1897, had created important legal rights for workers and their dependants in cases of accidents at work—which were so serious a problem at Dowlais and Cyfarthfa. But it was difficult for the individual worker to understand the Act's complicated provisions, and virtually impossible for him to enforce a claim unaided against

[28] Chambers, 'The Workers' Union', *Labour Annual*, 1900, p. 90.
[29] Ibid.   [30] Duncan, *Labour Leader*, 31 Aug. 1901.

powerful employers and their insurance companies. Many workers were thus scandalously cheated of their new rights. The Workers' Union offered full legal assistance in such cases, where necessary prosecuting the claims in the courts. By the end of 1899, four such cases had been won by the union locally; early in 1900 the rulebook was changed to provide its own benefits for injured members who were ineligible for compensation. In so hazardous an occupation the assurance of this support was clearly a powerful incentive to membership.

Towards the end of 1900 the situation changed; steel prices crashed, allegedly as a consequence of the 'dumping' of American products, and short-time working was introduced. Though membership fell, the numbers were still sufficient for Cauhlin's retention as the union's only remaining full-time district organizer; and when he resigned at the end of 1903 the district secretary, Sam Francis, was employed in his place. But in the following year the situation in the trade was further aggravated. The employers accused German and American manufacturers of 'reckless undercutting below cost prices'[31] and were forced to lay off several hundred men and extend short-time working. The effect on the union was now more serious. By the end of 1904 only five branches were functioning; early in 1905 Francis ceased to be organizer; and within a year little more than 100 members remained.

A new South Wales organizer was appointed in 1906, when membership locally was at its lowest since 1898. He was Matt Giles, a skilled engineer who was working as local organizer for the ILP. For several years Giles had been one of the union's elective Auditors, and the secretary of the Swansea branch—the only Welsh branch outside the Merthyr Tydfil district, and one which had never held more than a handful of members. Giles first consolidated the membership on Merthyr, reducing the number of branches to three, but increasing the number of members to 250 by the end of 1907. Although this number was reduced by the subsequent depression, it remained well above its earlier level. Giles' main success, however, was in organizing the metal workers in Swansea and the surrounding coastal area. By the end of 1907 the Swansea branch had grown to a membership of over 300—mainly spelter and lead workers—while

31 *Merthyr Express*, 10 Dec. 1904.

a branch of over 100 members had been created in Llanelli to the west, and two smaller branches in Cwmavon and Briton Ferry to the east. Despite the loss of membership elsewhere, in 1908 the Swansea branch reached a membership of 500, and became the union's largest. The South Wales district maintained its strength during 1909, and had by now re-established its position as one of the union's major centres.

Giles was able to resolve 'many difficulties in connection with working conditions and wages';[32] but as in Merthyr, the union's main achievement was in assisting members with claims under the Workmen's Compensation Act. In Swansea the main danger facing members was lead poisoning, which in 1907 was scheduled as an 'industrial disease' under the extended legislation of the previous year. As well as supporting members in claims for compensation, the union waged a continuing campaign against the long hours of work which were blamed for the increasing incidence of this killer disease.

The remaining centre of the union's initial organization was entirely different in character: the agricultural area of North Shropshire. One of its first branches was formed in the village of Ellerdine Heath, near Shrewsbury, by a former farm labourer named John Beard. His intention was to organize the low-paid ironworkers of the Ironbridge district; when this failed he and a fellow-member, John Simpson of Market Drayton, initiated a campaign among agricultural labourers. Both men began a correspondence in the local newspaper condemning in forthright terms the conditions endured by the farm worker, and both used their own names and addresses: an act of some bravery, particularly for Simpson, who was himself a farm labourer and was eventually victimized for his union activities.

After preparing the ground in this way Beard and Simpson arranged a series of meetings in April 1899, with Duncan as chief speaker. Many obstacles were placed in the union's way. In most villages the only meeting place was the public house or the Church school, and 'neither publicans nor parsons gave a very warm welcome to Trade Union organisers'.[33] At times meetings had to be held in the open air, 'the secretarial duties

[32] *Annual Report*, 1909.
[33] F. E. Green, *History of the English Agricultural Labourer*, 1920, p. 143.

being performed by the aid of a bicycle lamp'.[34] Some farmers threatened to dismiss any of their workers who attended the meetings. Nevertheless these proved an immediate success; many farm workers walked several miles to hear the speakers, and they joined the union in large numbers. By harvest time there were more than twenty branches in the area with a total membership of over a thousand, and Beard had been appointed full-time organizer. A programme of demands was drawn up, and in September 1899 it was reported that nearly a thousand members marched through Market Drayton to hear the union's national leaders.[35] But this display of strength was illusory, for the union's demands had to be put before the farmers by the members themselves. 'The men were brave enough at the meetings, but when it came to the point of bargaining they lost confidence and were broken up'.[36] A small number of farmers offered concessions which were gratefully accepted; but the majority refused, and few members were prepared to take strike action. Then with the harvest safely in the farmers commenced a counter-attack; workers were ordered to leave the union, and in one parish a general lock-out was enforced. In the rare cases when members stood firm they were dismissed and evicted from their tied cottages. Within a year all but three of the branches had been forced to close.

Despite this collapse Beard continued his efforts, opening a dozen new branches in 1900; but all had an ephemeral existence. Understandably, Beard was told in 1901 that the union could no longer afford to employ him; but at his own request he remained on a part-time basis, receiving a maximum of half the income of his district as wages.

In 1904 Morley made an organizing mission to Birmingham, and must have decided that prospects were hopeful; for the union's leaders decided to transfer Beard here, once more as a full-time organizer. The branch opened by Morley contained four members, employed in the Small Heath district. With the assistance of local members of the ASE Beard concentrated on this tiny nucleus, bringing in over fifty new members in the first few weeks. The new recruits were all machinists at the

[34] *Newport and Market Drayton Advertiser*, 20 May 1899.
[35] *Weekly Times and Echo*, 24 Sept. 1899.
[36] Beard, 'The Early Struggles of the Union', *Record*, May 1919.

Birmingham Small Arms (BSA) factory, a local pioneer of 'mass-production' techniques.

By the end of 1904 there were three branches in the city with a total membership of 100. In the following year progress was slower, but in 1906 six new branches were formed and membership rose to 600. In this year the union received a valuable campaigning issue when the Government announced the sale of its small arms factory at Sparkbrook to the neighbouring BSA company; the threat of redundancy stimulated recruitment among gun-workers at both factories. Another important source of new recruitment was at Cadbury's Bournville factory, where over 100 maintenance workers were brought in. By the end of 1907 Birmingham membership had reached 1,000, consisting mainly of labourers and semi-skilled workers in local engineering. The union's achievement received recognition with its admission to the local Engineering and Allied Trades Federation, which agreed on a scale of wages to be pursued by semi-skilled workers. At the same time, a District Committee formed from all local branches of the union decided on the objective of a 23s. minimum wage for all engineering workers. 'At that time the highest wage paid was 22s. per week, but generally the wage was 18s. per week, in a large number of cases less, and the labourer had less hope in his heart than wages in his pocket.'[37] Severe unemployment in 1908 and 1909 destroyed any hopes of translating this objective into reality. As it was, about a third of local membership was lost; and the effect might have been far greater, according to Beard, but for the high proportion of local members who had joined the union's out-of-work fund. In consequence, over 600 members remained at the end of the decade—more than in any other town in the country.

Other useful branches were opened in the Midlands towards the end of the decade—notably in Swadlincote, near Burton, among clay-getters and yard-labourers in the local pipe-works; and in Coventry, where organization among engineering workers was revived in 1906.

It remains to mention one further area of organization: Northern Ireland. Morley, a popular speaker at meetings of

[37] Beard, 'The Workers' Union in Birmingham', *Triennial Conference Souvenir*, 1916.

ILP branches, was invited to Belfast in 1907; his visit chanced to coincide with a strike of the local branches of the National Union of Dock Labourers. Morley took advantage of the unrest in the city to open two branches of the union for factory labourers, and on his departure a local organizer was appointed: Joe Harris, a leading member of the Upholsterers' Union. A membership of 500 was soon recruited, mainly composed of chemical workers and builders' labourers, and some improvements in wages and conditions were achieved. Numbers soon fell away again, but the losses were more than compensated by recruitment in the linen industry in County Antrim. Attempts were also made to organize in Southern Ireland, but these were frustrated by religious differences and inter-union rivalries.

THE RECORD OF THE FIRST TWELVE YEARS

In assessing the record of the union in the dozen years following its formation it is as well to recall the original objectives of its founders: a mass political movement, a fighting union to raise the status and conditions of the unorganized, and an all-embracing organization to unite workers of every skill and occupation. All presupposed the achievement of mass membership; they bore little relation to the options open to a tiny union of at most 5,000 members.

The justification for the intended political role was that the appeal of the Workers' Union would be far wider than to committed socialists alone; its membership would thus allow national activity on a scale beyond the resources of the Independent Labour Party or Social-Democratic Federation. Failing even to equal their combined membership, this objective was quietly forgotten. In the event the Labour Representation Committee (later the Labour Party) was formed in 1900 to fill the role originally intended for the Workers' Union. The union was represented at its inaugural conference, and was thereafter involved in national politics solely through this medium.

Though its leaders cherished Parliamentary ambitions, the Workers' Union was in no position to finance these. In 1903, following the decision of the ASE to sponsor five candidates, Duncan was successful in the Society's ballot. Morley was less successful; when the Ironfounders chose a single member to sponsor he came third. In 1904 Duncan was chosen to fight Barrow-in-Furness by the local LRC, and in the General Election of 1906 he was one of two ASE candidates elected. He was a conscientious member—a fact reflected by his election as a Junior Whip in 1908—but inevitably only a minor part of his Parliamentary activities was of any direct advantage to the Workers' Union.

Industrially too, the first grandiose objectives were quickly shelved. From dreams of marshalling a workers' army, the task of the union's leaders changed overnight to administering a tiny organization and struggling for its very survival.

In details of policy there was a corresponding adjustment to harsh realities. The proposal to enrol skilled and unskilled alike was never a whole-hearted objective of the union's founders. They doubtless felt that the rigid contemporary distinction between 'craftsmen' and 'labourers' had little practical justification, while the barriers of craft exclusiveness were objectionable as a divisive factor within the labour movement; but their forcible removal was out of the question. The 'One Big Union' was at most a distant ideal, and Mann had no desire deliberately to court the opposition of craft unionists to the Workers' Union. Thus the union's rules from 1908 made it clear that there was no intention of trespassing on craft unionists' preserves;[38] in industries where a union already existed for skilled workers, the Workers' Union enrolled only labourers, and its officials often expressed their gratitude for the craftsmen's co-operation.

Yet if craftsmen were not organized by the Workers' Union, neither were the mobile 'general labourers' whose predicament Mann had depicted when the union was formed. The most determined effort to enrol this class of worker was made in London in the union's early years, and although the numbers recruited bear witness to the energy and persistence of the officials, it was found impossible to establish any lasting organization. Where stable membership was created in these years, it was among workers who enjoyed some regularity and security of employment.

[38] 'The Union shall consist of any number of persons ... who accept the principles and methods of the Union, and who are not eligible to join a skilled Trade Union. ...'

In its internal government also the union experienced changes from the intentions of its founders. The original rule book displayed many of the features of the 'primitive democracy' of the nineteenth-century craft society, with central authority rigorously circumscribed. At local level, District Executives were to be formed where more than one branch existed in any town or district. Their secretaries were to be elected by a ballot of local membership, and they were to possess 'the fullest powers of local autonomy, subject only to the rules . . .'. Each such committee elected a delegate to a General Executive, in which was vested 'the management and control of the union'. Lest this body should act in an arbitrary manner it was in turn subject to an annual delegate conference which was empowered to decide any questions in dispute and determine the union's general policy.

These constitutional prescriptions necessarily conflicted with the realities of the union's limited membership and finance. At the end of 1898 the provision for a national conference was removed from the rule book, as being beyond the union's resources; in its place was specified an annual referendum, to which any branch might submit questions for the decision of the whole membership. It does not appear that this cumbersome procedure was ever operated.

The National Executive proved almost equally ineffectual. From the start its meetings were infrequent: the rule book prescribed an annual minimum of four, changed in 1901 to two, but even this minimum was not observed. In 1902 it ceased to meet altogether—presumably because the finances could no longer meet the fares and expenses of its members. The District Executives were at first more active (assuming that the meetings of the Merthyr and Dowlais committee, regularly reported in the local press, were at all representative), but here too there was a decline as membership fell. It appears that the district bodies also had ceased to function by the end of 1904.

With the demise of these executive bodies, authority necessarily shifted downwards to the individual branches and upwards to the national officials. Thus the General Secretary and President acquired effective autonomy over central decisions. This was clearly demonstrated in relation to the employment of full-time organizers—a subject on which the rule book offered little guidance. It appears that the first such officials acted largely under the surveillance of their District Executives (which may also have been responsible for their initial appointment). But the decision in 1901 to reduce the organizing staff appears to have been taken solely on Duncan's authority (in consultation with Mann), and it was he and Morley who determined new appointments after the recovery in the union's fortunes.

The rule book of 1908 brought further changes in the structure of authority. The District Committees—some of which had resumed meeting in the previous year—were now assigned only limited advisory functions. Significantly, the term 'Executive' disappeared from their title. The directly elected District Secretary also disappeared. At the same time, their power of collective control over the resurrected central Executive was removed; the latter was now composed of members directly elected on a geographical basis (which did not necessarily coincide with the area of any single District Committee). The rules now required only that the General Executive Committee (GEC) should meet once a year; evidently it was in no position to impose any serious constraint on the by now experienced national officers.

It has been suggested that every 'new union' which survived the years of depression did so by acting 'as a convenient "banker" for a multiplicity of local and sectional bargaining units'.[39] This was true of the Workers' Union, but with a major qualification. As has been noted, there were important sections of its membership for which it proved impossible to negotiate over wages and conditions of work; it is doubtful whether many sections really constituted 'bargaining units', and even these had other characteristics. Indeed, it is arguable that in periods of depression collective bargaining has at times ceased to be the primary function of trade unions; when unemployment and falling membership have reduced their bargaining power, or even lost them the recognition of employers, other aspects of their work have assumed greater importance for the trade-union member.

One such facet in the case of the Workers' Union was the

provision of financial benefits; this reversal of the attitudes of the union's founders has already been described. Another was the assistance provided in cases of industrial injury: a central feature of the work of the South Wales organizers, and one regularly emphasized by Duncan in his Annual Reports—particularly after the extensions to the Workmen's Compensation Act in 1906.

These 'subsidiary' functions were crucial in assisting the union's survival during these years. It entered a new decade with a membership of 4,500. Though little more than it had possessed ten years previously, this was enough to make it the fourth largest of the general unions—a sign of the ravages that all had suffered.[40] Thus the Workers' Union had at least endured. It had endured, thanks to the energy and determination of its officials, some of whose efforts have been described; thanks also to the dedication of many of its ordinary members: John Simpson, the Shropshire farm labourer, the strength of whose convictions won respect even from hostile farmers, but who lost his job for declaring too openly his allegiance to the union; Richard Wade of Manchester, who after a few months as an organizer was forced to return to work as a labourer, but still 'gave every moment of his spare time to the union';[41] Joe Walker of Farsley, whose branch was often on the verge of collapse, but who held it together because 'to have given up would have meant lowering the flag';[42] the sacrifices of these men, and many others whose efforts have gone unrecorded, maintained the Workers' Union throughout the years of endurance. Their dedication was to find a thorough vindication in the achievements of a new decade.

[40] The three leading unions were the Gasworkers, the Dockers, and the National Amalgamated Union of Labour.
[41] Duncan, Obituary of R. Wade, *Record*, Feb. 1923.
[42] *Record*, May 1916.

3

ACHIEVEMENT 1910–1914

'A NEW era is upon us', wrote Bob Morley in his President's Report for 1911. And indeed the four years before the outbreak of war were the most dramatic in the union's history. In a period when trade unionism generally achieved a vast upsurge in numbers,[1] the performance of the Workers' Union was outstanding; the mass membership envisaged by its founders was at last attained. One aspect of this pre-war 'revolt of labour' was a spate of industrial conflict which caused widespread alarm among the propertied classes. 'The essence of the cause of the Labour unrest', Morley explained, was 'the inadequate wage rate, the increasing pressure of workshop life, the increasing knowledge of the workers, and their intelligent and just demand for a "place in the sun".... I am glad it is with us. May it grow and prosper.' The Workers' Union played a worthy part in these turbulent industrial struggles.

The union's membership increased slowly in the first year of the decade, then in 1911 leaped from 5,000 to 18,000. After a slower increase in the following year, the advance in 1913 was again spectacular: a gain of 68,000, raising total membership to 91,000. This rate of growth continued to the outbreak of war, when numbers had reached 143,000. The Workers' Union was now closely challenging the Gasworkers for the position of leading general union; of all other British unions only the Railwaymen, the Engineers, and the South Wales Miners were larger.[2]

Mass membership brought a transformation in the union's finances. From its inception in 1898 to the end of 1910, total

---

[1] Total trade union membership rose in four years from 2,480,000 to 4,140,000. In the same period the combined membership of the four main general unions increased fivefold.

[2] Possibly also the Durham Miners. The Miners' Federation, as its name implied, was not a single union but a federation of largely autonomous district unions. So was the Amalgamated Weavers' Association, which also had a combined membership greater than that of the Workers' Union.

income had been little more than £20,000; in the single year 1913 it was £42,000. Higher income in turn allowed Duncan his first opportunity to achieve a substantial balance of funds; the reserves, reduced to less than £1,000 by the slump of 1908–9, were approaching £20,000 by the outbreak of war.

Duncan's concern to accumulate an adequate cash reserve was accompanied by a readiness to invest in further growth. One method adopted was a novelty in trade unionism: a publicity campaign using leaflets, posters, and regular insertions in the short-lived *Daily Citizen*. Advertisements composed by Duncan made liberal use of bold type and eye-catching slogans, and helped to gain the union a wide reputation as an energetic and successful organization.[3] Equally novel was the rapid increase in the union's staff. For ten years Duncan had been 'part Organiser, Secretary, Clerk and Office Boy',[4] then in 1910 John Barlow, since 1901 an elective auditor and Halifax branch secretary, was appointed clerk at head office; and within four years a staff of several dozen was employed. The expansion, which involved the acquisition of additional premises, was due both to the growth in membership and to the additional functions involved under the National Insurance Act of 1911; its result was to give the union 'a thoroughly business-like system in its work at Chief Office, which . . . has earned the Workers' Union the constant and highest of praises'.[5]

The increase in the number of organizers was equally marked. At the beginning of the decade there were six, in addition to the President and Secretary; but throughout the period there were new appointments made at frequent intervals. The primary function of the new organizers was normally that of recruitment, often in districts in which actual membership was small but the potential was considered good; an adventurous policy which paid handsome dividends. At the outbreak of war the union had over forty organizers; the Gasworkers, by contrast, with a slightly larger membership had only fourteen officers in the field.

[3] The advertisements were, according to the *Citizen* (22 Aug. 1913), 'of such virility and striking originality as not only to ensure their immediate success, but to extract eulogistic comments from the great advertising experts of London'. Certainly their impact on a modern reader is far greater than that of most commercial advertisements of the period.

[4] *Annual Report*, 1912.   [5] Ibid.

The period also brought changes at the top. Morley, who had been returned as President, often unopposed, in every election since 1900, was defeated by Beard at the end of 1913. Of the Trustees and Executive members in office in 1914, only one had held his position for more than two years without interruption. It does not appear that this turnover within the leadership represented internal conflict over union policy, as was the case in many trade unions at this time; rather it reflected the changing distribution of union membership. Morley had become President when his branch at Halifax had been the union's largest; by 1913 the Midlands district was dominant, and the bulk of its new members was willing to vote the local organizer into the Presidency. Within some Executive divisions, sitting members suffered a similar fate; others were appointed organizers and had automatically to resign their positions. Throughout these changes, Duncan's position as Secretary remained unshaken, and there can be little doubt that during this period his was the dominant influence on the Executive. The union's Vice-President, Tom Mann, who returned to Britain in 1910 and took a leading role as theorist of industrial militancy, was allowed no part in the formulation of union policy. His assistance was welcomed as a speaker during disputes and at recruiting meetings, but his position was otherwise purely honorary, a continued recognition of his past work as the union's founder. Duncan, who retained his seat at Barrow at both the 1910 General Elections, and held an essentially moderate view of the functions of trade unionism, was in no way receptive to Mann's conception of socialism, involving as it did the rejection of Parliamentary action and the use of industrial conflict for revolutionary political purposes.

In 1910 it would have made little sense to talk of the industrial structure of the union's membership, for its composition varied essentially on a geographical basis: metal workers in South Wales, lower-skilled engineering workers in the Midlands, textile workers in Northern Ireland, a range of 'general labour' in Yorkshire. At the time, the same was true of the sparse coverage of general unionism as a whole, (that is, if one excludes from consideration the stronger nucleus of organization among transport workers). Strong organization was still largely confined to two sections of the working class: craftsmen,

4—W.U.

whose trades were traditionally based on apprenticeship; and all or most grades of labour in a few industries lacking clear craft divisions, such as coalmining, textiles, the railways, and certain public employment. The rise of the general unions (which was to continue to the end of the decade) changed the picture markedly. Their main impact was in two areas of employment: they brought union organization to the lower-skilled in the traditional craft industries; and they tackled successfully a range of new mass-production industries—chemical, rubber, paint and oil-milling plants, breweries, flour-mills and other food-processing factories, brick and cement works, among many others—in which organization was previously almost non-existent, but in which a concentrated labour force with specialist abilities was ripe for trade unionism. In addition, the organizing zeal of the general unions often reached groups of workers who possessed none of the bargaining power or inherent solidarity of a factory proletariat.

The development of the Workers' Union followed these general trends. But its record in two areas of organization—engineering and agriculture—deserves more detailed examination.

THE UNION IN ENGINEERING

The union's most substantial achievement was without question in engineering: an industry (or rather, a complex of trades united less by a common technology than by shared collective bargaining institutions) which was indeed ripe for the intervention of such an organization as the Workers' Union.

Engineering had long provided a classic case of the rigid demarcation which was popularly made within the Victorian labour force. As a working-class author declared in the 1870s, '... there is no place where class distinctions are more clearly defined, or strongly, or if need be violently maintained, than in the workshop'.[6] On the one hand stood the skilled craftsman, a member of the country's largest and (until the lock-out of 1897-8) wealthiest trade union, and enjoying 'the higher wages, the greater respect, the other ponderable and imponderable perquisites of the "aristocrat of labour"'.[7] On the other, the

6 *Working Men and Women*, p. 11.
7 Hobsbawm, *Economic History Review*, 1949, p. 128.

unskilled labourer: 'as his title "unskilled" implies, he has no
handicraft and he has no union . . . though his work is hard, his
pay is always small'.[8]

At the heart of this stark distinction was the apprenticeship
system: the craft society enforcing a monopoly of skilled work,
to which only those who had 'served their time' were admitted.
But by the turn of the century this system of control was dis-
integrating. Two parallel developments were responsible.
First, changes in technology. There were two main categories of
craftsmen in nineteenth-century engineering: the turner, using
hand tools on a simple lathe, and requiring both accuracy and
versatility; and the fitter, carrying out at his bench the delicate
adjustments necessary to assemble the machined parts into the
finished product. But during the course of the century a range of
machines were invented to perform elements of the turner's
work—slotting, planing, shaping, boring—without the use of
hand-held tools; more accurate and versatile lathes were
introduced; and finally, automatic machine tools were derived
which, once set with the necessary jigs, could produce rapid
repetition work under the surveillance of a mere 'machine-
minder'. The accuracy with which these new machine tools
operated was such that components could now be assembled
directly without the need for the traditional fitter's skill. The
introduction of new machinery was associated with changes in
the organization of work and in the product itself. The traditional firm produced a wide range of articles in small batches or
one-off jobs; and to a large extent the employer relied on the
craftsman to use his own initiative in organizing his work. But
greater profitability lay in specialization, with the manufacture
of long runs of standardized products; this in turn required
large productive units and investment in expensive equipment.
This trend reached its logical conclusion in the mass-production
system, whereby the cost of the most advanced machinery could
be offset by its speed and accuracy; and such developments
made necessary a new and more positive form of management
to control and co-ordinate the process of production on the
shop floor.

Such changes occurred only gradually. By 1914 mass-
production techniques were prevalent only in the most modern

[8] *Working Men and Women*, pp. 105–7.

sections of engineering: small arms and ammunition, bicycles and motor vehicles, electrical equipment; elsewhere the traditional structure and methods of the industry remained largely unaltered. But the direction of progress was obvious; and the implications for the engineering labour force were enormous. Automatic machines could be run by a novice after a minimum of instruction; other, more complex machine tools could be operated by workers without a full craft training. Such developments struck at the roots of the craft system; as the Webbs noted, '. . . the youth or the labourer who begins by spending his whole day in "minding" the simplest driller or automatic lathe, may "progress" from one process to another with little further instruction until, by mere practice on a succession, the sharp boy becomes insensibly a qualified turner or fitter'.[9]

The reaction of skilled craftsmen was predictable. In the 1840s strenuous efforts were made, first to prevent the introduction of new machinery, then to reserve its operation for apprenticed men. With its defeat in the great lock-out of 1852 the ASE was forced to yield on this issue. Later still it felt compelled to abandon its opposition to the 'illegal' men who had progressed to skilled work without the recognized training; any who could prove their ability by earning the craft rate became eligible for membership of the Society. But this still left unorganized the far greater numbers of machine workers employed at lower rates of pay;[10] and from about 1890 this body of semi-skilled 'handymen' increased rapidly in size. The impact was soon felt by the fitters and turners of the ASE: unemployment among members reached 11 per cent in 1893. Resistance to changing methods hardened once more, and in several districts the demands of half a century earlier were again backed by strike action. This 'machine question' was the major cause of the embittered relationships which lay behind the national lock-out of 1897–8. For the second time in its history the Society conceded defeat; the Terms of Settlement established that

Employers are responsible for the work turned out on their machine

---

[9] S. and B. Webb, *Industrial Democracy*, 1897, pp. 471–2.

[10] A United Machine Workers' Association was formed for this class of worker in 1844; but its membership was concentrated largely in Lancashire, where it had its headquarters.

tools, and shall have full discretion to appoint the men they consider suitable to work them, and determine the conditions under
which such machine tools shall be worked. The Employers consider
it their duty to encourage ability wherever they find it and shall have
the right to select, train, and employ those whom they consider best
adapted to the various operations carried out in their workshops,
and will pay them according to their ability as workmen.[11]

In the following years the uneven process of mechanization
continued, and with it the growth of the semi-skilled. By 1914
they accounted for a fifth of the engineering labour force,
covering a wide range of machine operations; indeed, the gap
between such semi-skilled workers as the automatic stamper and
the universal driller was far greater in terms of skill than was
that between the driller and the fully-skilled turner. A whole
family of new engineers had become established, and their
advance could not now be halted.

A progressive minority within the ASE—including Mann
and Duncan—recognized the logic of this situation. Craftsmen
were being displaced on the new machinery because 'handymen' could be employed at far lower wages. Skilled engineers
would be able to control this competition by lower-paid rivals
only by admitting these to their own Society. In 1901, and
again in 1912, the ASE did indeed heed these arguments and
relax its membership rules; but the reforms were purely
nominal, for the fear of the handyman was so great that most
branches simply refused to operate the new rules. If the new
engineers were to be organized, it would have to be in a union
of their own.

The Workers' Union assumed this role as much by accident
as design. Its founders did not (as has sometimes been assumed)
see engineering as a major field of recruitment; on the contrary,
this would have conflicted with their aim that the ASE itself
should open its ranks to the lower-skilled.[12] Apart from the

---

[11] Despite this nominal surrender, in many areas continued shop-floor pressure
succeeded in maintaining traditional practices throughout the pre-war period.
Details are given in my original thesis; see also J. B. Jefferys, *The Story of the
Engineers*, 1945.

[12] Five years after the formation of the Workers' Union this was still Duncan's
view: 'The so-called unskilled man is already catered for by special unions, but all
skilled men and men working machinery should be within the ranks of the ASE . . .,
every mechanical operation and every machine tool should come within that
scope' (ASE *Monthly Journal and Report*, Feb. 1903).

abortive attempt to organize the Coventry cycle trade, the only engineering workers enrolled in the union's earliest years were labourers in the Halifax workshops and foundries.

The breakthrough came with Beard's transfer to Birmingham, described in the previous chapter. The BSA, with its predominantly semi-skilled labour force, was one of the largest factories in the city and an obvious target for Beard's attention. Yet he approached the task with little expectation of success. So potent still was the conventional dichotomy between craftsman and labourer that 'the class of semi-skilled machinists was not generally known and certainly not recognized'; they were indeed 'looked upon as impossible' to organize.[13] Beard's initial recruitment of fifty of these workers was therefore 'considered ... a tremendous achievement'.[14] Yet the machinists at the BSA formed a group whose stability and cohesion made them ripe for trade unionism;[15] and since the Midlands was the centre of many of the newest and most mechanized sections of engineering, they represented a key element in the local labour force. Once Beard—and the semi-skilled workers themselves—recognized the implications of this early success, the way was open to almost unlimited expansion.

By the outbreak of war the union had taken a major step towards realizing this potential, while officials in other areas (including those where more traditional forms of engineering predominated) were encouraged to seek membership in the industry. By 1914, fifty of the union's hundred largest branches were composed almost exclusively of engineering workers, and a further twenty contained at least a high proportion of members in the industry.[16] Even if the Birmingham district is

[13] Beard, *Record*, Sept. 1916.

[14] Beard, 'The Workers' Union in Birmingham,' *Triennial Conference Souvenir*, 1916.

[15] E. J. Hobsbawm (*Economic History Review*, 1949, pp. 138–9), has cited the career of a local Workers' Union member in arguing that the semi-skilled labour force was an unstable one. This may give a misleading impression: when Beard came to Birmingham the BSA has been operating mass-production methods for forty years, and many of the union's recruits had been employed there for a decade or more (and some of these had commenced their working lives there). In the 1890s, when totally unorganized, the machinists had shown sufficient collective consciousness to stage a protracted strike.

[16] These figures (which are in any case approximate) overstate the importance of engineering, since the giant branches were not fully representative of the union's membership as a whole. But they are the best index available.

excluded from consideration, engineering workers were still predominant in a majority of the largest branches. At the outbreak of war the Workers' Union could thus claim a national status in its representation of lower-skilled engineers.

By this date, other general unions had also established an important stake in the industry. But the Gasworkers and the National Amalgamated Union of Labour had their main strength among engineering *labourers*, in the traditional centres of the industry: Lancashire and Yorkshire, the North-East coast, Merseyside and Northern Ireland. The Workers' Union, by contrast, was supreme in the new light trades with their semi-skilled labour force. This difference was to be of crucial significance in determining the union's role within the industry.

Details of the rapid growth of organization at local level will be given later; here some more general comments on the union's work are in order. Before the war, engineering, like most industries, lacked any system of national wage determination. The Terms of Settlement of 1898 had provided a framework for national discussions, with regular Central Conferences at which the signatory unions—principally the ASE—could discuss with a panel of employers 'references' received from Local Conferences. But wages and conditions were still founded on the system of 'district rates', developed in the 1870s by the ASE. Each District Committee had determined a local standard and enforced this as far as possible, subsequently negotiating with employers for variation of these basic rates. Though local 'wage movements' now often resulted in reference to Central Conference, the 'fanatical attachment of the Engineers to an extreme local autonomy' would have prevented the development of a national wages policy even had the union leaders or employers desired this.[17]

Industrial relations were further complicated by the fragmented structure of trade unionism. In size the ASE dominated; but numerous smaller organizations, such as the Steam Engine Makers, the Patternmakers, and the Toolmakers, catered for sections of craftsmen who were reluctant to merge their identity and interests with the fitters and turners of the larger Society. Nationally there was no co-ordination between the

[17] S. and B. Webb, *Industrial Democracy*, pp. 96-7.

various organizations;[18] but when improvements in wages or conditions were desired, it had become customary for unions to co-operate in a local movement, often forming *ad hoc* committees which could become permanent. The ASE, as the strongest member, was however 'apt to assume the leading role, plan the operation, and then hustle the sectionals into acquiescence',[19] while the latter, however much they might resent such treatment, were finding themselves impotent in independent action. Where the Workers' Union wished to make any major move to change its members' conditions, this fact necessarily determined its tactics in its formative years in the industry; as a small and little-known union representing workers of no recognized skill, it could hardly hope to succeed by its own efforts when established societies of key craftsmen were finding this no longer possible. But while it was generally on such major movements that the union's officials made their reports, many lesser issues were of equal or greater importance to the membership than general wage claims, yet could at times be settled with little difficulty by independent action.

One such issue was overtime payment: while craftsmen received an increased wage, often time and a half, for work done outside normal hours, it was not unusual for labourers to receive the ordinary time rate whatever the hours they worked. This disparity could often be remedied by negotiation, providing a valuable increase in earnings at times. Payment by results affected the semi-skilled more than any other class of engineering workers; and though workers could benefit from such systems, these could also be used as a means of increasing the pressure of work while depressing pay, particularly in the absence of strong union organization. Where the union was able to adjust rates it could thereby obtain substantial improvements, particularly for new members who had previously been seriously exploited by their employers; while the conditions of other members could be defended against speeding-up or rate-cutting. More generally, much of the union's work consisted in standardization of conditions. Even the craftsmen's district

[18] A Federation of Engineering and Shipbuilding Trades, formed in 1890, did to some extent fulfil a co-ordinating role in shipbuilding; but in engineering it was ineffectual, since the ASE refused to associate on equal terms with sectional societies whose very right to exist it challenged.

[19] Clegg, Fox, and Thompson, *History of British Trade Unionism*, vol. 1, p. 131.

rates were rarely incorporated in formal agreements or universally observed; and while labourers' wages were customarily between 50 and 60 per cent of craftsmen's, considerable variation normally existed within each district. Clearly, the labourer who earned 2s. less than his fellows in neighbouring works suffered far more in terms of his standard of living than did the similarly placed craftsman; the union's efforts in eliminating such discrepancies were therefore of major importance. Of similar value to the semi-skilled was the work of obtaining uniformity in the rates which were paid to reflect their intermediate status; for machinists' wages varied considerably even within individual works, particularly when foremen fixed the rate of each worker in their section. In all these spheres, piecemeal treatment was possible and independent action often successful.

THE UNION IN AGRICULTURE

A second area of activity in which the union achieved considerable success presented a sharp contrast. In agriculture, as was seen in the previous chapter, the union obtained in its earliest years a membership which was localized and short-lived. Beard's efforts came at a time when British farming had endured a prolonged period of depression, and when 'nearly every vestige of a trade union had died out'.[20] Three farm workers' unions shared a membership of under a thousand, the bulk of these being in Scotland. The recruitment of over a thousand Shropshire farm labourers by Beard and his supporters was therefore a considerable achievement.

These first abortive attempts showed clearly the obstacles involved in establishing trade unionism in the countryside. Geographically isolated, and lacking (in most areas) any tradition of trade unionism, farm labourers were naturally suspicious of the union's approaches. Where a persuasive organizer was able to overcome these initial misgivings, the farmer—and often the other figures of authority in the village—had plenty of opportunity to rekindle them. And if this failed the employer could easily resort to coercion, holding the power to deprive the worker not only of his job but of his home as well.

[20] F. E. Green, *History of the English Agricultural Labourer*, p. 140.

Its initial failure appears to have cured the Workers' Union of all taste for rural organization. It returned to the task in 1912 in response to the initiative of the farm labourers themselves, who were beginning to react spontaneously to the decline in real wages which was provoking revolt in the cities.

The process began modestly enough when 'a few determined men' began a campaign in Herefordshire, much as Beard and Simpson had done in Shropshire a dozen years earlier.[21] Before long they decided to ask the Workers' Union for assistance. Morley visited the county during the autumn of 1912 and opened a dozen branches; the union then appointed as organizer one of the local leaders: Sidney Box, an independent-minded farm worker who had served as Liberal agent in the General Elections of 1906 and 1910. Box proved a vigorous and effective organizer, covering the whole of the county on his bicycle, holding meetings and opening branches. The farmers were evidently alarmed: many gave increases of up to 2s. a week, hoping to show that a union was unnecessary; but the effect of the tactic was the reverse of that intended. Others used more forceful methods: not only did Box receive the usual series of threatening and abusive letters to which trade union officials, in rural areas at least, had to become inured; on one occasion he was narrowly missed by shotgun fire while cycling home from a meeting. But violence also failed to inhibit the union's growth. By the beginning of 1914, some fifty branches had been opened in the county—nearly a tenth of all the union's branches.

Meanwhile, organization had been started in other rural areas. In the Midlands, a farm workers' union had been formed in 1912 by a former agricultural labourer with a long record of activity in the trade union movement, Robert Owen Hornagold. After experiencing the problems which confronted a solely agricultural union, Hornagold approached the Workers' Union, and was taken on in October 1912 as an organizer; his handful of branches in the Midlands was transferred to the union. An attempt was made to consolidate this initial membership, but with little success; it was therefore decided to extend the area of recruitment, and towards the end of 1913 a series of meetings was arranged in East Anglia. The campaign proved

[21] S. Box, *The Workers' Union in Herefordshire, c.* 1925, and *The Good Old Days: Then and Now,* 1955.

unexpectedly successful: within weeks, some thirty branches had been opened, the majority in West Suffolk but a number also in the adjoining counties. Subsequently Hornagold opened up organization further west, covering four counties in the area of the Cotswolds. In both districts, local organizers were then appointed to supervise and extend the new membership. Simultaneously, officials of the union began recruiting in Yorkshire, taking in parts of all three Ridings; and in Shropshire, aided in some cases by veterans of Beard's previous campaign.

Over the country as a whole, the union had some 150 agricultural branches by the beginning of 1914; though their average membership was well below that of industrial branches, they constituted over a quarter of the total number of branches in the union. After little more than a year's organization in the field—and during a period when its industrial expansion was so rapid—this was an impressive achievement; the union had reached a position when it could justifiably claim to be a national union for agricultural workers: 'Throughout England the rural labourers have caught the spirit, and we have now a foothold in at least fourteen counties'.[22]

Having established this groundwork the union could now seriously contemplate a confrontation with the farmers. In recognition of the widely varying conditions of work in each district, and hence the differing priorities of the members themselves, a series of conferences was held in each local centre in the early months of 1914 to draw up schedules of demands. In themselves these programmes had an important agitational effect, causing a notable increase in both the size and number of branches.[23]

From the farmers the response was less clear-cut. At first the union reported that 'there are indications that the Farmers' Union may be prepared to discuss a schedule of rates of wages and code of rules for the labourers'.[24] But if the conciliatory attitude of some enlightened farmers justified this optimism, it

[22] Hornagold, *Record*, Jan. 1914.
[23] Despite the rapid expansion in industrial areas throughout this period, over half the 250 new branches opened in the first six months of 1914 were for farm labourers.
[24] *Record*, Apr. 1914. Beard launched the *Record* at the end of 1913 as the monthly organ of the Midlands district. In 1916 it was adopted by the union nationally.

was soon clear that they were a small minority. In Suffolk the
union's demands led to a lock-out in two villages where wages of
13*s.* were said to prevail; elsewhere its proposals were generally
ignored. Three thousand separate schedules of demands were
then sent to farmers in the districts involved, but few even
replied to the union. Peaceful tactics had demonstrably failed,
and in some districts the membership was ready for more
militant action. As the summer advanced, strike action won
improvements in three counties—Hereford, Gloucester, and
Wiltshire; members in several others prepared to follow suit;
elsewhere the union's strategy was to consolidate its organization in readiness for a future confrontation. By August 1914,
farm workers appeared on the verge of their first national
struggle for forty years.

DISTRICT ORGANIZATION: THE ANATOMY OF EXPANSION

In 1910 the bulk of the union's membership was concentrated
in a handful of important branches. By the outbreak of war the
number of branches had increased from under a hundred to 750,
and of these some two dozen contained over a thousand members. Though these years brought the union the status of a
genuinely national organization, the advance was more
spectacular in some areas than in others. The Midlands was
outstanding: so rapid was the expansion here that by 1914
the region provided 40 per cent of the union's total membership.
In Yorkshire and Lancashire growth was sufficient to maintain
the relative position of the districts within the union. In the
London area and in Scotland, where membership had hitherto
been negligible, significant organization was achieved; while
pioneering work in other parts of the country, previously barely
touched by trade unionism, achieved some success. But South
Wales and Northern Ireland—which together had provided
40 per cent of the union's membership at the beginning of the
decade—could not match the pace of national expansion, and
both were reduced to minor outposts.

In detailing the union's development the Midlands must
receive pride of place. In 1910 progress was uneventful, but in
the following year organization was stimulated by two notable

disputes. The Black Country to the north-west of Birmingham was notorious as a graveyard of trade unionism; according to the local official of the Engineers '... the black country temperament does not incline much towards organisation; several people have broken their hearts over fruitless labour for the bringing together of the workers into the various unions. Revivals and spasmodic efforts are popular, but their effects wear off rapidly'.[25] Earlier sorties by the Workers' Union had proved fruitless; but in 1910 it was decided that Arthur Ellery (the leader of a small Bristol society of municipal employees who had joined the union as an organizer) should be transferred to Birmingham, and he began intensive propaganda work in the area. Early in 1911 a branch was opened in the town of Bilston; two months later the union's steward at a small firm of nut and bolt makers was dismissed, and other members were ordered to leave the union. A long and bitter lock-out ensued. The police were called in to intimidate the union's members (who were mainly women); these were arrested in a body as 'disorderly persons', and fifteen who refused to pay the fines imposed were sent to gaol. Meanwhile the firm replaced the union's members by blacklegs; and after six months it was necessary to admit defeat. But the struggle served a wider function: '... the insistent nightly propaganda achieved the ... purpose of educating the workers of that and the surrounding districts to the necessity of combination'.[26] Successful union action was stimulated in other local firms, and an impetus was given for the extension of membership throughout the Black Country.

The second dispute was at the BSA factories, where the union had the largest single section of its Birmingham membership. In October 1911 some 600 craftsmen began a strike over a complicated wage grievance. They were soon followed out by between two and three thousand lower-skilled workers, male and female, some of them Workers' Union members but the large majority unorganized. When it became evident that these workers had grievances of their own, Beard helped formulate a programme of demands and joined with the officials of the craft societies in the conduct of the strike.

[25] ASE *Monthly Journal and Report*, Nov. 1911.
[26] Beard, *Record*, Mar. 1917.

The dispute had two important parallels with the strike movement which was to follow in 1913. First, the unorganized workers were not eligible for union benefit, and had no savings to fall back on. Though a relief fund was hurriedly opened, this could provide only a few shillings for each of the many strikers, and they and their families were soon near starvation. The second feature was the attitude of the general public, which could read detailed reports of the struggle in the local press. 'Public sympathy for the semi-skilled workers was most marked. . . . The general feeling was . . . that workers "ought" not to be paid such low wages.'[27] This attitude almost certainly affected the settlement reached four and a half weeks after the strike began; the skilled workers gained little more than had been offered before the strike, actually suffering a slight reduction in hourly wages, but conditions of the other workers were improved considerably. Piece-workers in particular benefited; for the first time they were guaranteed a minimum weekly rate, and prices were adjusted to give the average worker 25 per cent above this.

As with the Bilston dispute, the strike stimulated membership in the surrounding area. The organizing staff also increased: George Geobey, Secretary of the District Committee and a former BSA worker, was appointed at the end of 1911; and Billy Adamson, a member of the Patternmakers, and Julia Varley, an organizer for a local women's trade union committee, during 1912. Varley, the first woman member of the union's staff, had assisted the union during the disputes of the previous year; her appointment is largely attributable to the widespread employment of female labour in the engineering and metal trades of the Birmingham area, often at sweated rates of wages. With its new accession of strength, the union felt able to revive its demand for a general minimum wage of 23s., this time as a serious immediate objective; and towards the end of 1912 it was endorsed by the Birmingham Trades Council. The scene was set for the Black Country Strike—a struggle which rivals in significance the more famous epics of the labour movement.

[27] A. Fox, *Industrial Relations in Birmingham and the Black Country* (Oxford, B. Litt. thesis), 1952, p. 352. I am grateful to Mr. Fox for providing a copy of the relevant section of his thesis.

The Black Country Strike began as a series of unconnected disputes and culminated in a vast wave of industrial action. There were three main phases. First there was a movement, largely successful, to win the 23s. minimum at the major engineering firms in Birmingham, Smethwick, and West Bromwich. Then came strikes in Smethwick and the Black Country which caused a chain reaction. Finally the strike fever turned into an epidemic, and for six weeks around 40,000 workers were affected.

The first movement began in Soho, the traditional heart of Birmingham engineering which took in parts of Handsworth, Smethwick, and West Bromwich. The Workers' Union had a few members at the weighing-machine factory of W. & T. Avery, well-known for their opposition to trade unionism. In November 1912 the secretary of the Winson Green branch was allegedly victimized. Four hundred workers immediately stopped work, and next day over a thousand were out, the majority being non-unionists. Beard took charge of negotiations, and within a fortnight a settlement was reached: the union was recognized, district rates and conditions were applied, an immediate minimum of 21s. took effect, and the union's claim for a further 2s. advance was negotiated separately. The dispute began a ferment among the low-paid workers in the Soho factories; as Geobey, the union's organizer, remarked later: '. . . all this awakening in the district of Smethwick had followed on the action of Avery's men; it was they who struck the first blow at poverty and misery existing in the borough'.[28]

The second blow came in February 1913 at the firm of Tangyes. The company was recognized as a good employer, and already paid a minimum of 21s. But the men wanted the 23s.; they were also aggrieved that many workers operating machines had not received the customary differential above the labourers' basic rate. The strike came as a surprise both to the firm and to the union, but a fortnight's detailed negotiations brought the men their full demands.

A third major dispute occurred at the beginning of April. Men at the West Bromwich firm of United Hinges stopped work on being ordered to work night shift; there was no bonus payment for night work, and since hours were shorter than on

[28] *Smethwick Telephone*, 1 Mar. 1913.

days they would have lost money. The strike quickly spread to
the firm's female workers and to neighbouring factories. The
Workers' Union had recently started organizing at these
factories, creating the enthusiasm which led to this spontaneous
outbreak; but of 1,500 strikers, only two had six months' membership and were eligible for union benefit. Beard and Varley
took charge of the dispute and found that the women's grievances were the most serious; the majority earned well under
10s. a week, and they were not paid for work until it was
dispatched from the factory—a rule which might involve a
delay of several weeks. A minimum demand for women
workers was rapidly formulated: at first 10s., but quickly
changed to 12s. at the age of twenty-one. Additional demands
were for regular methods of payment, adjustment of piece
prices, and—to cover the male workers' grievance—the 23s.
minimum, extra pay for night shift and overtime, and advances
for special classes of work. On 19 April, exactly two weeks after
the strike had started, a settlement was reached which conceded
virtually all the union's demands.

Meanwhile, these disputes had achieved a wider effect. 'The
industrial atmosphere at that time was charged with a new
feeling of excitement and determination. It seemed as if the
success achieved by a few firms' employees had set a standard
that all workers were determined to reach. Throughout the
workshops, in the local public houses when men were having
their evening drink, the question of the Union's organization
and the minimum wage campaign were the conversation topics
of the day.'[29] Following the victory at Tangyes, labourers at
many factories began to demand the 23s. minimum, and by the
date of the West Bromwich strikes this had been conceded by
at least ten of the main firms in the Birmingham district,
including the BSA and the giant Metropolitan Carriage and
Wagon Company at Saltley; this was achieved 'in the majority
of cases . . . by friendly negotiation', in the remainder by strikes
of one or two days' duration.[30] The process continued, and by
the end of April the 23s. had been conceded 'by most of the
principal firms' in Birmingham, Smethwick, and West Bromwich, bringing an average increase of 2s. to 10,000 workers. In

[29] J. Leask and P. Bellars, *Nor Shall the Sword Sleep*, n.d., p. 9.
[30] *Daily Citizen*, 9 Apr. 1913.

this district, the main struggle for the minimum wage was now, it appeared, almost over.

The second phase of the Black Country Strike began on Friday, 25 April with a stoppage among the night shift at the Smethwick works of the Birmingham Carriage Company, where the union had recently obtained members. By Monday nearly half the 2,000 employees were out, and the factory was closed. The immediate cause of the dispute is obscure; according to the local press there was 'an inner history'. The company claimed to have already applied the 23s. minimum, and the main demand which the union formulated was for a general advance of 2s. Negotiations were held for two weeks, but ended in deadlock. It was soon clear that the strike would be a long one.

As in the previous disputes, few strikers were eligible for union benefit. A relief fund was opened, with groups of collectors touring the local streets with barrel organs, and public support was generous. The managers of some theatres gave benefit performances, many tradesmen donated food or allowed extended credit; the Smethwick Council arranged for children of strikers to be fed at school, while the Mayor appealed to landlords to exercise restraint. Frequent meetings and demonstrations were held to sustain morale, while Varley arranged special meetings of strikers' wives to ensure their support. Even so, within a month the condition of most strikers and their families was pitiable: the relief fund could provide only between 1s. and 5s. a week per household, and many families went without food for days. Yet their determination did not weaken; they had, it was said, 'been "practising starving" all their lives, so that now they were called upon to suffer privations during a strike they were used to the ordeal'.[31]

As the Smethwick carriage workers began their dispute, the strike movement spread to the Black Country. The success of the minimum wage campaign in Birmingham led the Wolverhampton Trades Council (whose secretary, Harry Bagley, was later an organizer for the Workers' Union) to begin its own agitation. Then at the end of April women members of the union at a large local engineering firm began a strike which soon spread to several departments. The union first asked only

[31] Geobey, speech quoted in *Smethwick Telephone*, 24 Apr. 1913.

5—W.U.

for a general advance, then added the demand for the general minima of 23s. and 12s. Significantly, an official explained that several firms in the Birmingham district had conceded these minima only on the understanding that they would be extended to competitors in Wolverhampton. After a fortnight the strikers accepted an offer below these figures—a settlement to which the union refused to be a party—but the unrest which they had started had already spread to other local firms. Soon the whole of Wolverhampton's industrial east end was involved in disputes.

In the second week of May the movement spread more generally in the Black Country, when labourers at the John Russell tube works, Wednesbury, struck for a 2s. advance which had been given to workers in one department. Few of the strikers were organized, but the union convened a meeting and persuaded them to include the 23s. in their demands. The firm had its headquarters at the Alma Works in Walsall, and the Wednesbury strikers marched 3 miles to press the workers there to come out in support. The Walsall tube workers were almost totally unorganized—the union's local branch, recently formed, had only a dozen members—and were understandably reluctant; but on a second attempt they were persuaded to join the stoppage. Thereafter strikes spread rapidly among the tube and hardware workers of the Black Country, some 50,000 of whom had for years, allegedly, been sweated on wages below 23s.[32] By the last week of May, though estimates conflicted, the number that had stopped work must at least have been approaching 10,000.

The final phase of the Black Country Strike brought a rapid quickening of pace, and attracted national attention. At the end of May there was still no prospect of settlement at the Smethwick Carriage Works, and the strikers decided that it was essential to extend the dispute to workers in the same trade employed by the Metropolitan Company; this firm had works at Oldbury and Wednesbury, as well as its headquarters at Saltley where the 23s. minimum was already paid. On 28 May, nearly five weeks after the start of their dispute, 1,500 Smeth-

---

[32] *Daily Citizen*, 29 May 1913. At the Russell works in Wednesbury—one of the better paid in the town—wages were as low as 18s.; while in Walsall many of the workers earned only 16s. for a 54-hour week.

wick strikers marched in formation to Oldbury, where they persuaded the workers to 'come and be men, and join us', then proceeded to Wednesbury with similar success.[33] Two days later Beard called out 200 of the Saltley members, claiming that work was being diverted there from the strike-bound factories; and almost at once the firm retaliated by locking out 7,600 workers. Within four days, the Smethwick dispute thus involved more than 10,000 additional carriage workers.

The tube trade strikers were equally anxious to extend the scale of their disputes, and the topography of the Black Country allowed them to march from town to town, calling out more workers as they went. From Wolverhampton, Wednesbury, and Walsall the unrest spread through Great Bridge and West Bromwich to Halesowen, where 5,000 men at the Coombs Wood works of Stewart and Lloyd joined the strike at the end of May. By now, newspaper estimates of the numbers involved were little more than guesses, but they provide a good indication of the speed with which the movement spread; the *Times*, for example, reported the number of strikers on successive days as 17,000, 23,000, and 30,000.[34] Of this number, however, only a part represented workers demanding the 23*s*. minimum; some were higher-paid workers with grievances of their own, or showing solidarity with the lower paid; others were made involuntarily idle by the stoppages.

The dispute had by now swept in members of other general unions, and to co-ordinate activities Beard set up a Minimum Wage Council. This in turn published a comprehensive list of demands: in addition to the 12*s*. and 23*s*. minima, a general increase of 2*s*. on all day rates and a 10 per cent advance in piece prices.

The course of the dispute now fell into some sort of routine. Throughout June the number idle fluctuated between 30,000 and 40,000; there were constant reports of individual firms conceding the 23*s*., but new strikes broke out with equal regularity. The union at first welcomed all new recruits to the struggle, particularly when 3,000 workers came out at the factory of the General Electric Company, where conditions were alleged to be particularly bad. Soon however, officials were

[33] *West Bromwich Weekly News*, 31 May 1913.
[34] 29, 30, and 31 May 1913.

attempting to discourage further strikes. But to little avail: the disputes had from the start been spontaneous in origin, and they remained so. There was some justification for the sour comment of the local ASE organizer: 'The Workers' Union is not so much directing the strikes as following them, and is making members by the thousand.'[35]

The official pressure for restraint reflected the immense problems of organizing relief. Public contributions to the central relief fund and to local committees at first provided a shilling a week to single strikers, two shillings to married men, and a further shilling to those with children. Soup kitchens catered for strikers' children, and gifts of food from the Co-ops and local traders were also distributed. But the scale of the strike (which soon involved many workers who had contributed to the early appeals) became too great for local sympathizers. A national appeal launched on 1 June produced a gratifying response, but could do no more than maintain the existing meagre level of relief. Not surprisingly, by early June it was reported that strikers were beginning to die of starvation.[36]

Predictably, the struggle erupted into occasional violence. In Walsall, where destitute strikers had been forced to resort to Poor Law relief, the Talbot Stead tube works attempted to re-open without conceding the 23s.; a crowd estimated to be 3,000 strong soon gathered and attempted to rush the factory, and the blacklegs left hurriedly. Similar events occurred elsewhere in the Black Country; the strikers were no doubt encouraged by Tom Mann's advice 'to be loyal to their unions and not too mealy-mouthed over law and order'.[37]

There was every reason to believe that the situation would deteriorate further. Most of the firms involved in the strikes were 'non-federated' (since some refused to observe trade union conditions while others were in trades not generally recognized as engineering); these now combined to form a Midland Employers' Federation. Their sole purpose was to strengthen resistance to the union; the new body declared that it would not negotiate while the strikes continued. But popular opinion was strongly in favour of some concession by the employers; and

[35] ASE *Monthly Journal and Report*, June 1913.
[36] *Daily Citizen*, 11 June 1913.
[37] Ibid., 13 June 1913.

in the middle of June, following pressure from local dignitaries, the MEF reluctantly agreed to talks.

The discussions, however, were nominally with the Allied Trades' Federation, of which the Workers' Union was a member—presumably a means of avoiding direct recognition. And the employers offered little to bring a settlement nearer. They were prepared to apply the 23s. minimum in Birmingham itself—where almost all firms of any importance had already conceded this individually—but would pay only 21s. in the Black Country. The union officials saw no justification for this differential and were unanimous in rejecting the proposals; and to demonstrate the temper of the men the union arranged a ballot which gave the employers' terms a clear rebuttal.[38]

With the breakdown in negotiations, it appeared that the employers were determined to starve the strikers into submission. During the talks, the union also had remained prepared for a continued struggle. To publicize their fight, and obtain increased financial support, deputations of strikers were despatched as hunger marchers to appeal to trade unionists throughout the country. As the marchers left Birmingham, it was also announced that failing a settlement 10,000 higher-paid metal workers would hand in their notices to assist the 'fight for the bottom dog'. It was predicted that this would be 'the hardest blow the Midland employers have yet suffered',[39] and a further series of firms hastily conceded the 23s. But despite these individual settlements around 40,000 were still out at the end of June, and each day brought increasing distress. Conflict was heightened when several of the more intransigent employers tried to reopen their works. The MEF took the opportunity to allege that most strikers remained out only as a result of intimidation; while the Engineers' district organizer, whose sympathy for the bottom dog's struggle had long since evaporated, wrote that '. . . there is now a dangerous tendency among the marching crowds which are a feature of these strikes, and while many works are being stopped under compulsion, others

[38] The Board of Trade's *Labour Gazette* gave the vote as 4,717 to 99. Union spokesmen attributed the low total poll to the fact that most members thought such a ballot wholly unnecessary. Only strikers (not those involuntarily laid off) were allowed to vote.

[39] *Daily Citizen*, 18 June 1913.

are being closed down because of possible trouble.'[40] Certainly the allegations of violence were not unfounded. Thus at Fellows Ltd., Bilston, the scene of the strike of 1911, a large crowd of strikers tried to storm the works gates, stoned the hundred and fifty policemen who were posted there, and succeeded in inducing the blacklegs to stop work. By the beginning of July such reports were becoming increasingly common.

At this point the Labour Department of the Board of Trade[41] intervened. An official had been sent to learn the facts of the dispute at the end of May, and again at the beginning of June; but it was discovered that negotiations were to take place, and the official machinery was never used while an autonomous settlement appeared possible. Within two days of the announcement of the vote against the employers' offer, the Chief Industrial Commissioner, Sir George Askwith, arrived personally in Birmingham and almost immediately brought the two sides together. By now, the strength of the union's case for the 23s. had increased, for the first two days of July brought several reports of major Black Country firms conceding the demand. Those firms maintaining resistance were becoming increasingly isolated, and public opinion, as voiced through the local press, was now convinced that the metal trades as a whole could afford to pay a living wage. Though the bargaining remained hard, the MEF was now more conciliatory, and a draft agreement was reached on 7 July. In Birmingham, Smethwick, and Oldbury the 23s. was agreed without qualification; elsewhere, the minimum would be raised at once to 22s., and after six months to 23s. For women, the general 12s. minimum was conceded. Elaborate provisions for avoiding future disputes were also agreed.

The settlement was however notable by the absence of any concession to the demand for a general advance of 2s. and a 10 per cent increase in piece-rates. Thus the strikers at the Smethwick carriage works, who had been out the longest and had endured the greatest hardship, gained nothing; in the Black Country many of the semi-skilled workers, who had often played key roles in the dispute, were similarly placed.

[40] ASE *Monthly Journal and Report*, July 1913.
[41] The forerunner of the Ministry of Labour, established in 1916.

Understandably, jubilation at the settlement was not universal. In Walsall, a Mr Thickett advised strikers to smash the 'cursed agreement', and a mass meeting voted unanimously against its acceptance; elsewhere, union officials reported threats of personal violence.[42] Strenuous efforts were however made to overcome this opposition; it was pointed out that the cases of piece-workers and the semi-skilled could be negotiated directly with individual firms; the minimum wage demand had been the central element in the struggle, and it was the settlement of this issue which was the most urgent need. These arguments eventually had their effect—the agreement was accepted by a vote of 4,944 to 1,236; but the small number who participated perhaps indicates that a sizeable proportion of strikers remained dissatisfied.

Acceptance of the employers' terms was soon shown to be justified. The concession of the 23s. minimum brought increases of around 5s. to thousands of Black Country labourers; to have instructed them to stay out in support of the higher-paid could have caused a fatal loss of unity. As it was, the strikers returned as a body with the machinery available to continue negotiations. And indeed, it is clear from the number of increases recorded during subsequent months that the establishment of the 23s. minimum did have the effect of raising wages generally. The agreement, according to Askwith, 'created quite a new spirit in the Midlands',[43] while Beard could report that 'as far as the Midland Employers' Federation is concerned, we have hardly had a complaint, and when a case has cropped up it has been dealt with satisfactorily'.[44]

'A most remarkable strike'—one can scarcely quarrel with Arthur Ellery's comment as the dispute reached its height.[45] The central feature was of course the tactic of the minimum wage demand—an unprecedented step in this area, where labourers' wages varied considerably from firm to firm, and even within the same factory. To some extent the demand was a parallel to the craft unionists' district rate, as is clear from Beard's advice to the first tube trade strikers in Wednesbury: 'We pointed out the futility of an advance of a few shillings a

[42] *Times*, 9, 10, and 11 July 1913.
[43] G. R. Askwith, *Industrial Problems and Disputes*, 1920, p. 256.
[44] *Annual Report*, 1913.   [45] Quoted in *Daily Citizen*, 31 May 1913.

week without any minimum being established, and we convinced them that such a method of advance could produce only temporary results, as in less than six months many new hands would be found who had started at the old rates, thus menacing the new rates.'[46] But the novel feature was that the movement sought a *universal* minimum for workers in a range of diverse metal trades—one that would apply to the least skilled labourer, and also, at a lower level, to women and young workers. This tactic did not stem from any lack of confidence among the workers in their ability to pursue sectional demands. Special payments were already customary for work which required special aptitude, and two years earlier the union's District Committee had fixed a schedule of standard rates for a range of semi-skilled grades. Moreover, such key workers as boilermen had already learned their strategic power to bring a whole works to a standstill. During the Black Country Strike the Wednesbury case to which Beard referred was typical of many in which semi-skilled with a sectional grievance stopped work, only afterwards extending their demands, at the request of union officials, to include all their fellow-workers. In the end it was these workers, more highly paid than their fellows, who alone failed to benefit directly from the strike settlement, yet who were persuaded, albeit reluctantly, to accept the agreement. Thus the weakest sections gained large advances with the support—and perhaps even, in the short run, at the expense —of their stronger comrades. This was made possible partly by the skill with which the union's officials handled the struggle, and persuaded all sections to fight for one overriding objective; partly also by the genuine solidarity which the strikers displayed in preferring a living wage for all to special advantages for a few. How much this solidarity owed to the union's earlier work of education it is impossible to say; but certainly this aspect of the dispute was one in which its officials took a justifiable pride. 'In the Midlands', Beard wrote later, 'we can hold our own against craft and sectional prejudice, and we are able to declare that the Workers' Union stands for class as against craft'.[47]

As a consequence of the strike the union reaped a massive increase in membership, considerable in Birmingham, and even greater in the Black Country. In Smethwick, West Bromwich,

[46] *Record*, August 1917.   [47] *Record*, Nov. 1915.

Oldbury, Dudley, Wednesbury, Walsall, and Wolverhampton there was a combined membership of 250 in 1910; each town held over 1,000 members by 1914. By the outbreak of war, Birmingham and the Black Country provided a quarter of the union's total membership, while six full-time organizers covered the district.

Elsewhere in the Midlands major advances in organization occurred, though rarely on a comparable scale. The most notable achievement was in Coventry, where the union was able to recruit a considerable semi-skilled membership in the expanding cycle and motor vehicle trades. A claim for a minimum hourly wage of 6*d.*, formulated soon after the union's branch was reopened in 1906, became the basis of a serious campaign in 1912. Early in 1913 a strike was called, and 'after a short, sharp, well organised conflict', centred mainly at the Humber, Daimler, and Ordnance works, the union's demands were conceded in full: a minimum wage of 26*s*. 6*d*. for a 53-hour week, with overtime pay on the same basis as for craftsmen.[48] Shortly afterwards, the union signed the Provisions for Avoiding Disputes with the Employers' Association—its first such 'recognition' agreement with a local member of the Employers' Federation. This victory, though understandably overshadowed by the Black Country Strike, was in some ways even more spectacular; the three days' strike won advances larger both relatively and absolutely than those in the Black Country, and this despite the noticeable coolness of the established unions.

Other Midland branches which in the previous decade maintained a precarious existence expanded rapidly after 1910. The leading member of the Swadlincote clay and pipe workers, Joe Clark, was appointed a full-time organizer in 1911; not only did he increase local membership and negotiate important improvements in conditions; he was also able to organize the low-paid brewery workers in nearby Burton, recruiting a membership of 4,000 by 1914, and established a minimum wage of 23*s*. with other concessions. Similar progress was recorded in Derby. Elsewhere in the Midlands organization was established in completely virgin territory, with full-time officials covering the region from Stoke-on-Trent in the north

---

[48] Beard, *Annual Report*, 1913. The Coventry agreement established basic rate that were, with London, the highest in the country.

to Nottingham and Lincoln in the east and Gloucester and Swindon in the south.

In other areas the pace of growth was less dramatic but still remarkable. In Manchester the new decade brought rapid gains. In 1910 a branch was opened for permanent way workers on the Corporation tramways, and within a year substantial improvements in wages and conditions were obtained; this success led in turn to extensive recruitment among municipal employees. In 1911 there was a major advance among the engineering labourers who formed the original nucleus of local membership. A protracted strike, involving at its peak 3,000 workers, ended with the establishment of a minimum wage of 21s., higher rates for specified grades of workers, and a reduction in hours. As well as bringing wage increases of up to 5s., this was the first minimum wage agreement which the union obtained in any district.

This victory allowed George Titt, the local official, to recruit nearly 5,000 new members in the district. Subsequently the work of organization was extended through South Lancashire to Cheshire and North Wales. Expansion also occurred in the Preston area (which remained under the control of the union's Yorkshire office). Membership here was reputedly 'exceptionally keen',[49] and important concessions were won by militant action.[50] As in the Midlands, new organizers were appointed to cater for the expanded membership.

In Yorkshire, the Halifax branch remained predominant, but organization extended rapidly throughout the Calder valley. The membership in this district was perhaps the most varied in the whole union: improvements were negotiated for engineering, foundry, and boiler workers; gasworkers, roadmen, and other council employees; builders' labourers, brickmakers, and quarrymen; textile mill labourers and maintenance workers; brewery and malting workers; and many other categories. Local organization also extended to cover engineering workers in Leeds and Huddersfield, where full-time officials were ap-

[49] Morley, *Annual Report*, 1914.
[50] Most significant was an agreement that 'any labourer being put upon a semi-skilled job, he shall have 1s. per week advance three months after starting, and then nine months after that another 1s., and his wage advanced after that according to his proficiency'. This was almost certainly the first time that such a principle was formally established by any union.

pointed. Membership also increased in South Yorkshire, and new branches were opened for metal workers in Sheffield and Doncaster.

In South Wales the union had its share of spectacular disputes. At the Dowlais steelworks, twelve years of organization received its reward in 1911. Action was precipitated by a strike among the lowest-paid workers earning only 1s. 11d. a day. According to Giles '. . . we had to take our courage in both hands and advise the whole of the men to "down tools". . . . The men acted splendidly. On Monday a few men struck work—on Wednesday the huge steel works were silent; the following day I was sent for by the general manager, and on Friday an agreement was come to.'[51] The settlement brought recognition for the Workers' Union and other societies, a minimum day rate of 3s., and higher pay for all workers. In Swansea the union's main struggle was a strike which began at the end of 1912. Spelter workers had long objected to their seven-day working week, which increased the dangers of lead poisoning; but the employers insisted that a six-day week would be uneconomical. A serious campaign of agitation was launched by Matt Giles in 1912; and in the following year a number of workers who attended a Sunday protest meeting were dismissed. The nine weeks' strike which ensued failed to achieve the workers' main demand, but extra pay was conceded for Sunday work. The union was more successful at the Cardiff flour and grain mills. In 1911 the local branch, opened in the previous year, was swollen by a flood of recruits; over two thousand joined in a single week. A short dispute won higher weekly wages and special overtime rates; and in 1912 a longer strike gained further improvements. These dramatic events raised membership in the area to 12,000 by the outbreak of war; in itself an impressive achievement, but unable to compare with the progress nationally.

The record of the Irish branches was far more disappointing. The union actually lost membership in several districts, often after defeat in strike action. Joe Harris, the local organizer, blamed the explosive political situation. 'Local prejudice is very strong', he reported, 'and feeling runs very high. This is used by the employing and capitalist class to divide the

[51] *Annual Report*, 1911.

workers.'[52] By the beginning of 1913 it seemed that his task was hopeless, and he was therefore transferred to assist Giles in South Wales and the West of England.

One of the first assignments covered by Harris was in Cornwall. Organization in this area dated only from 1911, when several branches were opened in the St. Austell claymining district. A local organizer, C. R. Vincent, was appointed—'a bold step in the face of the general bitter hostility to trade unionism in the county at this time'[53]—and agitation commenced around the demand for a wage of 25s., in place of the existing rate of 18s. received by most workers. The employers ignored the application when it was submitted in 1912; but trade was booming, and several gave their workers an increase of 1s. 6d. in an attempt to forestall union organization. But workers joined the union in greater numbers, agitation increased, and in April 1913 Vincent obtained executive sanction to take strike action as soon as conditions appeared favourable. Still the employers refused to meet the union; but in June the largest clay company offered its men a further 1s. 6d. The wage of 21s. thus established was immediately taken up by the union as a minimum demand at all other firms, and a recruitment campaign was launched on the basis of this more modest demand.

The union was faced with a sudden dilemma when at the end of July a strike began at the small Carne Stents pit. Of some five thousand clayworkers in mid-Cornwall, only a small proportion had as yet been organized; yet if the union failed to support the strikers it would openly admit its impotence. A delegate conference resolved the problem, calling a general stoppage. Groups of strikers marched from pit to pit, and soon the whole area was at a standstill.

For a month the strike remained solid. But the employers clearly hoped to win the struggle by attrition; they refused to negotiate with the union, and rejected an offer of mediation by Sir George Askwith. Instead a number of employers announced

[52] Ibid.

[53] J. Ravensdale, 'The Workers' Union' (unpublished typescript). I am grateful to Mr. Ravensdale for the loan of a copy of this account of the clayworkers' organization, and for other information concerning the dispute of 1913. Geographically isolated, and in a glutted labour market, the Cornish workers had been unorganized since the 1870s.

that they would re-open their works for any employees who wished to return. They had misjudged the mood of the strikers; only in Bugle was there any significant blacklegging, and here a few violent incidents occurred.

This was enough to persuade the local authorities (which of course reflected the class interests of the employers) to intervene, and a large body of extra police was called in from South Wales. This brought a new element to an already explosive situation. Within days of their arrival the new police made an apparently unprovoked attack on Beard, who with other union officials had come to assist in the dispute; according to his own statement he was in a picket with five strikers when a group of police sprang on him, knocked him down, and kicked and punched him. Hours later, a large detachment of the Glamorgan police made a baton charge against a peaceful group of strikers; according to an eye-witness, 'a struggling, seething crowd was reduced to dazed and startled units as one by one they fell bleeding and groaning to the ground amid the shrieks and screams of the women onlookers';[54] among the wounded were Vincent and Julia Varley. This incident led to widespread protests within the labour movement, including an emergency resolution at the TUC expressing 'its deepest indignation at the brutal conduct of the police'; while locally it was widely reported that the police had been liberally supplied with beer by the employers, and anger was sufficiently widespread for the 'Glamorgans' to experience a general boycott by local tradesmen.

The police violence brought the dispute national publicity, and helped swell the strike fund; while a ballot, held to disprove the employers' claim that most strikers were now willing to return to work, showed a majority of 2,258 to 558 for staying out. But this show of determination was deceptive, for there was a slow but continuous increase in the amount of blacklegging; as union officials had feared at the outset, the clayworkers' experience of trade unionism was too brief for unity to be maintained throughout a protracted dispute. By the beginning of October, ten weeks after the start of the strike, the employers felt strong enough to announce their intention of a general re-opening of work; ten days were offered during which strikers

[54] *Cornish Guardian*, 5 Sept. 1913.

could return without victimization. Another delegate meeting was held, and the officials advised that it would be useless to continue the dispute. The men returned to work with their organization intact, admitting 'a reverse, but not a defeat'.[55]

The wisdom of this decision was soon demonstrated. Harris stayed on to take charge of Devon and Cornwall as a separate organizing district, and membership among clayworkers continued to increase. The employers were clearly impressed; in January 1914, three months after the end of the strike, the principal company announced a conference of workers at which unionists might be represented by their officials. The result was an agreement giving substantial increases in pay and other improvements. The example of the leading firm caused others to follow suit, conceding recognition and advances; and by the summer of 1914 the union had established almost complete organization among the clayworkers.

Two other new organizing areas were opened during this period. In December 1911 George Kerr, a Glasgow organizer for the ILP, was appointed to extend the union's Scottish membership—then numbering 250 and contained in five branches.[56] By 1914 he had succeeded in building up forty branches with 9,000 members. Most of the growth came in Glasgow; among those organized were foundry and building trade labourers, railway shopmen, and brewery workers. Elsewhere, the union's outstanding success was among the herring barrel makers in the East Scotland fishing ports. Though coopering was a skilled occupation, the men were wholly unorganized—possibly because many were migratory workers, travelling to England when the summer fishing season ended in Scotland. In the spring of 1913 Kerr began recruitment, and by the autumn an almost complete organization was established. A programme of demands covering time and piece rates, hours of work, and overtime was put to the employers; under threat of strike action the union obtained almost complete satisfaction. By the end of the year the Workers' Union claimed 3,000 members in the

[55] Giles, quoted in *St. Austell Star*, 9 Oct. 1913. A more detailed account of the 'White Country Strike' than is possible here is given by Ravensdale, loc cit. An unpublished memoir was written in 1963 by Mr. F. Greet, a member of the original strike committee; a lengthy ballad written in 1913 also exists.

[56] Previously, Morley had had to travel from Yorkshire whenever this tiny membership required assistance.

trade, with eleven branches in Scotland and three in England, and with their own full-time official.

The other new organizing district was London and Southern England. The collapse of the union's initial London membership has already been described; at the beginning of 1910 there were only four branches in the London area—Kennington, Rotherhithe, Erith, and Colchester—sharing a membership of under a hundred; no other branch was nearer London than Swindon and Coventry. When a local society in Portsmouth joined the union in 1910, the new branch had to be placed under the charge of Giles in Swansea; and when Colchester members were involved in a strike in the same year, Titt had to come down from Manchester to settle the dispute.

Subsequently there was some improvement in the London situation, with organization among South London engineering workers boosted by the amalgamation of a small trade society at Woolwich Arsenal. The new membership was keen to receive material assistance from the union's Executive; but 'the GEC were exceedingly sceptical. They were not very anxious to give us money or organisers. . . . It had been tried before and failure had resulted.'[57] In 1913 the union's leaders eventually yielded, appointing as organizer George Dallas, a Scottish socialist who had previously worked for the National Federation of Women Workers. This investment paid rapid dividends. Progress was judged sufficient for four further organizers to be appointed by the summer of 1914, and for the London area to be constituted a separate Executive division—a privilege for which several other districts pressed unsuccessfully.

In Essex there was also a rapid advance, following a strike at Chelmsford in May 1913. Unorganized workers at the Hoffman ball-bearing factory, some of whom were said to earn as little as $3\frac{1}{2}d$. an hour, struck work, and the dispute soon spread to almost all the 1,800 employees. Dallas was asked to assist, and organized the men into a Workers' Union Branch, helping to formulate a demand for a 5d. minimum. The strikers were supported by collections in the surrounding towns and villages, and after a fortnight they achieved success. The publicity attracted by the dispute helped spread organization through the surrounding area. In Braintree, a large branch was formed from silk

[57] C. W. Gibson, *Record*, Oct. 1919.

workers at Courtaulds and metal workers at Crittalls, and substantial improvements were conceded by both firms after strike action. Important achievements were also recorded in Colchester; while the Eastern Counties generally were a major centre of recruitment for farm workers during 1914. Organization was also extended further west into Bedford and Oxfordshire, notably at the Witney blanket mills.

INTER-UNION RELATIONS

From the outset, the Workers' Union was committed to the aim of closer unity within the labour movement. In its first year it affiliated to the Trades Union Congress; in 1899 it joined the newly-formed General Federation of Trade Unions. But such were the union's financial straits that the modest affiliation fees proved too heavy a burden, and in 1900 it left both bodies (though it maintained an unbroken membership in the Labour Party).

The GFTU never again attracted the union's interest; but membership of the TUC offered more evident advantages, and in August 1913 the union's executive decided to investigate the possibility of re-affiliation. Three months later a formal application was submitted; but the union found its approach rebuffed. The Parliamentary Committee (forerunner of the present General Council) shelved the application; and there the matter rested until July 1914, when the union withdrew its request in disgust.

The treatment which the Workers' Union received reflected the displeasure which its very success had caused among a number of established members of the TUC. There were two main objections to the union's activities, and in subsequent years these were heard with increasing regularity. First, the Workers' Union was accused of recruiting members of other societies; it was, according to its critics, 'notorious for poaching'.[58] Certainly, charges of this nature were occasionally substantiated; but there is little evidence to suggest that such poaching was part of a deliberate policy. General unions were particularly vulnerable to allegations of this kind: by their

[58] A. Pugh, *Men of Steel*, 1951, p. 84. Cf. G. D. H. Cole, *Organised Labour*, 1914, p. 92.

nature they competed for membership with many other societies, among workers who often moved from job to job and from union to union. However careful an organizer might be, it was easy to poach members of other societies as much by accident as by design; and in all unions there were some officials, lay and full-time, who were not always careful about such matters. But it was rare indeed for a charge of deliberate poaching to be substantiated, and there is no evidence that the Workers' Union was any worse an offender than the other general unions.[59] Almost certainly its special notoriety was the direct result of its dramatic rate of growth; so great was the union's success that it was easy to believe that its methods *must* have been unfair.

More complex was the frequent complaint that the union recruited workers who, while not already trade unionists, ought properly to have been left to other organizations. The union, according to such critics, possessed 'oecumenical ambitions',[60] and acted as 'a sort of embryonic Industrial Workers of the World with all labour for its province'.[61] Certainly there is evidence to support such a view. The ideal of 'One Big Union' to unite all workers (which dated back to the Owenite movement of the early 1830s) was revived by the Social-Democratic Federation when Mann was still a member, and the same objective was frequently expressed when the Workers' Union was established. The slogan 'One Big Union' was itself later adopted (somewhat self-consciously) by the union's leaders; and their expansionist attitudes, as will be suggested later, were an important element in their success.

But in general the union's actions scarcely matched such ambitious pretensions. From the outset—as was seen in the previous chapter—it shrank from any policy which might offend established craft societies, disclaiming the original intention of recruiting skilled workers; and throughout the pre-war period the union's leaders continued to describe their organization as catering for the lower-skilled. Some conflicts

---

[59] During the twelve years that the union was subsequently affiliated to the TUC, only ten formal complaints were laid against it, and only four of these were found to be justified.

[60] Hobsbawm, *Economic History Review*, 1949, pp. 136–7.

[61] Cole, *Introduction to Trade Unionism*, 1918, p. 17.

were indeed inevitable: in a trade union movement containing craft, industrial, and general organizations there were bound to be serious problems of demarcation. But these applied to all general unions; there was little basis for special criticism of the Workers' Union.

However, in two industries the role of the Workers' Union could be distinguished from that of other general unions. It alone was involved in agriculture (though other general unions had in the past tried their hand here; and the 'industrial' union of farm workers which was formed in 1906 showed few aspirations at this time to organize on a national scale). More important was the union's status in engineering, which was in some respects distinctive. It has been seen that the union differed from all other general unions in its strong core of membership among semi-skilled production workers; the implications of this fact for relations with established unions were considerable. An organization based on unskilled labourers held little inherent bargaining power, and was almost wholly dependent on the goodwill of the craft societies.[62] When craftsmen went on strike, both they and their employers normally assumed that they would eventually reach a settlement and return to their jobs; but if labourers stopped work it was far easier for an employer to find replacements off the streets, and they knew this. But the situation of the semi-skilled worker who had become proficient on a complex machine tool was closer to that of the craftsman than to that of the labourer; he was difficult to replace quickly, and his employer suffered heavy losses if expensive mechanized plant was standing idle. There could have been no more convincing demonstration of this fact than the rapid success of the Coventry strike in 1913. Moreover, the semi-skilled could lend their own strength to the demands of the labourers, when both sections were organized in the same union; this was shown clearly in the Black Country Strike, and indeed in many other districts where the Workers' Union had members.

The semi-skilled machine-workers did not appreciate their own strength in many cases until long after they had become

---

[62] Thus the NAUL and the Gasworkers were members of the Federation of Engineering and Shipbuilding Trades, having given undertakings satisfactory to the craft societies.

organized; nor did the union officials, for the conventional opinion was that such workers were mere labourers. It seemed obvious that nothing could be achieved without the support of the craft societies, and the union acted accordingly. This strategy came into question only when the craft societies themselves ruptured the existing cordial relationships. One example occurred in Birmingham in 1911. The craft societies had admitted the union to their Engineering and Allied Trades Federation, and when at the end of 1910 this body took advantage of the improved trade to launch a wage movement, the union helped formulate the demands—'the first time', according to Beard, 'that the Workers' Union has ever been involved in such a movement'.[63] But when an advance was agreed in the following year, the employers insisted that only the higher-paid workers should benefit, and the skilled unions accepted this position. Beard later argued that the event convinced him of the need to build an organization strong enough to act independently. In Coventry, a breach occurred over the machine question; the craft societies demanded as the price of their support that Workers' Union members should refuse to operate machines which were claimed for skilled workers. The branch refused to submit to the principle 'that the lower-paid must remain the lower-paid, mere fetchers and carriers and tea-brewers';[64] and its members had perforce to rely on their own strength.

Friction could also occur over recruitment. On one occasion, indeed, an official of the ASE alleged that 'fitters, turners, smiths, etc.' had been enrolled by the Workers' Union: 'men who have resisted all inducements to join the skilled unions for which they are eligible are paying their shilling entrance fee and consider themselves trade unionists as soon as they can get a button in their coats'.[65] No evidence was offered to substantiate this colourful indictment; indeed the union at this date was still scrupulously applying its own rules and turning away any workers it thought eligible for a craft society. Nevertheless, a genuine basis of conflict did exist. With the growth of

[63] *Annual Report*, 1910.
[64] Beard, *Record*, Nov. 1918. This breach occurred at some date between 1910 and 1912.
[65] ASE *Monthly Journal and Report*, June 1913.

mechanization and the declining importance of apprenticeship, the borderline between skilled and semi-skilled was becoming increasingly arbitrary; and it was in the Midlands that technological advance had made this problem most acute. It would have been understandable if an ASE organizer had included a wide range of machine tools within the skilled category; but Beard—who unlike most Workers' Union officials at this period had himself no craft background—may have drawn a different boundary. It is not hard to imagine the recriminations which could result from such differences.

The union's growing strength was in itself a cause of apprehension within the ASE. The strike of Manchester labourers in 1911 had put a thousand craftsmen out of work—an uncomfortable reversal of traditional roles. The Coventry dispute of 1913 had alarmingly narrowed the customary differential between the pay of skilled and semi-skilled. No wonder that some craftsmen felt their status threatened: 'when the membership of a semi-skilled union rises from 5,000 to 65,000 in less than four years, and nearly trebles in less than twelve months, we get dictatorship'.[66] It must be emphasized that in 1914 it was only in a small minority of districts that the Workers' Union found itself in conflict with the craft societies, or had even contemplated acting independently of them; in most areas members still accepted without question their status as lower-skilled workers in a subordinate union.

Nationally it is apparent that the union saw its status as analogous to that of other general workers' organizations, for it was an active participant in schemes to achieve closer unity among them. As early as 1902 it took part in an abortive attempt to amalgamate twelve general unions; six years later it helped establish a General Labourers' National Council, designed to ease inter-union relations by arranging the mutual recognition of cards and transfers of membership. Through this body it was involved from 1910 in new efforts to achieve amalgamation (efforts which were to show a marked lack of any sense of urgency on the part of the various societies involved); and a ballot held in 1911 showed the membership overwhelmingly in favour of the principle of a merger of all general unions.

[66] Ibid., Jan. 1914.

The Workers' Union, through Duncan, made an important proposal for consideration by the other participants in the discussions. So far amalgamation had been conceived in terms of a straightforward and complete merger; but this involved two difficulties. First, the differing contributions, friendly benefits, and financial reserves of the various unions had to be combined in a manner acceptable to the membership of each; second, the law required the consent of two-thirds of the members of each union involved—and to persuade so high a proportion of a union's members to cast their votes at all was, then as now, a herculean task. Duncan's suggestion was that, as a first step, the unions should agree on a partial amalgamation. A common fund should be established, to which each should contribute on the basis of membership, and which would be used to pay dispute benefit and all the expenses of organization. A joint executive would control the fund, direct the whole work of recruitment and bargaining, and sanction all disputes. But until a complete merger was achieved, each union would remain responsible for its own friendly benefits. Such a scheme would not be viewed legally as an amalgamation, and could therefore be implemented by an ordinary majority of those voting in each union. Duncan's aim, he explained, was to create 'a slippery slope on which, once a union embarked, there would be no drawing back, excepting at a very big financial sacrifice'.[67]

The Workers' Union demonstrated the strength of its commitment to the eventual aim of a single general union, by offering to finance secretarial assistance to co-ordinate subsequent discussions. But this offer was not taken up, and lengthy delays ensued. By 1913 a further complication had emerged: the National Transport Workers' Federation also decided in favour of an amalgamation of its member unions; and since several of these were also affiliated to the GLNC, it was necessary to unite the proposals of both bodies. Further talks led to a joint conference in July 1914 at which thirty-one unions were represented, and after lengthy discussions a common scheme of amalgamation was agreed. A rapid consummation was now

[67] C. Duncan, *Statement Relating to the Question of Amalgamation*, dated 13 Nov. 1916. Published by the Workers' Union, London, probably for internal circulation only.

expected: but within a month the war had nipped all amalgamation efforts in the bud.

What explains the tremendous success of the Workers' Union in these four pre-war years? In part it benefited from conditions which helped all trade unions extend their coverage: full employment which increased workers' bargaining strength, and rising prices which were a spur to organization.

General unions did particularly well for a number of reasons. They covered sections of workers who at the beginning of the decade were so badly organized that spectacular advance was possible; such feats of organization were clearly not open to unions which were already well established, and were restricted to specific groups of workers. When sections of workers had been hitherto unorganized, they were typically uncertain of their own collective strength, whilst their employers were bitterly hostile to attempts to introduce trade unionism; these obstacles could normally be overcome only by a decisive demonstration of strength—membership *had* to increase explosively. At the same time, such a feat was extremely difficult; so the factors which assisted other unions were of crucial importance in allowing them to make this breakthrough wholesale. And whereas the explosive upsurges of general unionism which occurred on several occasions in the nineteenth century involved hastily improvised organization, in 1910 general unions were already established and able to take immediate advantage of favourable conditions.[68] Finally, the development of large-scale mechanized production in a range of manufacuring industries was of great importance. The emerging process workers were seen as mere 'labourers', but events showed them to possess great potential as trade unionists, while the fact that they earned labourers' wages often allowed a wide margin for successful trade union action.

While all these factors applied to the Workers' Union, there

[68] Any large trade union requires an elaborate structure of organization, with officials—local and national, lay and full-time—who are competent in administration and negotiation. For unions of relatively unskilled and uneducated workers this could present major problems; any union which had to develop such an organization spontaneously was particularly handicapped.

were three additional reasons for its exceptional performance. First, there was an element of chance: its existing foothold among Midland engineering and metal workers allowed it to exploit a vast reserve of unorganized production workers; without this initial basis it might never have acquired a national membership in this industry.

Secondly, the structure of organization in the Workers' Union contributed to its success. In the Gasworkers, the basic unit of organization was the semi-autonomous district; the full-time District Secretaries, together with a lay representative from each district, formed the central executive. To open a new district was a major step, involving the staffing of a new district office and the adjustment of the central machinery. The executive members showed themselves extremely reluctant to agree to so large an investment or to dilute their own authority with the creation of a new district. In the NAUL, authority was held by a lay executive drawn from the union's original centre of organization on the North-East Coast; this showed an extreme reluctance to delegate responsibility to full-time officials or to increase administrative expenses. The appointment of a new full-time organizer was therefore a major policy issue which could involve months of debate. The structure of the Workers' Union was far more flexible. It was possible to open a new district or appoint new organizers without rule book restrictions and without affecting the structure of government. Organizers for the most part worked from their own homes without secretarial assistance; new appointments thus involved no important expense beyond the official's own wages; and they could be made in the first instance on a probationary basis. A proposal by the President or Secretary to open a new area, or a request by an existing organizer for assistance in his district, could therefore be discussed solely on its merits, and was normally agreed without dissent.[69]

A final distinguishing characteristic of the Workers' Union was its attitude to growth. Such unions as the Gasworkers and

---

[69] In this period the Executive met with increasing frequency, a larger membership bringing more numerous problems; by 1914 meetings were held at least once a month. But there was a rapid turnover in E.C. membership, and the executive as a whole normally accepted without question the guidance of the far more experienced national officers.

the NAUL in 1910 already possessed a sizeable national membership, and with it a position of standing in the trade union movement. By reckless action these assets might be lost; and the machinery of both unions was dominated by members still affected by the trauma of the disastrous losses of the 1890s which followed the heady years of rapid growth. For nearly twenty years their officials had been obliged to concentrate on those sections of workers who had proved their value as steady trade unionists; and the siege mentality remained. The main rivals of the Workers' Union were thus 'almost pathetically cautious. They hoarded their funds, appointed new officers only with extreme reluctance, and absolutely refused to alter their structures'.[70] But the Workers' Union, at the start of the decade, had virtually nothing to lose. It had been formed in 1898 to bring trade unionism to the mass of unorganized workers, and despite the subsequent reverses its leaders had not abandoned this objective.

Like the officials of other general unions, Duncan and Morley had themselves endured the cycle of growth and collapse, and had no illusions that future conditions would be easy. But they remained committed to expansion, and were ready at the outset to exploit the favourable circumstances of a new decade. In making their union the biggest advertiser in the trade union movement, or in appointing organizers in areas where no membership as yet existed, they showed an unprecedented willingness to invest in growth. The vigorous image which the union presented was assisted by such spectacular successes as the Black Country Strike; while its very name proved an advantage, for potential members could have no doubts whether the union covered their job or not: 'they were workers and therefore eligible to join; it was as simple as that'.[71] The vigorous approach of the union's leaders proved infectious; the rank and file were urged to become amateur organizers, and many responded to the call. The union clearly believed that no section of the working class was incapable of organization; determined effort must eventually succeed. At times this

---

[70] H. A. Clegg and A. F. Thompson, *History of British Trade Unionism*, vol. 2 (draft typescript). I am grateful for the opportunity to consult this at present unpublished volume.

[71] R. Sargood, 'Notes re the Workers' Union' (MS., 1965).

approach led to failures; but it also meant that the Workers' Union could achieve success where other unions refused to make any serious attempt at recruitment.

Thus the summer of 1914 saw the union in its fourth year of rapid growth, and still expanding at a spectacular pace throughout the country. For members and officials alike this was seen as merely the beginning. 'The fringe has only yet been touched', wrote Duncan, 'of the possibilities latent in the present industrial situation. . . . Let us stick to the task . . . , and we can build a monument by our industry that the world will admire'.[72] The form that subsequent expansion might have taken, but for the outbreak of war, is one of history's many might-have-beens.

[72] *Annual Report*, 1913.

4

CONSOLIDATION 1914–1920

THE First World War and the immediate post-war years formed a crucial stage in the development of the modern trade union movement. Numerically, the change was striking: though the war had an initially disruptive effect on membership, this soon gave way to expansion, and by 1920 the number of organized workers was double its pre-war level. Equally notable was the new status of the trade union movement, 'radically enhanced almost overnight'.[1] The twin demands of military recruitment and war production made the co-operation of organized labour essential to the Government; in consequence, through representation on official committees and by direct consultation trade unionists were persuaded to support Government policy on labour questions, and could in turn press their own demands on the Government. Trade unionism's new-found respectability was further emphasized by the Whitley Reports of 1917–18, which stressed the desirability of union recognition and proposed permanent joint machinery in every industry— machinery which would not only determine wages and conditions but also consider 'matters affecting the progress and well-being of the trade'—and by the National Industrial Conference of 1919, convened by the Government to formulate proposals for the regulation of post-war industrial relations. Finally the nature of collective bargaining altered markedly during these years. The almost continuous rise in prices—which at their peak in 1920 stood at almost three times their pre-war level—was national in incidence and created a demand for standard national wage advances; and these were generally provided, during the latter half of the war, under the system of compulsory arbitration. This sytem also led to an extension of organization amongst employers, and allowed negotiations at national level to take place in many industries for the first time.

[1] H. A. Clegg and T. E. Chester in A. D. Flanders and H. A. Clegg, *The System of Industrial Relations in Britain*, 1954, p. 330.

Following the Whitley recommendations, the formation of Joint Industrial Councils made national bargaining over wages and conditions increasingly the norm.

All these trends were clearly reflected in the development of the Workers' Union. Membership rose from just over 140,000 at the outbreak of war to 379,000 at the end of 1918, and was claimed as 500,000 at its post-war peak. In absolute terms, this growth exceeded that of any other British union; while in percentage terms the wartime increase was behind only a few societies whose pre-war membership had been insignificant, and that of the two post-war years was among the best.

The union stood up well to the first months of war, when many sections of industry were dislocated, and unemployment was the main fear of the labour movement. Demands on the union's out-of-work fund rose only briefly; and though losses of membership occurred in some areas, these were outweighed by new recruitment in the expanding war industries. The pre-war pace of expansion was cut drastically; but the Workers' Union was one of the few British unions to record any increase (some 20,000 members) in the last five months of 1914. In the following year the union continued to grow at a similar rate; membership reached nearly 200,000, far above that of the rival general unions. But there was an ominous feature to this progress: over 40,000 members lapsed during the year. The turnover problem deteriorated rapidly; as a result, while recruitment of new members did not slacken in 1916, total membership remained static. In the following year 200,000 new entrants were enrolled—a number equalling total membership at the start of the year—but the net gain was little more than 30,000. By contrast, the Gasworkers (or the General Workers, to use the union's new title) nearly doubled in membership during 1916 and 1917, overhauling the Workers' Union; while the NAUL and the Dockers also grew rapidly.

The union's serious losses of membership were due largely to the operation of conscription; but it is not clear why it fared so much worse than other general unions. Because of its previous rapid growth the union's active membership was no doubt predominantly young and thus particularly liable to conscription, and this may have caused serious disruption at branch level. It is possible that differing procedures for recording membership may have exaggerated the contrast between unions.[2] Also important was the deteriorating relationship between the Workers' Union and the Amalgamated Society of Engineers; in many areas skilled workers attempted to frustrate the union in its recruitment and to aid its rivals.

The poor performance of 1916 and 1917 could not have been due to any structural weakness; for in 1918 the union's rate of growth recovered dramatically. The number of new members was at least 240,000—greater than the union's total membership at the start of the year—while the rate of lapsing was reduced. The net increase was 150,000, the largest gain in any year of the Union's existence. Once more it attained the position of the largest general union, and of all trade unions it was now second only to the Miners and Railwaymen. In the following year, the transition from a war economy caused some dislocation of membership and turnover increased. But the number of new entrants was even higher than the record level of 1918, and total membership reached 495,000. The Workers' Union was now the largest single trade union in the country.[3] But by 1920 the end of the post-war boom was becoming apparent: recruitment fell, lapsing increased, and total membership remained static.

As before, increased membership brought the union a pleasing financial progress. By 1918 the weekly income averaged over £5,000—more than was received in the whole year 1910—and two years later this had again doubled. Though expenditure increased, it did so at first more slowly; in particular, war conditions limited members' claims for benefits. The growth in the union's assets was therefore spectacular: a balance of £18,000 at the end of 1914 had increased to £280,000 four years later. The end of the war brought a sharp rise in expenditure, and the annual surplus was drastically reduced; nevertheless, the balance of funds reached £300,000 in 1920. Continued numerical and financial growth brought further increases in the organizing staff: the number of officials more

---

[2] At the start of the war the Workers' Union, unlike most general unions, included in its returns members on active service; this minimized the apparent loss of membership. It is possible that this procedure was subsequently altered, exaggerating the apparent rate of turnover.

[3] The membership of the Miners' Federation remained higher; but this was a federal body rather than a single union.

than doubled during the war, reaching 100 by the end of 1918, and in 1920 reached a peak level of 160; 'our organising staff', wrote Duncan, 'far exceeds that of any Union in this country'.[4] The union was able to acquire, at a cost of £10,000, extensive new premises at 'Highfield', Golders Green Road. A further important result of the improved finances was that the union's revised rules, adopted in 1915, provided for a Triennial Conference of members; the first of these took place in June 1916, and the second in September 1919.

The union shared in the movement's enhanced status. In the pre-war period its organizing work frequently aroused bitter hostility, not merely among employers directly affected. Two notable examples may be given of legal cases which demonstrated such antipathy. In June 1914 a leading Burton member, Vale Rawlings, was arrested while holding a meeting of women workers, apparently for obstruction; later he was accused of assaulting a policeman a foot taller than himself and over twice his weight. Despite obvious inconsistencies in the police evidence, and numerous defence witnesses, Rawlings was convicted and received a three months' sentence. A month later the union's South Staffordshire organizer, W. M. Adamson, was accused of assault on a blackleg during a dispute at Walsall. Again a magistrates' bench composed of local employers convicted, against the weight of evidence, and Adamson was gaoled for refusing to pay a fine. With the war, such occurrences became far less frequent. The new mood was set by Duncan's appearances on the platform at army recruiting meetings—behaviour that could not fail to earn the support of the patriotic middle classes. In March 1915 Beard and Duncan were among the trade union leaders called to hear Lloyd George at the Treasury Conference; in September 1915, Duncan was one of those appointed by the Government to the Central Munitions Labour Supply Committee. At local level organizers and lay members were appointed to a range of official committees, often working with local dignitaries whose hostility to the union had previously been undisguised. Soon, union members were themselves to be appointed as magistrates. The needs of war thus brought respectability.

[4] *Annual Report*, 1919.

With the war the union's leaders, who in their early years had stood well to the left of the labour movement, adopted an uncompromisingly right-wing stance. Beard demonstrated his patriotism by joining his local Volunteer Force, adopting the habit of attending meetings in uniform; at the beginning of 1915 he resigned from the ILP in protest at its attitude to the war. Duncan, like most Labour M.P.s, fully supported the Government's involvement in the war; with Beard he later favoured conscription, and Labour participation in the Coalition Government. Both were connected with the British Workers' League, which towards the end of the war opposed the growing demands for a negotiated peace; Duncan was until 1918 a Vice-President, resigning only when the League insisted in supporting Parliamentary candidates against Labour nominees. On industrial questions Beard's editorials in the *Record* expressed a similar line. The Munitions Act, to most unions an unfortunate necessity, was welcomed almost unreservedly. Beard regularly urged that the union's attitude to employers should be conciliatory, and indeed businesslike; not surprisingly, he gave his support to the 'Alliance of Employers and Employed' which was formed towards the end of war. At the same time he denounced in vehement terms those militants who joined in unofficial stop stewards' movements, took unauthorized strike action, or advocated workers' control. In 1920, when the labour movement showed unusual unanimity in endorsing direct action to prevent the danger of war with Russia, he was one of the few who expressed reservations at this 'unconstitutional' action. Beard's views, generally well argued, would have been typical of most union leaders a decade later; but his consistently right-wing attitudes were uncommon at a time when most trade unionists allowed themselves at least the occasional left-wing enthusiasm.

Though there was left-wing opposition within the union—particularly in the London district, which in 1916 launched a monthly magazine as a rival to Beard's *Record*—Beard and Duncan both retained their positions without difficulty in the biennial elections. It is not surprising that the internal opposition, which centred on the issues of the Munitions Act and conscription, proved unsuccessful. The Munitions Act and the associated changes in workshop practices were in many ways advantageous to the lower-skilled membership of the Workers' Union; and while conscription did indeed have a major impact on the union's members, those who suffered were in no position to affect its internal politics thereafter. A co-ordinated revolt against official policies would in any case have been unlikely; for the great increase in the union's organizing staff robbed the rank and file of its most able activists. In fact the main rebuff suffered by the leadership came from outside the union. Duncan's views had roused the anger of industrial militants (mainly ASE members) in his constituency at Barrow, and the local Labour Party refused to support his candidature in 1918; as a result, he was narrowly defeated. Until 1922 the union's only representative in Parliament was Neil Maclean, a member of one of the Glasgow branches, who was successful as ILP candidate in Govan in 1918; from 1919 he represented Scotland on the union's executive.

Industrially, the union's composition in these years matched the changing priorities of the national economy. War brought an increasing concentration in engineering, with a major growth of membership in most munition centres. With the armistice, the importance of engineering declined, and the pre-war trend towards organization in a range of new factory industries was resumed. The post-war period also brought an unexpected growth of membership in agriculture, following the creation of statutory wage-regulating machinery under the Corn Production Act of 1917.

THE UNION IN ENGINEERING

In 1914 engineering was already a central focus of the union's industrial activity; this now became even more marked. War was to create two insatiable demands: men and munitions. These twin requirements dominated the political and industrial life of the nation, and bore with particular urgency on the trade union movement. In engineering the two demands combined to create problems of peculiar intensity.

The demand for war materials had an immediate effect on engineering production. There were four main areas of influence. First, the structure of the industry: there was a rapid transfer of existing productive capacity to armaments, and new munition factories were constructed by the government.

Within a year of the outbreak of war over 70 per cent of workers in private establishments were employed on government contracts, and by 1918 the proportion had reached 90 per cent; while the new 'national' factories employed half a million workers by the end of the war.

Second, the urgency of war requirements accelerated the previous developments in technology. The process of mechanization continued apace, making further inroads into the craft content of direct production work. The increasing tendency was for work of the highest skill to be confined to indirect employees engaged in tool-making and setting.

A third change was in the composition of the labour force, swollen by a massive influx of new workers. Total employment in the engineering and allied industries rose by nearly 60 per cent during the war period. The most notable feature of this expansion was the use of female labour. Before 1914 some 170,000 women were employed in the engineering complex, but the great majority worked in distinct 'women's trades', often at sweated rates; less than 20,000 were in general engineering and machine shops. By 1918 there were 600,000 women working in these industries, with a high proportion (170,000) in ordinary engineering shops. In addition, they formed a clear majority in the new government establishments.

The structure of the labour force was also affected by the military demand for manpower. When conscription was introduced in 1916, official policy was at first that skilled workers should not be recruited. As the army's demands became more insistent the government changed its priorities, and craftsmen were recruited where replacements were available who were unsuitable for military service. The ASE (whose members were in general far more easily replaceable than those of the smaller craft societies) fought a vehement campaign to retain the earlier exemption; a major unofficial strike movement took place in the North towards the end of 1916, and the ASE subsequently threatened a repeat performance. Though the Engineers eventually backed down, it was inevitably the lower-skilled who bore the brunt of conscription in engineering; this 're-sulted in the removal of most of the fit and eligible members of the less skilled male grades of labour'.[5]

[5] G. D. H. Cole, *Trade Unionism in Munitions*, 1923, p. 137.

The fourth and most explosive development was in the manning of machinery. From the outset the employers, with vigorous backing from the government, demanded that craft unionists should abandon all remaining resistance and permit the maximum use of lower-skilled and female labour on machine tools. Official agreement was reached in 1915 that such 'dilution of labour' would be permitted on all war work, after an undertaking was given that pre-war conditions would be restored when hostilities had ceased. But the ASE maintained a successful opposition to dilution on private work (an attempt to force the issue caused a wave of strikes in May 1917); and even in munitions there was prolonged unofficial resistance to the process. For this reason the wartime changes in the use of labour were less radical than at first sight appeared. Female machinists for the most part worked either in the government factories (in which employment was drastically reduced after the armistice) or on specialized equipment in private establishments (which left them unqualified for the different requirements of post-war engineering). Because of conscription, those lower-skilled male workers who advanced to highly skilled work were in the main the old, the sick and the wounded; these were at an obvious disadvantage in the peace-time labour market. Legislation passed in 1919 further assisted in restoring pre-war practices in the workshops. It is therefore arguable that the war did not accelerate but delayed those changes in the deployment of engineering labour which were apparent long before 1914.

The war had a more lasting impact on industrial relations in the industry. By 1914 the Procedure 'for avoidance of disputes', instituted by the Engineering Employers' Federation, had been in existence for sixteen years. But only the ASE and two smaller unions made regular use of it; many societies, including all the general unions, were not party to any national agreement and relied solely on their local strength in district bargaining. On the outbreak of war the unions declared a voluntary Industrial Truce; they then found themselves faced with rapid price inflation but with no weapon to enforce their wage claims. One consequence was a great increase in participation in the national machinery; another was the intervention of the state to determine issues which remained unresolved. A Committee on

7—W.U.

Production (originally appointed to propose means of increasing the output of armaments) was constituted a voluntary arbitration tribunal early in 1915; shortly afterwards the Munitions Act outlawed all strikes on war work and made the Committee's awards mandatory.

A further important change occurred in 1917. District bargaining had developed at a time when trade commonly fluctuated on a local basis; but now engineering was working at full volume in every district, and prices were rising nationally also. A monotonous routine thus developed: largely identical claims were formulated in each district (there were some forty local Associations affiliated to the EEF), passed unresolved through Local and Central Conference, and resulted in identical awards by the Committee on Production. Trade unionists complained bitterly at the lengthy delays involved; the government, and the Committee itself, wished to simplify the procedure; while even the employers could not have relished the time spent on purely formal negotiations. An agreement was therefore reached in February 1917 to suspend all district applications (except that claims might still be made in individual cases where wages were 'unduly low') in place of general wage claims to be made before the Committee at four-monthly intervals.

National wage negotiation provided advances which allowed engineering workers to keep abreast of the rising cost of living; though not all succeeded in recovering the ground lost between 1914 and 1917, engineers did far better than most sections of the working class. The lower-skilled fared particularly well, since all the Committee's awards were for a flat-rate money sum. But all sides appeared reasonably satisfied with the arrangement, for after the armistice an indefinite extension was agreed. Feelings soon changed, however; the Committee now proved far less generous than previously. The craft unions in particular complained that their wages were lagging behind those in other industries, even though engineering profits and share prices were booming. In August 1920 a conference of unions therefore agreed to end the National Wages Agreement of 1917 (though the general unions, having fared best under arbitration, were reluctant to take this step). The unions still intended to submit their demands at national level; but they would now, they believed, be able to achieve more through direct negotiation and industrial action than was forthcoming through arbitration. The collapse of the post-war boom soon destroyed such expectations.

The impact of war on the engineering trades provided the Workers' Union with an unexpected opportunity to consolidate its previous achievements. The inflated labour force allowed a great expansion of membership in the munition centres, first among male 'dilutees', then among the women workers who replaced male labour in many sections of production.

The union possessed little more than 5,000 female members at the outbreak of war, most of these in the Midlands; and though the number had risen to 10,000 by the end of 1915, Duncan could correctly insist that 'so far, the organisation of women and girls in the industrial centres of this country is undoubtedly a colossal failure'.[6] Most officials had too much on their hands to give much attention to this task; and though Varley had begun touring the country, acting in effect as a national organizer, she could make only a short-term campaign in each district. Moreover, active co-operation was not always forthcoming from male members; Beard alleged that many had not 'lived up to the rules'.[7]

Duncan proposed that the union should commence a serious campaign to recruit a female membership, and this was soon under way. In the last three months of 1915, four new women organizers were appointed; more were added in the succeeding years, and by the end of the war twenty female officers were employed. The exhortations of the union's leaders also encouraged the rank and file to assist, particularly as conscription led to the replacement of male members by female dilutees; only in this way could solid organization be maintained. Despite fierce opposition from many employers—open intimidation of young female workers was common—and the ignorance of many of the dilutees themselves of industrial life and trade union objectives, the union's vigorous approach paid handsome dividends. By the end of the war there was a female membership of over 80,000: more than in any other general union, and nearly a quarter of the union's own total membership.

With recruitment among new entrants to munition work, the predominance of engineering in the union's membership

[6] *Record*, Sept. 1915.   [7] Triennial Conference, June 1916.

was further accentuated. By 1918 it appears that eighty of the union's hundred largest branches were based primarily on engineering; it is reasonable to assume that around 200,000 members—just over half the total—worked in the industry. Though all general unions made rapid wartime advances in this field, the Workers' Union held an undisputed lead.[8]

The end of wartime production had inevitable repercussions on the union's organization. This was most noticeable in the case of women: total female membership had fallen by over a quarter by the end of 1919, and this suggests a massive loss as munition workers left the industry, partly offset by gains in other industries and in the traditional 'women's sections' of engineering. Even though female membership recovered in 1920, the importance of engineering in this total was much reduced. Among male workers, engineering seems to have contributed little to the post-war growth which raised the union to its peak of success; in some sections there was indeed an expansion, but the evidence suggests that this did little more than match the decline in munitions. By 1920, only sixty of the hundred largest branches were based on engineering; given the rise in total membership, it may be assumed that the numbers in engineering remained near the 1918 level.

From 1914, the most pressing problem for the union, as for all others, was the rapid and continuous rise in the cost of living. 'It soon became apparent that wages would have to be substantially altered if the workers were to keep level with pre-war conditions, however low those conditions may have been.'[9] But though improvements were urgently necessary, the union's freedom of action was circumscribed by the voluntary Industrial Truce; and in this situation its existing relationship with the employers proved inadequate. In most districts the union

[8] One further aspect of the union's wartime membership deserves mention. With the arrival of refugee Belgian engineers to work in British munition factories, their organization—the Belgian Metal Workers' Union—sought arrangements to maintain union membership during the war period. Talks with the ASE failed to result in a satisfactory arrangement; the Workers' Union was then contacted and an agreement reached. A special section was opened, under the charge of a Belgian organizer, and several thousand engineers recruited; at the end of the war trade unionism among Belgian engineers thus remained intact and a proportion of the contributions paid was returned to the Belgian organization. This arrangement was a notable gesture of international trade union solidarity.

[9] *Record*, May 1923.

remained formally unrecognized; where local recognition did exist, the failure to reach agreement on a claim raised by the union alone left no means of peaceful settlement open; and when the union participated in a joint movement, 'it had no standing when a wages question left a local conference, and its case had to be put to central conference by the skilled workers'.[10] The problem was of course a new one; the union had signed its first local recognition agreement only a year previously, and was in general content to depend on the threat of direct action to obtain concessions. It was soon clear that it was unsafe to rely on other societies to fight the union's battles at Central Conference: a joint claim for the London district resulted in agreement that gave nothing to the lower-skilled. A new application (submitted jointly with the Gasworkers and the NAUL) brought an acceptable local agreement—clear evidence of the fact that general unions might gain most through independent action (a lesson already learned by the Workers' Union in the Midlands).

The problem was resolved at the end of 1914 when the Coventry employers, during the discussion of a wage claim, suggested that it would be desirable if the issue could be referred to Central Conference. It was agreed that the local Association should recommend national recognition of the Workers' Union, and these formalities were quickly completed.

The union thus became the first general workers' organization to become nationally recognized—an achievement which officials saw as final confirmation of its established status in the industry. Since effective use of the new procedure required specialized negotiating skill, the union appointed W. T. Kelly, one of the London organizers, to present its case at all Central Conference hearings. Kelly had previously served ten years on the full-time executive of the ASE, until the overthrow of the entire body in a palace revolution in 1913; it was an amazing stroke of fortune that the Workers' Union now had on its own staff an official so experienced in engineering negotiations.

With the development of compulsory arbitration, Kelly's functions were soon enlarged. Most cases referred to the Committee on Production had previously been taken through the engineering procedure; it was thus natural that he should

[10] Beard, ibid., Sept. 1916.

be made responsible for representing the union at all arbitration hearings. The importance of the union's membership in
engineering was such that it was involved in more such hearings
than all the other general unions combined; the volume of
work was therefore soon so great that a special Arbitration
Department was created by the union under Kelly's control.
The department served effectively as both a research department and a central clearing-house for collective bargaining—a
remarkable innovation in contemporary trade unionism.

It was not long before the union recognized that piecemeal
applications on a district basis, or at the level of the individual
firm, were inadequate. By the summer of 1916 the cost of living
was some 50 per cent above its pre-war level, but few members
had received even 20 per cent increases in their wage rates.
The union therefore announced its intention of launching a
'National Movement', explaining that its main concern was
with day-workers who were not employed on direct production
work: '. . . such classes of workers as labourers, slingers, crane
drivers, belt men, oilers, men in stores, viewers, etc., . . . do not
get bonuses, nor are they able to get increased wages by working
piecework, although engaged upon the most important work
of the factories'.[11] The notorious 'leaving certificate' system
introduced by the Munitions Act tied engineering workers to
their existing employers;[12] and firms were unwilling to transfer
experienced indirect workers to machine work, where earnings
were often higher. The union's campaign, backed by signs of
serious unrest among munition workers, soon achieved results.
In July 1916 the Committee on Production (which since the
beginning of the year, on government instructions, had been
imposing a 'wage freeze') commenced a series of pace-setting
awards for time-workers only. But the awards were necessarily
still on a district basis; and with inflation continuing, the union's
voice was soon among those calling for some form of national
settlement.

Under the existing system of district applications the Workers'
Union normally acted either independently or as part of an *ad*

[11] *Record*, Apr. 1916.
[12] This system, introduced to control competition between firms for scarce
labour, prevented munition workers from moving between firms without the formal
sanction of their existing employer.

hoc joint movement. National negotiations quickly led to more formal links between the general unions. In July 1917 the loosely constituted General Labourers' National Council was replaced by a stronger body, the National Federation of General Workers; in contrast to its predecessor, the Federation was able to take the initiative in co-ordinating at national level the bargaining activities of its members. In engineering the size of its membership qualified the Workers' Union for a leading role, and from the outset it was Kelly who presented the Federation's case in the hearings before the Committee on Production. The choice was inevitable not only because of the union's position within the industry, but also because of his personal experience of national negotiations and his position as virtually a full-time national engineering officer.

A major triumph for the general unions was the adherence of the Committee on Production—at times in the face of opposition from the craft societies—to the principle of flat-rate increases. In this way the lower-paid made the highest relative gains, and traditional differentials were thus narrowed. But on one occasion the government itself overturned the principle of equal advances and caused a wave of unrest.

Just as the Workers' Union had complained of the predicament of its time-worker members, so the craft societies voiced a similar grievance. Such craftsmen as toolmakers, they argued, who were among the highest skilled in the trade, were earning less than semi-skilled machinists with no engineering experience. This was almost certainly an exaggeration: just as today, tales of the fabulous wages of piece-workers were part of the national mythology. A minority of machinists were indeed able to take advantage of 'loose' piece rates and obtain exceptional earnings; but most semi-skilled earned well below the average craftsman. Even so, the craftsmen's sense of grievance was understandable. In consequence, when the government yielded to trade union pressure and announced that the hated leaving certificates would be abolished, it feared a massive transfer of craftsmen to lower-skilled production work. To forestall that, a 12½ per cent bonus was applied by Ministerial order in October 1917 to all fully-rated and qualified engineering time-workers. The response should have been predictable. The definition of eligibility for the award was inevitably fairly arbitrary, and great unrest ensued among those excluded; as a result the bonus was rapidly extended among all higher-skilled grades.

The reaction of the lower-skilled was equally predictable. According to Beard, 'the skilled workers have some small cause for putting up this grievance, but the grievance affects to a larger extent the day-working unskilled and semi-skilled workmen'.[13] Official protests received added force through a wave of unofficial strike action in Sheffield, in which Workers' Union members played a leading part. Fearing the extension of this movement the government capitulated; and agreement was signed directly between leaders of the NFGW and the War Cabinet (in itself an unprecedented step) applying the bonus, backdated to October, to all time-workers in munitions. After further unco-ordinated pressure the $12\frac{1}{2}$ per cent was conceded by one means or another to all workers on time rates in the engineering and metal trades (and in many other industries also) who were well organized enough to get it. But now it was the turn of the lower-paid piece-workers to erupt in anger. Leaders of the general unions had already given undertakings not to press for increases in piece rates; and Beard had insisted that such action on a local level would be 'unfair, unworthy, and unbrotherly'.[14] But the union's organizer in Sheffield— where the problem of low-paid piece-workers appears to have been particularly acute—led to a further unofficial campaign at the start of 1918. The pressure was sufficient for the government to meet the piece-workers' demands more than half-way: on the advice of the Committee on Production they were awarded a $7\frac{1}{2}$ per cent bonus.

The union was involved throughout the period in efforts to defend and improve the conditions of its female members in engineering. In January 1916 the government assumed powers to issue orders prescribing the pay of women munition workers. Before this date the Workers' Union was able to negotiate district agreements setting minimum rates for women in federated firms, which improved the conditions of many such workers. Thereafter the union participated in the special arbitration machinery set up to hear the women's claims; from 1917 it co-operated with other general unions, and a joint committee was established. The advances obtained were in

<hr/>

[13] *Record*, Nov. 1917.   [14] Ibid., Dec. 1917.

absolute terms far below those awarded to male workers; but because of the low level of their pre-war wages the relative improvement was greater. The comparative weakness of trade unionism among female munition workers caused special problems; for some employers were encouraged to ignore the statutory minimum rates, while others did so out of ignorance. The union's Scottish organizer alleged that he 'could point out to shops where no single order has been observed. . . . In one district we discovered not one single shop where the women were being paid the proper rates'.[15] In the absence of any official inspection machinery it was only through trade union pressure that such situations could be redressed, if necessary by means of legal action.

GOVERNMENT EMPLOYMENT

Special problems were involved in the representation of engineering workers in War Office establishments and Government dockyards. The union's organization in this field dated back to 1909, when a branch was opened for contractors' labourers in Devonport; a similar branch was opened shortly afterwards in Pembroke, and a small Portsmouth union covering this class of worker amalgamated. Apart from a limited membership in the engineering and shipbuilding craft societies, trade unionism among employees of the Admiralty itself was confined to weak localized organizations, normally covering only a single occupational section, which charged small contributions, had no full-time officials, and acted as little more than friendly societies. Shortly before the outbreak of war the dockyard branches of the Workers' Union began to recruit these workers, and the wartime increase in employment gave a great stimulus to this effort. By the end of 1915 new dockyard branches had been opened at Chatham, Sheerness, Woolwich, Deptford, Rosyth, Crombie and Invergordon, and membership had increased correspondingly. The growth continued throughout the war, assisted by the absorption of many of the local societies, and raised dockyard membership to a peak of some 25,000. Numbers declined as employment was reduced after

[15] Kerr, *Record*, Mar. 1918.

the armistice, but this loss was offset in 1920 by the amalgamation of the largest of the sectional societies, the Portsmouth-based National Union of Government Employees.

War office employees were first organized by the union with the amalgamation of the Woolwich Workers' Union in 1912. Again, the war brought an opportunity for rapid expansion, both through vigorous recruitment and through the absorption of various local organizations. The peak membership achieved was probably also 25,000, derived principally from the three Royal Factories in the London area (Woolwich Arsenal, Enfield Lock Small Arms Factory, and Waltham Abbey Gunpowder Factory). As in the dockyards, membership inevitably fell after the armistice.

The union found that wages in government employment were determined in a deplorable fashion. District rates were paid to craftsmen, but in the absence of recognized rates for lower-skilled workers each department could prescribe unilaterally the minimum (and in some cases the maximum) payment for the various grades. Advances for individual workmen were given on an apparently arbitrary basis; and alterations in maxima and minima were made without any form of collective bargaining. The Admiralty 'more than any other Government Department . . . lived in an atmosphere of detachment from the outside world, and . . . conducted its affairs with an air of autocracy'.[16] Under 'a most humiliating system of approach by the men to their employers',[17] the Lords Commissioners of the Admiralty made annual visits to each yard, and received from deputations of workmen 'humble petitions' requesting improvements. Their decisions were made known after lengthy delays—often a year or more—and were usually unfavourable. Conditions in War Office establishments were little better. Workers were of necessity 'constantly going "cap-in-hand" for some small increase; where piecework operated rate-cutting was common, and 'it was a rare thing to know what rate a man was entitled to or by what means he should reach the unknown maximum, and . . . many men were afraid even to ask for that to which they were entitled'.[18] The system encouraged the

---

[16] E. Colston Shepherd, *The Fixing of Wages in Government Employment*, 1923, p. 27.
[17] *Record*, June 1921.   [18] Ibid., Aug. 1921.

development of the sectional organizations, which in turn acquired a vested interest in its perpetuation. Though weak and sectional unions were the norm in large areas of private industry also, there at least most employers too were small and disorganized; but government workers, faced by the resources of the country's largest employer, were particularly impotent in their divided condition.

From the outset the union recognized that these procedures were incompatible with genuine trade unionism, and in the war years it launched a vigorous campaign for the adoption of more acceptable methods. One reform came quickly: the Admiralty suspended the system of petitioning, to which the union took special exception, in the interests of war production; instead, the Financial Secretary to the Admiralty, Dr. Macnamara, agreed to receive deputations (which could include trade union officials) at any time. But this change was intended to be only temporary; and other basic grievances common to all departments remained. The government did not pay sweated wages, but neither was it a model employer. In the dockyards, wages at the outbreak of war had risen only two shillings since 1906, despite the rise in prices. At its establishments in rural areas the War Office 'had taken the wages of jobbing blacksmiths, agricultural labourers, and gardeners' as the basis on which its own labourers were paid.[19] Where private engineering works and government factories existed in the same district, it was often argued that the rates of labourers and machinists were not comparable because of the 'special conditions' of government employment. Not only basic wage rates were affected by this argument: provisions for overtime payment and piecework guarantees, increasingly common among similar workers in private employment, were rarely as favourable for government workers. There could be little hope of remedying these general grievances with the traditional methods of local and sectional applications, and through the procedure whereby government departments, themselves subject to close Treasury control, might receive deputations and announce their replies but made no approach towards real negotiations.

Throughout the war the union's central struggle was with the Admiralty. In War Office factories its field of action was

[19] Dallas, Triennial Conference, June 1916.

circumscribed by the powerful organization of the engineering craft societies, whose members did not suffer from the same grievances as the lower-skilled. In the dockyards, craft unionism was far weaker; for much of the skilled work was performed by special categories of 'skilled labourers' who received little more than the basic labourers' wages and were largely unorganized. The union's first task was to establish itself as a national organization of dockyard workers. It criticized forcibly the various Government Labourers' Unions as divisive organizations, financially too weak to afford officers independent of dockyard employment or to call a dispute when their claims were rejected, and thus forced to rely on petitions. It urged workers instead to join or transfer to the Workers' Union, with its staff of experienced organizers and a representative in Parliament. Soon it could claim to be 'undoubtedly . . . the strongest and most powerful organization the Government worker has ever had at his back'.[20] In September 1915 it felt ready to call a national conference of delegates from the dockyard branches, and a series of general demands was drafted. In November, the first national wage claim in the history of dockyard employment was placed before Dr. Macnamara; as a result, a general increase was announced a month later.

Genuine collective bargaining, however, was still little nearer. Though raised to a national level, the system was still one of petition: the union submitted a claim and awaited the department's reply, which was intended as its final decision. Further improvements could be gained only by a convincing threat of strike action, with or without the union's official support.[21] This was an unpleasant position for the union's officials, reluctant as they obviously were to sanction stoppages on war work; and by the end of 1917 the difficulty was eased by the readiness of Government departments to apply to their industrial staff the national engineering awards of the Committee on Production. In the latter period of the war, therefore, sectional grievances were the main source of contention. In

[20] Dallas, *Annual Report*, 1915.
[21] Only the imminence of a major strike at Chatham made the Admiralty agree to apply in Mar. 1917 the advance awarded by the Committee on Production to munition workers. At Woolwich Arsenal in 1915, a similar situation was allowed to develop before the War Office paid its labourers an increase conceded by the local Engineering Employers.

1916 the union found that when deadlock occurred on any claim the Admiralty and War Office could refuse to accept a reference to arbitration. Thereafter Duncan raised the issue regularly in Parliament.[22] Government departments, he argued, 'had it both ways', for while they could avoid the obligations of compulsory arbitration imposed on private employers by the Munitions Act, their workers were bound by the leaving certificate provisions of the same Act. The official response was that while the Act was not binding on the Crown, departments did in fact allow 'reasonable' claims to go before the Committee on Production. But the fact remained that they were able to refuse arbitration whenever they saw fit, and could thus 'still abide by the old-time old-fashioned methods, and . . . defy all the machinery that has been set up and snap their fingers at the law'.[23]

While controversy over this issue remained intense, the first recommendations of the Whitley Committee were published; but though the Government approved their application to private industry, it showed no intention to extend them to its own employees. This reticence led the Committee in its second Report to issue a mild rebuke: 'we have formed the opinion that the expression "employers and workmen" in our reference covers State and Municipal authorities and persons employed by them. Accordingly, we recommend that such authorities and their workpeople should take into consideration the proposals made in this and our first Report. . . .' In December 1917, when this recommendation was as yet unpublished, the union too pressed that the Government should 'have the recommendations in the [first] Report put into operation in all Departments of the State employing men on weekly wages'.[24] The initial response was however wholly unsatisfactory. In May 1918 the Admiralty published proposals of its own which clearly reflected its officials' previous attitudes. Its projected machinery, based on shop and yard committees elected from long-established employees, 'would have made negotiations, for every dockyard, separate and distinct, and would have excluded

[22] *House of Commons Debates*, vol. 85, cols. 1827, 1850, 1262; vol. 90, col. 1758; vol. 94, col. 602; voll 97, col. 1328; vol. 104, col. 54.
[23] *Record*, Mar. 1918.
[24] Duncan, *House of Commons Debates*, vol. 100, col. 1950.

from such negotiations the officials of the unions'.[25] Understandably the union condemned this as 'an insult to labour', and reported that there was 'much disaffection in the dockyards, owing to the attitude of the Admiralty in refusing to treat direct with the unions'.[26]

The government was taken aback by the widespread criticism of its proposals; and in July 1918 it gave way, announcing that the Whitley recommendations would be adopted in principle. Further delays ensued while detailed proposals were formulated and were discussed with the unions concerned; agreement was finally reached in February 1919. In the following months, Joint Industrial Councils were established on a departmental basis to discuss detailed issues relating to working conditions. General wage negotiations were the responsibility of four Trade Joint Councils (for engineering, shipbuilding, building, and 'miscellaneous' trades) which straddled departmental boundaries. Unresolved differences, the government finally agreed, should be referred to arbitration.

Under the new system, serious grievances concerning wages and conditions remained; but union members and officials alike recognized that industrial relations in government employment had been transformed. 'The days had gone when the Government workers had to beseech the Lords of the Admiralty to grant their petitions'.[27] A large share of the credit for this achievement must go to the Workers' Union for its long and determined pressure for reform.

THE UNION IN AGRICULTURE

While the war gave a major stimulus to the union's growth among some sections of industrial workers, in agriculture the initial impact was wholly disastrous. As a parallel to the Industrial Truce, all plans for strike action were dropped, and with them the farm workers' hopes for improved conditions. Many labourers sought a new means of escape from their feudal situation, and provided the Army and Navy with willing recruits. Inevitably, these included the bulk of the young,

---

[25] Shepherd, *The Fixing of Wages in Government Employment*, p. 142.
[26] *Record*, July 1918.
[27] Tom Macnamara, speech quoted in *Record*, May 1919.

active workers who had led the union's advance in the villages; and in every area organization collapsed. In the summer of 1914 there had been some 250 branches of the union composed wholly or predominantly of agricultural workers. By the end of the year, less than 100 were still in existence. During 1915 the total fell to 40; and the decline continued, though more slowly, in 1916. And not only were the branches reduced in number; the membership of the survivors was in many cases seriously depleted.

Despite the obvious problems of maintaining organization under war conditions, the severity of the collapse is at first sight surprising. Despite the wholesale loss of branch officials and rank and file members to the forces, the bargaining position of those who remained was soon enhanced. For while the supply of agricultural labour was reduced, the demand for domestic food production was greatly increased; with prices rising the worker needed higher wages while the farmer could well afford to pay them. As a result a rival organization—the Norfolk-based Agricultural Labourers' Union—suffered only a slight fall in membership during this period.[28]

The explanation for this difference in fortunes would seem to be that the membership of the ALU was geographically concentrated, and branch organization was comparatively easy to maintain. But the Workers' Union had covered a wide area of the country by dint of the intensive attention of a band of full-time organizers. With the war this situation changed. Hornagold, the union's main agricultural official, reached the age of sixty-five and retired. Several other organizers themselves joined the forces. But most important of all, many urban officials had previously devoted time and energy to organization in the villages; now they were forced to concentrate on the urgent industrial problems which the war created. The rural branches were therefore neglected at the very time when official attention was most urgently needed.

In one area the union did prove that successful organization was still possible. In 1916 Jack Shingfield, one of the union's

---

[28] Official returns by the ALU itself recorded a rise in membership between 1914 and 1916, but it seems clear from other sources that its figures were exaggerated: see R. Groves, *Sharpen the Sickle!*, 1949, p. 245; M. Madden, *National Union of Agricultural Workers* (Oxford B. Litt. thesis), 1956, p. 299.

London officers and himself a farm labourer's son, succeeded in establishing a chain of branches in the small industrial towns of Essex and Suffolk. In the following year he launched a campaign to extend recruitment to the villages. Rank-and-file members were persuaded that while low wages persisted in local agriculture their attempts to improve their own conditions would be handicapped, and they gave valuable assistance; and the response from the farm workers themselves was most encouraging.

This local achievement foreshadowed the revival of organization at a national level. With food imports sharply affected by war conditions, the government was anxious to reverse the long-term trend of falling domestic cereal production. Protracted deliberations resulted in the introduction in April 1917 of a Corn Production Bill, which became law four months later. The central aim was to induce farmers to bring more land under the plough by providing price guarantees for cereals; but a subsidiary provision—intended to reduce losses of experienced farm workers to industry, and as a concession to labour interests —was for statutory wage machinery to be established. An Agricultural Wages Board for England and Wales[29] would define minimum wage rates for farm workers in each county, together with the hours for which these were payable and the rates for overtime; it would itself receive recommendations from thirty-nine District Wages Committees. All bodies were to comprise an equal number of farmers' and workers' representatives, together with a number of 'neutral' members to hold the balance.

Such machinery provided the union with a new opportunity to win improvements for the agricultural labourer. It also presented a challenge: if it was to be able to claim representation on the new bodies, it would have to achieve a rapid reconstruction of its rural membership. This was at once recognized by George Dallas, chief organizer for London and the Home Counties, who launched an appeal for the rank and file to take the message of the Workers' Union into the countryside. 'Comrades', he wrote, 'let us buckle to and show the farmers and landlords that the workers of England mean to end the tyranny of the countryside'.[30] The call brought an immediate

[29] Separate machinery was established for Scotland and Ireland.
[30] *Trade Union Worker*, Sept. 1917.

response. Members were rapidly recruited throughout the Home Counties, particularly in East Anglia where firm foundations had already been laid by Shingfield. A parallel revival occurred in other districts—in the West Midlands and Yorkshire—which had been covered before the war, while organization also spread into new areas—notably Northumberland, where most farm workers were specialist stockmen and earned wages far above the average in agriculture. Two amalgamations further extended the union's coverage: in 1918 the National Farm and Dairy Workers' Union, with members in Lancashire, Cheshire and part of North Wales; and in the following year the Anglesey Workers' Union.

Total membership rose dramatically. At the start of 1917 organization was almost extinguished. In May 1918 the union claimed that 400 of its branches covered agriculture, with a membership of 30,000.[31] In the summer of 1919 it was suggested that numbers had reached 125,000; by the end of the year it was possible to speak of 150,000.[32] The highest claim which the union published was 160,000—a figure given by Beard in April 1920.[33] Undoubtedly all these claims involved considerable exaggeration; even so, it seems possible that the union at its peak may have represented over 120,000 farm workers—a quarter of its total membership.

This rapid expansion was made possible by a continuing policy of additions to the union's organizing force. By the summer of 1920, when the union employed 137 organizers, about forty catered mainly for agricultural workers; almost all had been appointed after the Corn Production Act. Over half worked in the large Home Counties division; here every county had at least one full-time official by 1920. The scale of the union's investment compares favourably with that of the rival farm workers' organization; the ALU, with a slightly higher membership (its official returns claimed a peak of 180,000—a figure doubtless as inflated as those recorded by the Workers' Union) employed only thirty organizers.

It was of course on the basis of union membership in 1917 that the composition of the wage determining machinery was

[31] TUC Parliamentary Committee *Report*, 1917-18.
[32] *Record*, Aug. 1919; *Times*, 6 Jan. 1920.
[33] Speech quoted in *Record*, June 1920.

8—w.u.

decided. The members of the central Agricultural Wages Board were appointed in November 1917. Of the sixteen workers' representatives, half were appointed by the Board of Agriculture, six were nominated by the ALU, and two—Beard and Dallas—by the Workers' Union. Of the eight appointed, four became associated with the union. The first task of the new body—the allocation of seats on the District Wages Committees —involved long and acrimonious disputes between the officials of the two unions. When after six months these were resolved, the Workers' Union obtained 120 out of a total of 320 workers' representatives.

The process of wage regulation fell into two stages. During 1918 orders were issued defining minimum wages for each county, on the basis of the recommendations of the District Committees. The pattern was set, perhaps unfortunately, by Norfolk—traditionally a low-wage county. Its minimum rate of 30s. was widely followed; few county minima were significantly above this level, though none was below. In most areas these initial orders did no more than restore the pre-war level of real wages; the most important gain was that the hours to which these wages applied became legally defined, and overtime pay was introduced—a remarkable innovation for most farm workers.

Subsequent adjustments to the district minima took place largely on a national basis, through negotiations on the central Wages Board. After three national advances wages reached their peak in the summer of 1920, with minima of 46s. in the lowest-paid counties; in addition, standard hours had been reduced. The over-all effect was to bring a significant improvement in real wages; in relative terms farm labourers did better than the average industrial worker. But understandably, widespread dissatisfaction remained. The size of the gains reflected the poverty of the pre-war agricultural worker, not the adequacy of his new wages; it was felt that he deserved more, and that farmers could afford to pay more.

Anger was particularly strong in the Workers' Union, which had launched a campaign for a national minimum of 50s. at the start of 1920. And unlike its rival, the union was not averse to using direct action to back up its pressure on the Wages Board. Its view was explicit: the sole purpose of the statutory machinery was to set a legal minimum to protect the weakest sections of farm workers; but it was perfectly legitimate to seek higher wages by negotiation, and to use strike action in support of its demands. In some areas this policy achieved concrete results. In Lancashire and Cheshire in 1919, a vigorous campaign resulted in an agreement which established rates nearly ten shillings above the legal minimum; and a system of conciliation committees was set up, apparently designed to bypass the whole Wages Board machinery. Similar action was also taken in Northumberland.

But in general the farm labourer was badly placed to take effective industrial action. In arable areas it was only at harvest time that a strike could seriously embarrass the employer; and concerted action was particularly hard to achieve because of the isolation of the worker and his exposure to victimization. Even when economic conditions were favourable, militancy succeeded for the Workers' Union only in very specific circumstances. First, the union was able to restore the traditional regional differentials in pay, which had been drastically reduced by the Wages Board. This explains its successes in the north of England; an attempt in 1920 to organize a strike for the 50s. in Essex—traditionally lower-paid—ended in total failure. Second, its achievements usually consisted in applying to a whole district conditions which some farmers were prepared to concede voluntarily. When faced by the united opposition of the farmers—as when Cheshire members struck for a wage of 60s. in 1920—defeat was almost inevitable.

DISTRICT ORGANIZATION IN WAR AND PEACE

During the war the union's organizing structure—which had developed in a completely unplanned manner—was finally rationalized. In 1910 the position had been that a few districts, their boundaries often imprecise, were assigned to individual organizers; the rest of Britain was covered by Morley, who also assisted the other officials when the need arose. Of the appointments made thereafter, some were to cover a portion of the districts of existing organizers, others further reduced the area of Presidential responsibility. When Morley's tenure of the office ended, he was left in charge of Yorkshire, North Lancashire, and—somewhat surprisingly—Herefordshire;[34] Beard assumed no territorial responsibilities apart from the large Midlands district which he already controlled. At the end of 1915 the structure of authority within the growing staff of organizers was formalized by the establishment of a system of Divisional Organizers, each with over-all control (subject only to the Executive) of a large area in which a number of subordinate officials operated. Those appointed were the six organizers of longest standing—Beard, Morley, Giles, Titt, Harris, and Ellery—and in addition Kerr and Dallas, whose districts had an obvious claim to the status of separate Divisions. By 1920, five further Divisions had been created.

In the Midlands area the union's existing membership in engineering formed the basis for rapid wartime expansion, notably in Birmingham and Coventry (in the heavy metal trades of the Black Country there was less opportunity for growth). The return to peacetime production occurred smoothly, and there was little change in membership in the post-war period; the main new sources of membership were the Courtauld artificial fibres plant at Coventry, and the mid-Warwickshire cement works (where 100 per cent membership was achieved).

The district to the south-west of Birmingham, which Arthur Ellery was sent to supervise shortly before the outbreak of war, was detached from Beard's control in 1915 and made a separate organizing division. While strong branches were composed from engineering workers in Gloucester and Worcester, the greatest progress was made in the smaller towns of West Wiltshire. The union's first branch in this district had been formed as the result of a strike of unorganized rubber workers at Melksham in November 1911; Ellery had been the nearest trade union official that the strikers could contact, and after enrolling them in the union he negotiated a satisfactory settlement. Though trade unionism was virtually unknown in this rural area, a firm foothold was soon obtained among local rubber, textile, and

[34] Morley had been personally responsible for the development of local organization, and the county was not an integral part of Beard's district; but from 1916 it was assigned to the West Midlands division under Ellery. North Lancashire came under Titt's control in 1918.

food-processing workers. During and after the war this formed the basis for rapid expansion. Further east, a substantial membership was recruited at the Swindon railway workshops. By 1920, total membership in the West Midlands had reached about 30,000.

The war brought mixed results in the North Midland district, where Joe Clark was organizer. Membership fell sharply in the union's existing strongholds: slackness in the building industry affected the Swadlincote pipe trade, while restrictions on drinking hit the Burton breweries. But existing branches in Derby and Loughborough, based on engineering workers, grew rapidly; while in Leicester a full-time organizer, Syd Taylor, appointed in 1915, was able to recruit a large membership from the local engineering, textile, and rubber trades. These branches continued to expand in the post-war period, while membership quickly recovered in Burton and Swadlincote. In the area as a whole, membership was well over 30,000 at the end of the decade.

Further east, a district based on branches in Newark, Lincoln, and Grimsby grew rapidly after the appointment of a local organizer, George Deer, in 1915. At the end of the war it was constituted the centre of a new East Midland division under W. M. Adamson, previously Irish Divisional Organizer. Also included was Nottingham—where membership doubled in the two post-war years, mainly through the recruitment of lace workers—and Peterborough, where branches catering for engineering and brick workers grew to a membership of 2,000. In Lincolnshire itself the post-war growth was slower, and the whole division was in 1920 the union's smallest, with little more than 10,000 members.

Over the period the original Midlands district, now divided in three, had increased its membership to some 170,000—a third of the union's total. The division remaining under Beard's control—the Birmingham area and the North Midlands—contained a quarter of total union membership. With this impressive concentration of organization, the division remained easily the union's largest; even so, there had been a relative decline, for Birmingham and the Black Country alone held this proportion of membership before the war. No doubt this may be explained by the extent of the union's success before the war:

fewer sources of recruitment remained to be exploited than in areas where the union was less well established.

The Lancashire division, controlled by George Titt, maintained its position within the union throughout the war. There was continued growth in the Manchester engineering shops, and a significant consolidation of organization in the surrounding towns where this had hitherto been weak. The improvement was most notable in the Rochdale district; the local woollen workers had always been ignored by the Yorkshire union which covered their trade, but the Workers' Union achieved a strong organization. After the war there was little further expansion in Manchester itself; the only notable progress was among Corporation employees. Among the woollen workers of Rochdale and district membership doubled in the two years; elsewhere in Lancashire the only branch to expand notably was at the Prescot cable works. In Cheshire and North Wales intensive organization of agricultural workers was obtained following the amalgamation, in 1918 and 1919, of the Farm and Dairy Workers' Union, and the Anglesey Workers' Union. The most striking development, however, was in the Isle of Man, where before 1917 trade union organization was virtually non-existent. In that year a group of Douglas workers led by Alf Teare, a printing worker, opened a branch of the union, and by the end of 1918 it held well over a thousand members; branches had also been formed elsewhere on the Island, and all local industries were covered. This organization was used to gain a dramatic victory benefiting the whole Manx working class; demands for a bread subsidy similar to that operating in England culminated in July 1918 in a general strike, led by the union. After a day and a half the demand was conceded by the Lieutenant-Governor of the Island. This success brought a further expansion of membership, raising the total in the Island by 1920 to between three and four thousand. In the whole division, membership had now risen to around 40,000.

In Yorkshire the pattern of development was varied. In Sheffield, which obtained its first organizer in 1916, several new branches were formed, and a membership of some 4,000 was recruited from the local munition trades. It has already been seen that these members played an important part in unofficial wartime strike movements; shop stewards of the general unions were in close contact with the Sheffield Workers' Committee, led by ASE members, and the Workers' Union organizer, William Allen Byrne, supported their militant activities. There was a similar growth of membership among munition workers in Doncaster. But in the original South Yorkshire branches based on the welded boiler trade there was a fall in numbers during the war. In the post-war period, with the end of munition work and the revival of peacetime industries, the experience was reversed: there was a decline in Sheffield and Doncaster, and renewed expansion in the Rotherham district.

In the other main area of organization around the Calder Valley the record was similar. In Halifax and Leeds there was rapid expansion in a range of munition trades; but the most notable development was in Huddersfield, where numbers increased from a few hundred to some four thousand, drawn mainly from chemical works. In several other Yorkshire towns the union succeeded in organizing chemical workers, gaining an important status in the industry. But here too the end of war conditions did not permit further progress. Thus the Yorkshire division as a whole failed to expand over the period as a whole as rapidly as the union nationally. Even so, with nearly 50,000 members it still contained a tenth of the union's total, and was the third largest division.

Easily the most dramatic expansion of the union's organization occurred in London and the Southern Counties; of minor importance in 1914, the area contained over a quarter of the union's membership by 1918, and a third by 1920. At Woolwich Arsenal the union already possessed a major foothold, and with the appointment of the branch secretary, Tom Macnamara, as organizer just before the outbreak of war, it was well placed to take advantage of the massive wartime increase in employment. Membership grew rapidly, reaching 15,000 in 1918; this made Woolwich the largest branch in the union, and almost certainly in the entire trade union movement. With considerable membership in other local munition factories, the area by 1916 accounted for nearly half the membership in the London and Home Counties division. It was then detached, Macnamara becoming Kent Divisional Organizer. At the time the only important centre of organization outside Woolwich was at Chatham, where a branch of dockyard workers was opened in

1915. One of the union's Devonport members, Alf Edmonds, was sent here as organizer in the same year; he succeeded in building up membership not only in the dockyards but also in local civilian employment. By the end of the war there were twenty-two branches in the district of Chatham, Gillingham, and Rochester, with a total membership at least equal to that in the Woolwich area.

With the end of the war, membership in Woolwich fell to half its peak level. But employment in the Chatham dockyards was not greatly affected, and the union's organization was sustained. At the same time, new sources of recruitment were exploited. The most important sections organized were workers in the East Kent brickyards and cement-fields; strong organization was also achieved among the county's agricultural workers. The altered distribution of organization in the county was recognized on the death of Macnamara in 1919; he was succeeded as Divisional Organizer by Edmonds, and the Divisional Office was transferred to Gillingham. At the end of the decade, the division held some 40,000 members.

In London itself, there was a rapid growth of membership throughout the years 1914–20. The most intensive organization remained in South London, where numbers grew during the war from 1,500 to 8,000. This membership was extremely heterogeneous, deriving from a variety of engineering and other factories; two sources of organization were however prominent: a shell factory in Battersea, and the naval victualling yard at Deptford, each providing a thousand members by the end of the war. In North London, wartime growth was spectacular. Most notable was the development of the Enfield Lock branch, formed by the amalgamation at the end of 1914 of a small union at the Royal Small Arms Factory; within a year membership had reached 3,000, and by 1918 it was 4,000. Other branches of engineering and munition workers at Ponders End, Waltham Abbey, Edmonton and Walthamstow together contributed a similar membership: considerable progress in an area where the union had possessed no organization whatever before the war. War production aided the formation of several strong branches in West London also; by far the largest covered the White City factory of Waring and Gillow, where tents and gas masks were manufactured; in 1917 a four-day strike of members, largely female, won recognition of the union and improved wages and conditions, and raised membership allegedly to 6,000. Finally, a large network of branches was developed in East and Central London. One interesting success was at Liptons, where the union had suffered defeat in its early years; some of the firm's employees were enrolled in the City branch in 1917, and advances of wages were obtained almost immediately; by the end of the war the branch held over a thousand members. At the Army and Navy Stores, the scene of another early struggle, a success was also registered: in the course of a campaign to organize the London furniture removal trade the firm's removal workers were organized, and advances were won after a strike. Other large branches in the district contained skilled workers in the cloth-finishing trade, and 'minor grades' of workers in government offices; the latter were first recruited in 1916, and by 1918 provided some 2,500 members in three Whitehall branches.

In 1919, London was made a separate organizing Division under the control of Beard—who already held the posts of President and Birmingham Divisional Organizer.[35] With the return to peacetime production, the solid organization among munition workers in North and West London was considerably depleted; but in other districts where war production had been less important—particularly East London—membership increased. The net result was a London membership numbering some 30,000 in 1920, with a composition more diverse than in any other of the union's divisions; the coverage included engineering, metal, rubber, and other manufactures, brewing and food processing, government and municipal employment, building trades, and a range of service industries. While the union scarcely succeeded in achieving its objective of organizing the 'teeming millions' of the metropolis, this still represented a major extension of trade unionism to the lower-skilled.

[35] The change was almost certainly a reflection of the union's internal politics. It is scarcely probable that Dallas relinquished control of London voluntarily to Beard; in later years their relationship was certainly extremely embittered, and already there were important differences of political opinion between them. It appears that Beard's dual positions as Divisional Organizer for London and Birmingham were largely nominal; subordinates exercised routine control in both divisions, while Beard concentrated on his national role as President (which was not, in theory, a full-time office).

Growth was even more rapid in the remaining section of the original London organizing district: the Home Counties division. In the eastern area of the division, the pre-war agricultural membership was largely lost in the first years of war; but after the appointment of Jack Shingfield as Local organizer in 1916 there was a rapid expansion. By 1920 there was hardly a village in Essex, and parts of the adjoining counties, without a Workers' Union branch; total membership in the Eastern Counties had risen to 35,000.

Further west, the war brought strong branches of engineering and munition workers in Luton and Bedford, but the armistice caused some losses. In Witney, membership was affected little either by the outbreak of war or by its conclusion. The armistice however brought a growth of membership among sections where organization had been interrupted by the war: agricultural workers generally, and brickworkers in Bedfordshire and Buckinghamshire. By 1920 the north-western section of the Division held nearly 20,000 members.

In the Southern Home Counties, pre-war organization had been minimal; but following the appointment of a Portsmouth organizer, George Rogers, in 1915, considerable progress was made. Some twenty branches were opened for various sections of dockyard workers and membership, reaching over 2,000 by the armistice, continued to expand and in 1920 stood at some 5,000. This was then boosted by the amalgamation of the local Government Employees' Union, with some 7,000–8,000 members; its secretary, Arthur Gourd, was taken onto the union's staff with the status of Divisional Organizer. Further east, the later years of the period saw the growth of a number of branches in the Sussex coastal resorts, catering mainly for municipal workers. As in the rest of the division, many farm workers were recruited in Hampshire, Sussex, and Surrey after 1917. By 1920 there existed a membership of over 20,000 in an area which before the war held only some 1,000 members. The whole Home Counties division was now second in size to Birmingham, containing a sixth of total union membership.

The remaining areas of Britain were of less importance during these years. In Devon and Cornwall the war seriously disrupted the china clay industry, which provided the bulk of local membership. In the second half of the war Cornish organization was revived with recruitment among tin miners and munition workers in Camborne and Redruth. The small Devonport branch led the union's advance in the dockyards; by the end of the war 6,000 members were claimed. With the armistice, this pattern of development was reversed. Discharges by the Admiralty caused a heavy loss of membership in Plymouth and Devonport, while the end of war demand caused the closure of many of the Cornish tin mines. But the clay industry once more expanded and membership recovered; postwar conditions in the industry were satisfactorily determined by a Joint Industrial Council, formed in 1918. Branches of North Devon lace and glove workers, opened during the war, also grew rapidly, providing several thousand members by 1920. Total membership in the division was then somewhat above 20,000.

In the remainder of South-West England, covered by Matt Giles, efforts at expansion were less successful. The Dockers' Union was already well established in the area—it had virtually driven the Workers' Union out of Bristol in 1910; and though the Divisional Office was moved here from Swansea in 1915, the results in terms of membership in the city were disappointing. From 1916 a chain of branches was opened in Somerset by Ruby Part, the first (and one of the youngest) of wartime female organizers; the new members were mainly women glove-workers in isolated rural districts, and their organization was a considerable achievement. Membership was also recruited in Bournemouth and Poole, first at an Admiralty ammunition factory, then among building and municipal workers. But it is doubtful whether the total membership in the Bristol division was ever far above 10,000.

Progress in South Wales was no better; the only significant expansion over the period was among the metal workers of the Swansea district. At the end of the war the Executive sent the union's Stoke organizer, Hugh Lawrie, to take charge of the area as a separate division; but there was little to justify this step.[36] At the beginning of the decade South Wales had provided 20 per cent of the union's membership, but by now the proportion had fallen to 2 per cent.

[36] It seems likely that internal politics were involved. Lawrie was the union's most senior organizer without Divisional status.

In Scotland, the war provided the opportunity for rapid expansion—concentrated, as before, in the Glasgow area. Considerable membership was achieved among female dilutees in the Clydeside munition factories, and the local tube trade—unsuccessfully tackled by the union before 1914—was thoroughly organized. Elsewhere in Scotland, new areas of organization were opened; notably in Rosyth, where a naval base was built, and among textile workers in the Border Counties. But with the armistice, the union's membership in munitions disappeared; and gains elsewhere could merely compensate for this loss. At the end of the decade, membership in the division thus remained around its 1918 level of 30,000.

In Ireland there was a considerable improvement on the pre-war situation. In 1914 there had been no local organizer and little more than a thousand members. But in 1915 the union's South Staffordshire organizer, Billy Adamson, was transferred to Belfast; on his return to England at the end of the war he was succeeded as Divisional Organizer by a local member, James McKeag. By 1920 a membership of nearly 20,000 was achieved, drawn mainly from the shipyards, the linen industry, and—in the post-war period—the building trade.

The last years of the decade saw the extension of the union's organization outside the British Isles. Following its success in organizing Admiralty employees at British dockyards, the union was approached by a small society in Gibraltar, and absorbed 'the whole of the organised Government workers . . . numbering 2,000'.[37] Giles was given the responsibility for these new members, and he subsequently opened a branch of 500 dockyard workers in Malta, and another in Tangier. In 1919 it was decided that the union should organize in South Africa, and an ASE member, George Kendall—one of the Rand deportees of 1913—was appointed to take charge of this work. The choice was unfortunate, for 'owing to Mr. Kendall's drinking habits and neglect to carry out his engagements' the funds which the union expended were wholly wasted.[38] Despite the hopes of international coverage, only 3,057 overseas members were returned at the end of 1920.

[37] *Annual Report*, 1919.
[38] Duncan, letter to Madeley, 22 Jan. 1921.

The structure of the union's membership at the end of the decade may be compared with that of the other main general unions. The General Workers had its two strongest districts in London and the South and in Lancashire; there were also important sections in Yorkshire, Scotland, and North-East England. The NAUL had originated on Tyneside, but subsequently developed major centres in Liverpool, South Yorkshire, and Northern Ireland. Both therefore had the bulk of their organization in the traditional centres of British manufacturing. The Dockers' Union was of course based principally on the major sea-ports, notably London and Bristol; its main industrial coverage was in South Wales and the West of England. The Workers' Union was by contrast most prominent in those areas—the Midlands and the South—where British industry was expanding most rapidly.

THE GOVERNMENT OF THE WORKERS' UNION

The period saw important changes in the structure of authority within the union. Control was formally vested in the General Executive Committee; but before 1914 this body met infrequently, was composed mainly of inexperienced members, and made little attempt to develop its own policy; this task was left to the President and Secretary. Central direction was in any case limited in scope; the main issues requiring decision at this level were the appointment of organizers and the administration of the union's benefit funds. Industrial relations remained very much the prerogative of the rank and file at local level. Collective bargaining (a somewhat grand title for the processes which applied to most members in the pre-war years) was normally confined to the individual factory or department. 'Deputations of workmen' were a common channel for the presentation of collective demands; more formal applications and negotiations might be conducted by the branch secretary; the occasional 'trade movement' on a district basis would be co-ordinated by the local District Committee. Where a local full-time official existed his task was to recruit new members rather than to control existing ones; he would normally be involved in negotiations only after deadlock had been reached domestically, and often after the members had stopped work. The rules did indeed prescribe that the Executive should sanction all strikes, but this was merely in order to regulate the payment of union benefit; it was apparently accepted that members would often stop work 'unofficially' and only afterwards seek Executive approval. Such indeed was the origin of almost all the disputes which constituted the Black Country Strike.

The growth of membership, the wartime Industrial Truce, and the development of formalized bargaining procedures, all led to a transformation in this situation. With the official renunciation of strike action on war work, the concept of an unofficial dispute became for the first time a clear one; and the union's leaders were determined to prevent such outbreaks occurring. Thus it was necessary for the growing staff of organizers to become involved in negotiations *before* deadlock was reached. The extension of formal recognition by employers accelerated this development; the union had now to specify clearly who had the right to negotiate, and to undertake that members would observe agreements made on their behalf. The rule book of 1919 bore the imprint of this new situation. It became explicit that the Executive Committee had the power 'to inaugurate and conduct all trade movements', 'to settle disputes that may arise between the members and their employers', and 'to declare strikes, to order and direct the members of the Union to withdraw their labour and to fix the date of such withdrawal and to return to work and to fix the date of such return'. Branch initiative was limited to the right to suggest trade movements for Executive endorsement.

This change was merely one aspect of a broader process of increased central control. Before 1910, with Duncan the union's sole employee at Head Office, it was inevitable that authority was largely decentralized. By the outbreak of war the situation was quite different; there was a central staff of some two dozen to cope with the needs of the increased membership. At the end of the decade an elaborate administrative machine existed, employing a hundred workers. A Chief Clerk had general responsibility for office management; a separate Accounts Department operated under a Head Clerk; and an Executive Clerk took minutes for the GEC, kept it serviced with information, and saw to the implementation of many of its decisions. In addition the Arbitration Department, created during the war, supervised all details of the union's industrial work at national level.

But the most significant change was in the status of the Executive. The war brought a substantial increase in the amount of business conducted, and it soon became customary to hold fortnightly two-day meetings. Following the Whitley Reports, the union secured representation on some fifty Joint Industrial Councils and similar bodies; and though most representatives of the Workers' Union were full-time organizers, GEC members (who were responsible for the appointments) sat on the Councils of any industry of which they had special knowledge. Most members took seats on at least two such bodies; in addition, all occasionally attended engineering Central Conferences. By the end of the decade Executive members thus normally spent two or three days a week on union business (receiving payment for loss of earnings); and for provincial members, who required additional travelling time, the position became effectively a full-time one. Before the war, EC members had been elected annually. In 1915 the term of office became two years, half the members retiring each year; and in 1919 this was extended to three years. In itself this ensured that the Executive became a more experienced body; it also gave members time to make themselves well known within the division which they represented, thus enhancing their prospects of re-election. Finally, the 1919 rule book extensively amplified the formal powers of the GEC. The new rules appear for the first time to have been drafted under close legal guidance, and the Executive's monopoly of authority was established unambiguously. Its powers had been set out in less than a page of the previous rule book; now over four pages were required.

Against this extended central authority there existed only limited countervailing power. The national conference, first held in 1916, was assigned no policy-making powers; it was solely a talking-shop, and one at which organizers and Executive members often took more than their fair share of the discussion. Its powerlessness was demonstrated when the first conference was held: a motion criticizing Beard and Duncan for their attitude to conscription and the Munitions Act was carried by 33 votes to 12, but both officials declared that they would ignore the resolution.

Attempts to restore to the District Committees some of the powers they had enjoyed when the union was first formed were equally unsuccessful. Beard's main opponent for the Presidency in 1915 championed the cause of local autonomy, and the conference in the following year endorsed this demand. But instead the authority of the DCs was still further reduced. At the time of the 1916 conference there were 30 Committees operating; many covered a significant proportion of the union's membership. But by 1920 the number had increased to 150; this inevitably diluted the influence of each separate DC. The rules of 1919 finally made clear that the functions of DCs were confined to 'consultative purposes or propaganda work'; and the GEC was given powers to open or close them and to prescribe their constitutions.

The electoral process itself imposed only limited constraints on the use made of the increased powers of the Executive. Before the war there was a regular turnover in EC membership; but this was less a verdict on the record of sitting members than a reflection of the upheaval in the geographical basis of organization, with branches rising from obscurity and voting their local leader into office. But after 1914 the structure of organization became more stable; and as has been seen, the EC members obtained a three-year term of office. By the end of the decade each member represented an area which covered on average about twenty DCs. Sitting members of the Executive enjoyed the extremely advantageous facility of visiting, at union expense, all DCs in their area in order to report and explain GEC action. This kept them in contact with the active branch members who could exercise considerable influence in the branches at election times. Sitting members were further assisted by the secrecy which increasingly shrouded Executive business. Printed minutes were sent to branches after each meeting, but from 1914 these became progressively less informative: no indication was given of the attitudes of individual members on contentious issues, and soon all reference to controversial items of business was excluded. Thus the rank and file had little basis on which to judge the record of their representative, apart from the reports which he himself gave.

The most important source of alternative authority was in fact totally removed from the formal structure of union govern-

ment, arising from the growth of unofficial workshop organization. The rule book prescribed the appointment of branch
collectors to collect contributions from members working in the
same establishment. As in many other unions, this official often
acquired a negotiating role for which there was no provision in
the rules. Even before the outbreak of war it had been noted
that 'upon him frequently falls the duty of acting as spokesman
for the others, in discussion with Foreman or Works Manager';[39]
and the title of shop steward had come to signify this new role.
The war greatly increased the number of shop-floor grievances
requiring speedy settlement, and the number of shop stewards
increased rapidly—leading in 1917 to a national agreement
with the Engineering Employers' Federation providing for their
incorporation in the industry's disputes procedure. But the
stewards were never integrated within the union's own structure;
indeed their title never appeared in the rule book. The method
of their appointment varied from district to district: some were
elected by the branch, other on the shop-floor; some acted as
collectors, others did not. Thus stewards were only partially
susceptible to control from above. In some districts (notably
Sheffield and Coventry) this relative autonomy was reflected in
participation in left-wing rank-and-file movements with
stewards from other unions; occasionally it was demonstrated in
strike action against the instructions of a national leadership
which was increasingly averse to militant action. Though the
rules gave the Executive the authority to impose discipline in
such cases, it had little effective power against shop floor
representatives who enjoyed the confidence of their members.

INTER-UNION RELATIONS

Continued growth brought the Workers' Union a new status
within the trade union movement. This was demonstrated by
its eventual affiliation to the TUC. A second application to join
was made in 1916, but was rejected on the grounds that the
union was 'encroaching on the membership of other societies'.[40]
But in the following year a third request was accepted, appar-

---

[39] Ellery, *Record*, Jan. 1914.
[40] TUC Parliamentary Committee *Minutes*, 24 May 1916.

ently without opposition. Needless to say, its methods of organization had not changed in the intervening period; but its continued exclusion had become increasingly ridiculous.

The union's introduction to Congress in 1918 was scarcely a happy one. The Agricultural Labourers' Union, which had once shown little desire to organize outside Norfolk and the adjoining counties, had by now developed national ambitions and sharply attacked the Workers' Union for recruiting farm workers. When Beard attempted to justify the union's position he received a hostile reception from the delegates, many of whom were sympathetic to the objective of industrial unionism. Earlier in the same year the TUC Parliamentary Committee had arranged meetings between representatives of the two unions in order to improve relationships; but while the Workers' Union was willing to accept a demarcation of areas of organization, the ALU refused to consider any compromise which would dilute its claim to exclusive representation of farm workers. Thereafter, open conflict between the two unions was never far below the surface.

The years after 1914 also saw increasing inter-union friction in engineering. The war brought into new prominence such issues as the nature of engineering skills, the position of the lower-skilled worker, and his rights as against those of the craftsman. Thus the conflicts which had previously been smouldering in a few districts now erupted at a national level. While all general unions were obliged to take issue with the craft societies, the Workers' Union because of the nature of its membership was most centrally involved.

At first, relations at national level were cordial enough. At the beginning of 1915 discussions were held between the Executives of the Workers' Union and the ASE to arrange a working agreement. This resulted in April in a memorandum proposing joint negotiating and recruiting activities; on the vexed question of demarcation it was suggested that skilled members of the Workers' Union should be permitted (but not obliged) to transfer to the ASE, that the union would not attempt to recruit workers eligible for full membership of the ASE, and that semi-skilled machinists might join either organization. But a month later the policy-making body of the ASE, the Delegate Meeting, rejected these recommendations. Fearful of inroads into traditional craft prerogatives, the delegates refused to consider closer relationships with a mere general union.[41]

This aloofness was soon reflected in the Society's bargaining strategy; its officials refused to submit claims jointly with the Workers' Union at engineering Central Conferences or before the Committee on Production. At local level, the ASE seceded from joint negotiating bodies which included the Workers' Union, taking the other craft societies with it; while in centres where the union was not yet a member its applications for affiliation were rejected. On occasion, even more drastic action was taken to frustrate the union's work: a policy which, according to Duncan, 'almost made him look back with regret upon his 27 years' membership of the ASE'.[42] This hostility was not directed at the Workers' Union alone, though it was the first to suffer; all general unions experienced similar treatment. The Society's antipathy apparently derived both from a resurgence of craft consciousness, and from a belief that craftsmen would gain a sectional advantage by pressing their claims independently, where possible in advance and even at the expense of those of the lower-skilled.

An issue which accentuated inter-union conflict was the organization of female dilutees. The ASE did not itself accept female members, yet it was anxious that women's wages should be subject to trade union control; but its major fear was that these new entrants to engineering might remain as competitors *after* the war. Apprehensive at the interest of the Workers' Union in recruiting women munition workers, in June 1915 it signed an agreement for joint action with the National Federation of Women Workers, a purely female union. As the price of ASE assistance with recruitment, the Federation agreed that at the end of the war it would withdraw its members from all those occupations claimed for male craftsmen. Accordingly, in July 1915 all ASE districts received a circular from their Executive urging them to oppose Workers' Union attempts to represent women workers and instead to assist the NFWW.[43]

---

[41] This reversal of policy reflected a serious conflict of opinion within the ASE itself at this time. Craft traditions retained their strongest hold in the North, where the Society still had the bulk of its membership.

[42] Speech quoted in *Woolwich Pioneer*, 20 Aug. 1915.

[43] Cole, *Trade Unionism in Munitions*, p. 204.

As a result, attempts were made in several areas to sabotage the
union's efforts, and at times it was subject to violent abuse.
Some Workers' Union officials were stung to reply in kind.
Beard was particularly incensed; the concern of the ASE for
the conditions of female workers was, he declared, 'more to
protect men's craft interests, and it is to some extent incidental
that the women benefit.... If there were no menace to the
craft interests, many men who today are declaring their undying
love for the women's cause would see them hang before lifting a
finger'.[44]

This conflict had wider repercussions. Previously the ASE
had ostracised all general unions; now the Workers' Union
attracted its special hostility. Soon it was prepared to co-operate
with other general unions if this would work to the disadvantage
of the Workers' Union. This was demonstrated in September
1916 when it signed an agreement with the Gasworkers (now
entitled the National Union of General Workers) defining
spheres of interest, along the lines of the abortive memorandum
with the Workers' Union a year previously.

But the earlier general hostility between the craft societies and
the unions of the lower-skilled was soon revived. The operation
of conscription caused widespread unrest at the end of 1916
with the recruitment of skilled workers, and a hasty agreement
was reached in November between the ASE and the government authorizing the Society to issue a card of exemption to its
skilled members engaged on war work. Immediately the other
craft societies demanded similar treatment, and the 'Trade
Card' scheme was extended piecemeal.

The general unions were furious, for the government's
action gave official recognition to craft distinctions which were
already crumbling. The ASE, in many areas at least, was no
longer a 'pure' craft union, since it contained members who
were not, on any realistic assessment, fully skilled. Yet though a
strict application of the scheme would have excluded such
workers from exemption, as members of the ASE they were
receiving their Trade Cards. Meanwhile members of the
general unions, many of whom were carrying out identical
work, received no protection. The Workers' Union was
particularly concerned because of its strong representation of

[44] *Record*, Aug. 1916.

machine workers, who in some cases had been able to progress
to skilled operations. 'We can prove right up to the hilt,' wrote
one of the London organizers, 'case after case where WU men
have had to show ASE men how to do their work, thus proving
themselves just as capable as the so-called mechanic. . . . The
Workers' Union is going to fight this out until we have either
got the same treatment as the ASE or have burst the whole
scheme'.[45] To make matters worse, in some districts it was
reported that the ASE was taking the opportunity to 'poach'
members of the Workers' Union, telling them to 'join our
union and you won't have to go into the army'.[46] Even in
areas where semi-skilled membership was small, the Engineers'
attitude caused intense resentment:

> Don't send me in the army, George—I am in the ASE.
> Take all the bloody labourers, but, for God's sake, don't
> take me.
> You want me for a soldier? Well, that can never be—
> A man of my ability, and in the ASE![47]

From the outset the Workers' Union led all general unions in
demanding equal treatment. When an approach to the government for protection for their members 'doing skilled work in
the engineering trade' failed to yield concrete results, an
extensive campaign of protest was launched. There were bitter
attacks on the pretensions of the 'so-called craft unions'; and
even Beard, despite his previous unimpeachably 'patriotic'
attitudes, was prepared to endorse threats of strike action. This
agitation achieved its effect; in April 1917 the government,
which by now fully regretted its introduction of Trade Cards,
abolished the whole scheme. But conflict between the ASE and
the general unions was not easily eliminated; for with the
progressive extension of conscription throughout the war, the
Society's pressure for special privileges continued to exacerbate
relations.

It was in the post-war period that resentment in the Workers'
Union reached its height. As the price of its acceptance of
dilution in 1915, the ASE received a government pledge that all

[45] C. W. Gibson, *Trade Union Worker*, Feb. 1917.
[46] *Record*, Jan. 1917.
[47] An 'amateur poet' quoted in the *Sheffield Daily Independent*, 18 May 1917. I am
grateful to Mr. James Hinton for this reference.

changes in working practices would be reversed after the armistice. Though there was a smooth reversion to the pre-war situation in much of engineering, this remained incomplete, and the Society pressed the government to make good its undertaking. The resulting Restoration of Pre-War Practices Bill was accepted as inevitable by most general unions, though they hoped to persuade the craft societies 'not to operate the Act harshly as against our members'.[48] The Workers' Union alone voiced its opposition to the measure; the proposed legislation, according to Beard, 'tries to convey a return to a condition of things which did not exist. It pretends to protect crafts that lie in the limbo of lost things. . . . It is the last effort to keep going a mere fiction'.[49] Up to now the union had maintained some attempt to avoid outright confrontation with the craft societies; it still retained its rule that skilled workers might not become members, and in 1915 it had been willing to allow members promoted to skilled work to transfer to the ASE. Such restraint was now formally abandoned. Craft unionism, according to Beard, was now 'mean little Toryism . . . one of the sinister features of the present trade union movement, which must be fought'.[50] And with the new rule book of 1919, all restrictions on the enrolment of craftsmen were removed.

The tendency to act independently of—and even in opposition to—the craft societies had been discernible before 1914; the process was now fully developed. Yet the other main general unions still sought an amicable relationship; they were members of the Federation of Engineering and Shipbuilding Trades,[51] and were eager for a working arrangement with the ASE (as the General Workers had indeed achieved). The reason for this difference was that the Workers' Union was in its strongest districts the largest union in engineering, and was not prepared to accept a relationship of inferiority (which the ASE demanded of its associates). And though other general unions, as a result of the war, contained sections of higher-grade machinists, the Workers' Union had the highest proportion of

---

[48] National Federation of General Workers, *Executive Minutes*, 28 June 1919.

[49] *Record*, May 1919.

[50] Triennial Conference, Sept. 1919.

[51] The Workers' Union itself applied for affiliation in 1918; but it was asked to agree that members promoted to skilled work would be required to transfer to a craft society, and refused to give this undertaking.

workers capable of skilled work; and thus it was far less willing formally to accept the status of a lower-skilled organization, or to give any undertakings which might jeopardize their interests. This defiant independence had wider repercussions. The ASE was keen to extend its 1916 agreement with the General Workers, and made several approaches to the NFGW; but the Workers' Union blocked any such arrangement. According to Beard, 'we know the conditions on which we can have an agreement—those conditions do not satisfy us'.[52] On the machine question, the union pressed successfully for an uncompromising line by all general unions; while the craft unions proposed a rigid rating of machines which would have given them an effective monopoly of their operation, the NFGW insisted 'that our people shall have the right to progress where they show capacity'.[53] With the Workers' Union acting as militant defender of the rights of the lower-skilled, other general unions were reluctant to appear too ready to compromise. The Workers' Union thus gave institutional form to the conflicts of interest which existed within the engineering labour force. Its efforts hastened the breakdown within trade unionism of rigid craft divisions which were incompatible with the developing structure of the industry. In the long run, all sections of engineering labour benefited.

THE NATIONAL AMALGAMATED WORKERS' UNION

If the war period brought increasing friction with the craft societies, it also saw closer unity among the general unions. The creation of the NFGW permitted, for the first time, effective common action in collective bargaining. In addition—though the ambitious pre-war plan for a mass merger was shelved—all the major general unions were involved in more modest amalgamation discussions.

Since war conditions made a successful amalgamation ballot virtually impossible to achieve, it was necessary for the 1914 scheme to be abandoned for the duration of the war. But rank and file activists soon became impatient at this delay, and in 1916 the Workers' Union decided to pursue independently

[52] NFGW Annual Meeting, Aug. 1921.
[53] Central Conference, 28 Oct. 1920.

Duncan's earlier idea of a partial merger. An approach was made to the third largest general union, the National Amalgamated Union of Labour, and lengthy discussions followed. Subsequently a third union joined in: the Municipal Employees' Association, a body which because of the restricted scope of its organization had been excluded from the TUC and the Labour Party, and which now saw amalgamation as a means of regaining the recognition of the labour movement.

At the end of 1917, detailed proposals were agreed by the Executives of the three unions. A National Amalgamated Workers' Union would be established, controlled by a Joint Executive (with five representatives from the Workers' Union, five from the NAUL, and three from the MEA, together with the three General Secretaries). Each union would pay to the federal body from its central funds 3s. per member, and $1\frac{1}{4}d$. weekly thereafter; this fund would be used to finance all organization and trade benefits. Ballots in each union endorsed these proposals by a comfortable majority; the wisdom of Duncan's idea was fully demonstrated, however, for the numbers voting fell far short of the legal requirement for a complete amalgamation. On 1 January 1919 the National Amalgamated Workers' Union formally began its existence.

Official reactions within the Workers' Union—both to the operation of the new body, and to the concurrent preparations for complete amalgamation—were almost lyrical. 'Already one can discern the new spirit within the vast membership beginning to feel its way to better things. The old suspicions and jealousy are beginning to flicker out. . . . Doubt and distrust are dying, division is passing away, and the days of closer unity are stealing quietly into our midst.'[54] As far as the Municipal Employees were concerned this was no exaggeration. 'The Executive machinery is now working smoothly', the MEA reported.[55] Its representatives joined the Workers' Union delegation to conferences of the labour movement; while in some areas its branches were placed under the control of Workers' Union organizers and were even described as Workers' Union branches.

With the NAUL, however, relations within the new body were far less happy. The reason was a total conflict in trade

[54] Duncan, *Record*, May 1919.   [55] MEA *Annual Report*, 1918.

union philosophy. The constitution of the NAUL was modelled on the 'primitive democracy' of the old local craft societies, and was designed to overcome the danger that full-time officials might further their own interests to the detriment of the membership. Decisions of policy required the sanction of a Delegate Meeting or referendum of members. The Executive Council was elected from members living within 16 miles of the Newcastle Head Office, and was thus able to meet regularly outside working hours. Organisers, known as District Delegates, were elected from the rank and file and subject both to close Executive surveillance and to triennial re-election. This machinery was a valuable instrument of democratic control for a small and localized organization, but far less suited to the needs of a national union with a combined membership of over half a million. So while the NAUL remained committed to its own ideals of trade union organization, both the Workers' Union and the MEA believed that some sacrifice of democracy was essential in the interests of efficiency, and thus of the members themselves.

From the outset these differences bedevilled the functioning of the NAWU. The presence of Beard—a full-time official—on the Joint Executive was bitterly criticized. The appointment of new organizers by the Workers' Union caused an almost hysterical reaction. Proposals for higher salaries for officials (at a time when workers in every industry were receiving wage increases) were fiercely resisted. Finally, the insistence of the Workers' Union and the MEA that while organizers' wage sheets should be available for inspection, these should not form part of the agenda at Executive meetings—there were over 200 organizers in the three unions—was received with horror: 'the other parties to the Amalgamation were going to have all their own way, and were going to act without regard to either rules, regulations or anything else; but simply make a condition of things that would make the Officials masters of the situation'.[56] A section of the NAUL Executive had from the outset been lukewarm about the amalgamation, and such issues provided ample opportunity to present the Workers' Union in an unfavourable light. This campaign extended to angry attacks on alleged 'poaching' by the Workers' Union; but

[56] NAUL *Executive Minutes*, 18 Aug. 1919.

there is little to suggest that such complaints (which were indeed far more frequent *before* the amalgamation) were the primary cause of the differences between the two unions.[57]

Understandably, when the constitution of a complete amalgamation was discussed there was deadlock on the rules which should cover officials. The MEA and the Workers' Union both favoured appointment by an elected Executive; the NAUL insisted on direct election. Unable to maintain an effective opposition indefinitely, the NAUL sought a new ally: the General Workers. In 1919 this union was negotiating for an amalgamation with the Dockers; but by the beginning of 1920 these plans had fallen through, and it agreed to hold discussions with the NAWU. A joint sub-committee was established, and throughout 1920 a plan of amalgamation was hammered out.

The entry of the General Workers into the discussions created the prospect of a merger of all three main general unions—resulting in 'by far the largest and most powerful trade union organisation in the world, with over 1,250,000 members'.[58] But it also introduced yet another viewpoint into the conflicting approaches to the desirable structure of government in the new amalgamation. In addition, it brought new problems of personality. Bell, for twenty years the General Secretary of the NAUL, enjoyed a considerable standing within the movement as a result of his work in the Labour Party and the Federation of General Workers. But because of the size of his union it was inevitable that whatever the formal provisions he would take second place to Beard and Duncan in a complete amalgamation (though the status of Beard, a full-time official, as Workers' Union President caused some resentment in the NAUL). But the General Workers had long been accustomed to the position of leading general union, and even now was only closely behind the Workers' Union in terms of membership.

[57] The worst trouble was in Belfast; but here the poaching occurred before the amalgamation and was the fault of a branch secretary acting without official union knowledge. Complaints by branches in Barrow and Liverpool seem not to have been particularly serious. The Sheffield organizer of the NAUL referred to 'persistent efforts of other unions to steal our membership unblushingly' (ibid., 5 Sept. 1919), but gave no evidence; for political reasons he was already strongly hostile to the Workers' Union, and his district had been the main centre of opposition to the amalgamation within his union.

[58] *Annual Report*, 1920.

Thorne, its Secretary, was one of the most prominent 'elder statesmen' of the labour movement; Clynes, its President, had served in the wartime Coalition government and had also acquired a reputation far more prominent than either Beard or Duncan. It was improbable that they would accept anything less than the leadership of an amalgamation. Though optimism remained high, these problems were eventually to prove too great.

THE UNION IN 1920

So ended a decade in which the Workers' Union had increased its membership a hundredfold, to become the largest single union in the country—'a record of continued expansion and growth . . . unequalled in the history of Trade Unions'.[59] The six years from the outbreak of war had seen, in absolute terms, by far the major part of this increase. Yet in an important sense the natural process of pre-war growth had been distorted. The conditions of the period were essentially artificial: wartime inflation and compulsory arbitration gave all general unions abnormal advantages; and their recruitment was drawn predominantly from a temporary labour force in munition trades. This led inevitably to post-war disruption; and though the losses were more than made up in the short-lived boom which followed, the new and extended membership had dangerously shallow roots. Less favourable circumstances were to show that the foundations of the union's achievements were weak indeed.

[59] *Annual Report*, 1919.

5

DISASTER 1920–1929

At first sight there was no reason to doubt that the remarkable achievements of the years before 1920 might form the basis of even greater success. Such was indeed the expectation of the union's leaders: 'if we stick to the task we can easily surpass our best'.[1] But closer examination might have shown good cause for disquiet. By the end of the decade the dislocating effects of the return to peace-time production had been absorbed, yet membership turnover was so high that the union's expansion had ground to a halt. The financial position was equally ominous: the union's large reserves had been accumulated almost entirely in the war period when expenditure, in proportion to membership, was abnormally low. With the end of the war, demands on the funds rose rapidly; indeed, the accounts for 1919 showed a deficit. If such instability could exist in years of economic prosperity, the prospects for less favourable times were scarcely rosy.

The depression years of the 1920s demonstrated only too clearly this instability underlying the union's recently acquired strength. The history of the previous decade was reversed: then, expanding membership had brought increased income, allowing greater expenditure on organization and leading in turn to further growth; now, reduced membership and income necessitated economies in organization, causing new losses of membership. Financial and numerical decline thus interacted in a cumulative process of disaster.

The decade may be divided into three main periods. Between 1920 and 1923 there was a spectacular collapse. Membership fell from nearly 500,000 to 140,000—a drop of over 70 per cent to the level of August 1914. Financially, these years were even more catastrophic. At the end of 1920 the balance sheet showed assets exceeding liabilities by £300,000; a year later this balance had been reduced to £125,000, and by 1923 it had

[1] *Annual Report* 1919.

fallen almost to £80,000. Office property was valued at £50,000; excluding these highly illiquid assets, the reserves in fact fell from £250,000 to £30,000. For the next three years it appeared that the tide had turned. The fall in membership was halted, and a slow but definite increase ensued. The annual deficit in the union's finances was sharply reduced, and in 1925 was transformed into a small surplus. But the last years of the decade saw renewed decline. The General Strike marked the turning point: benefit payments to members in 1926 were 50 per cent higher than in 1925, and the balance of assets was halved. The downward spiral began once more; by the beginning of 1929, membership had fallen almost to 120,000, and the balance sheet showed a surplus of under £30,000—less than the value of premises included as assets. Bankruptcy and total collapse loomed perilously near; only the amalgamation with the Transport and General Workers' Union, which took effect in August 1929, saved the Workers' Union.

This disastrous record is largely explained by the drastic change in economic circumstances. At the end of 1920 the post-war boom suddenly collapsed, prices tumbled, and unemployment soared to unprecedented levels. Official returns showed 17.8 per cent of insured workers unemployed by the summer of 1921; for over a decade it was rare for the proportion out of work to fall below 10 per cent. The economic crisis led to a wholesale attack on workers' conditions, and in many areas of industry mass unemployment was accompanied by the disintegration of established bargaining procedures. The whole trade union movement suffered grievously: total membership fell by 35 per cent in three years, and by the end of the decade the loss was 42 per cent. The collapse was worst among those organizations—notably the general unions—which had made the greatest gains in the previous decade; by 1923 the NAUL had lost 65 per cent of its membership and the General Workers 60 per cent. 'General workers' were for the most part new recruits to trade unionism, and in addition were particularly vulnerable to unemployment and employer attack under adverse economic conditions. So there was nothing surprising in the scale of the decline.

The Workers' Union suffered worst of all the main general unions in the early 1920s. To some extent, this was merely paying the price of its exceptionally rapid growth in the previous years. But the union was also at a disadvantage by virtue of the industrial composition of its membership. In engineering, which had long been its main area of organization, economic conditions were worse than in most other industries, and wage reductions—particularly for the lower-skilled—were more savage. In agriculture, which at the turn of the decade provided the union's second largest section, demoralization and disorganization were even greater; indeed the National Union of Agricultural Workers (as the ALU was now called) was the only major British union to lose an even higher proportion of its membership during the decade than did the Workers' Union.

There was also an internal reason for the magnitude of the initial collapse. The Unemployment Insurance Act of 1920, which made insurance against unemployment compulsory for almost the whole working population, permitted trade unions to administer the state scheme for those members who contributed to their own out-of-work funds. (An analogous provision had been contained in the National Insurance Act of 1911.) The Workers' Union Executive decided to exploit this new opportunity by making the union's own scheme more attractive. Under the rules of 1919, members could contribute 6*d.* weekly to the fund;[2] after a year's payments they became eligible, in the following twelve months, to benefits of £1 for up to six weeks and 10*s.* for a further six weeks.

In September 1920 the Executive announced an offer 'unique in its generosity':[3] full benefit would be payable for the whole twelve weeks per year; members joining the fund before December would become immediately eligible for benefit; even those currently out of work would qualify after eight weeks' contributions. The reasons for the change are obvious. The union's leaders were clearly worried at the high rate of turnover—no less that 600,000 members had lapsed in three years; if more members were eligible for friendly benefits their commitment to the union would be stronger. Other general unions were now launching unemployment funds, and the Workers' Union was determined to offer best value for money.

[2] It was also possible to pay lower contributions and receive proportionately lower benefits.
[3] *Record*, Oct. 1920.

In addition, the new scheme was seen as an important means of stimulating recruitment.

But the Executive—and Beard and Duncan, who appear to have suggested the new offer—were gambling with the union's future; and it was a gamble in which the cards were stacked heavily against them. In the past the out-of-work fund had shown a long-term surplus; but the balance was small, and the expenses of the fund's administration were carried by the union as a whole. Recent years showed that the fund, even on its existing level of benefits, rested on very shaky foundations. In twenty years to the end of 1918, only £26,000 was paid in benefit; in 1919 alone claims amounted to £25,000, and in the following year they more than doubled. In both post-war years the fund showed a loss. On any realistic assessment, the union's provisions were already over-generous. The immediate benefit provision, together with the increased benefits, was enough to guarantee that the fund would lose money whatever the economic climate. This could be seen without the benefit of hindsight. In London, full-time officials 'went to great lengths to organize protests by the membership.'[4] Dallas led a deputation of Home Counties organizers to warn GEC members that they would 'cut their bloody throats.' In other parts of the country also there were protests from officials. But all objections were brushed aside.

The consequences of the new benefits exceeded the most pessimistic of predictions. The great publicity given to the offer of 'a pound for sixpence' provided the expected boost to recruitment; in some areas 'queues were formed . . . by workers to join the union',[5] and among the new entrants were many who expected soon to be out of work. Even among those whose employment was apparently secure, many were quickly overwhelmed by the onset of depression. Weekly contributions to the out-of-work fund had averaged £600 in September 1920; by January 1921 they had increased to £2,000. Payments, meanwhile, reached almost £12,000 a week. A single quarter thus saw the loss of a sum equal to a third of the union's total assets—and this when unemployment had as yet reached only half its peak level.

4 R. Sargood, 'Notes re the Workers' Union', (M.S.), 1965.

5 C. E. Akroyd, letter, 6 July 1965.

The response of the union's leaders was too little and too late. At the beginning of February the Executive imposed a weekly levy of 2*d*. on every member (officially to build a 'fighting fund' to resist wage cuts), hoping that this would suffice to support the unemployment benefits. By March it was clear that more drastic action was needed: benefits were reduced to the former scale, and a year's contributions became once more necessary before full benefit was payable (though a new clause was introduced providing for half benefits after six months). Criticisms from some officials that the cuts did not go far enough were rebuffed by the Executive, but were soon proved correct. In April the new scale of benefits was slashed by more than half; and in place of the 2*d*. levy, introduced as a temporary measure, all members were required to contribute at least $1\frac{1}{2}d$. to the out-of-work fund.[6] Even now, though the deficit on the fund was greatly reduced, solvency was not immediately restored; only with the gradual improvement in employment during 1922 was a consistent surplus achieved. In the whole year 1921 the fund lost £140,000; between September 1920 and April 1921 the loss was £185,000. Even under the 1919 rules, the heavy unemployment of 1921 would have caused a serious deficit; but the 'immediate benefit stunt' must have added well over £100,000 to the loss. But for this disastrous episode the Workers' Union might still, in the view of some surviving members, exist today.

For the Workers' Union, wrote Duncan, 'the year 1921 has not been a year at all, it has been a nightmare.'[7] Membership had been halved, falling to 247,000; and there had been a similar drop in income. Despite some attempts to limit organizing costs, and the abolition of the union's rule permitting branches to retain 5 per cent of members' contributions for local purposes, the year's accounts showed a serious loss over and above the deficit on the unemployment fund. All liquid assets were exhausted, and an overdraft of £100,000 was created. 'A few more months', Duncan told his Executive, 'will easily knock the bottom out of the Workers' Union.'[8]

[6] Members in industries not covered by the 1920 Act (notably agriculture) were exempt.

[7] *Annual Report*, 1921.

[8] Report to GEC, 4 Jan. 1922.

In this desperate situation it would be surprising if Duncan
did not recall his struggles two decades earlier, and his response
was similar to that in his first years as Secretary. Considerable
savings were enforced at Central Office, but the main economies
had to come in organizing costs. Natural wastage had reduced
the number of full time organizers only slightly below the peak
level of 160, and their wages and expenses had come to consume
almost half the dwindling income of the General Fund. 'If we
increase the staff rapidly during busy times, then we must like-
wise reduce the staff just as rapidly when income is reduced',
argued Duncan. This may have been good business logic, but
there was opposition from those who thought a trade union
should be run on different principles. At a meeting between the
GEC and Divisional Organizers at the end of 1921 a compromise was agreed: a 15s. reduction in salaries,[9] tight curbs on expenses, the dismissal of some 25 'inefficient' organizers, and the
relegation of others to a three-day working week. The total reduction in organizing costs was somewhere above 20 per cent—
about half what Duncan had proposed. During 1922 there were
further cuts in salaries (totalling 20s. 6d.), and additional though
less drastic dismissals; among other economies were the de-
motion of two Divisional Organizers to subordinate status.

But these savings were largely vitiated by the continued decline in membership and income. Membership fell by over
100,000 during 1922, while the accounts for the year showed a
deficit of £30,000. Duncan was therefore soon urging further
economies. Organizers' expenses, he argued, were in many cases
'out of all proportion to the income of the district', and there
was still 'a very urgent necessity for some reduction in the organizing staff'.[10] The union still employed over 120 organizers,
though membership was a mere 30 per cent of its peak level.
Yet if from a financial viewpoint the union was overstaffed, its
officials were scarcely underworked. Negotiations to prevent
wage reductions were far tougher than those in previous years

[9] The union's first organizers received 30s. a week; this remained the basic rate
until 1914, though senior officials were paid up to 50s. During the war pay
approximately doubled; as with industrial workers, flat-rate increases were
normally given. In 1919 and 1920 there were further rapid increases: Divisional
Organizers' pay reached £8. 15s., the basic rate for ordinary officials £7. 2. 6d.,
and the probationary rate for new appointments £5. 15s.
[10] Report to GEC, 17 Jan. 1923.

to win advances; preventing weaker members from lapsing demanded more effort than their original recruitment; arranging relief for out-of-work members, and representing them in claims before Unemployment Committees, was a new and time-consuming duty. The danger was only too real, given the composition of the union's membership, that further economies would result in yet more loss of membership.

For this reason, Beard opposed Duncan's proposals. 'More saving may in the long run be pure waste'; if the Workers' Union was ever to recover its strength, a full staff of organizers would be needed; even to prevent further decline, constant recruitment was necessary. The officials had already accepted large wage reductions in order to keep dismissals to a minimum. 'To scrap men now will be brutal. It may also be foolish and bad economy and produce in the rest a feeling of insecurity under which no man can work.'[11] The latter view appears to have prevailed. The number of organizers fell by only eight during 1923, at least partly as a result of natural wastage. One reason for this moderation was the realization that the depression had—for the moment—passed its most acute stage; Beard pointed out that the recruitment of new members at the start of 1923 was once more showing an increase, while the persistent fall in income had almost ceased.

Soon there were more general signs of recovery. In 1923 the gap between recruitment and lapsing was closed, membership remaining stable at 140,000; in the following two years there was a steady growth to 152,000. Expenditure in 1923 was brought within £11,000 of income; in 1924 the deficit was further narrowed; and in 1925 the union achieved a modest surplus. With the gradual realization of the union's less liquid securities, the overdraft was slowly reduced, and by April 1926 there was a small credit on the bank account—the first for five years. The progress was admittedly small, but so was the economic improvement; the unemployment rate remained above 10 per cent.[12] It was, according to Duncan, a time 'of small things. Slight improvement in trade, slight improvement in trade union finances, slight increases in trade union membership, but

---

[11] Report to GEC, 13 Feb. 1923.
[12] With the exception of a brief period in the summer of 1924.

a dull dead load of unemployment dragging along.'[13] The union's growth compared favourably with the stagnation of trade unionism generally and was more rapid than that of the unions which in 1924 merged to form the National Union of General and Municipal Workers (though it failed to rival the success of the new Transport and General Workers' Union, with its younger leadership and its concentration in more sheltered industries).

In 1926 the brief period of recovery came to an end. The turning point in the union's fortunes was marked by the mining dispute and the General Strike. Beard, since 1920 a member of the TUC General Council, was involved in the decision to lend the support of the whole trade union movement to the miners' fight against longer hours and lower wages.[14] Following the temporary victory of 'Red Friday' (in July 1925, when the government offered a nine-month subsidy to permit further investigations and negotiations), Beard made clear that the union endorsed this policy: 'Our wholehearted sympathy and moral support goes out to the miners. . . . Throughout the discussions between the TUC and the Miners' Federation we have given active support to the miners in their fight. . . . We could not permit, as trade unionists, the miners accepting the dictates of the mineowners.'[15] In April 1926, when the mining dispute came once more to the crisis point, the union shared in the common decision to hand over full powers to the General Council.

It seems likely that Beard was personally opposed to the decision to call a General Strike. Given his previous political opinions he might have been expected to resist action which, however innocent in intent, could be construed as a 'challenge to the constitution'. Certainly he was highly critical of the miners for refusing to consider terms which the General Council thought acceptable, and strongly supported the decision to call off the strike: 'I am not prepared to put everything our unions have into pawn and feel that it is not appreciated by those people.'[16] But if its President was an unwilling participant in the General Strike, the union as such showed no special reluct-

[13] *Annual Report*, 1925.
[14] Julia Varley was also a member of the General Council when the dispute first arose, but lost her seat shortly afterwards.
[15] *Record*, Aug. 1925.   [16] Lord Citrine, *Men and Work*, 1964, p. 200.

ance. In terms of membership it was firmly committed to the
struggle: 58,000 came out (nearly 40 per cent of total membership) in metal and chemical production, engineering, building,
and power stations. Though some unions were more fully involved, the Workers' Union clearly made a significant contribution to the abortive national dispute.

For the trade union movement as a whole, the long-term
effects of the General Strike may have been slight; but for the
Workers' Union its impact was far more severe. In the years
1923–5 the union had paid on average £8,000 in dispute benefit
and £14,000 in out-of-work benefit; in 1926 the sums were
£32,000 and £26,000. There was a deficit on the year's accounts equal to the increased spending on the two benefits. This
was almost the union's death-blow: the balance of funds was
halved, all realizable assets were long since exhausted, and the
union was once again burdened with an overdraft amounting
to £35,000.

Though economy became once more the order of the day, the
scope for further savings was limited. Duncan pressed once more
for further reductions in the organizing staff, but Beard remained critical. Again there was a compromise: over three
years the number of organizers fell to a hundred, there was a
new squeeze on expenses, and wages were reduced further. But
total expenditure was reduced only to the level of 1918; and
meanwhile, membership and income was continuing to fall. In
1927 all the gains of the brief period of expansion were lost,
numbers declining to 140,000. In the following year losses were
even greater, while by the summer of 1929 only 95,000 members
were returned.[17] The Workers' Union had clearly ceased to be
a viable undertaking: the only alternatives to bankruptcy were
amalgamation, or economies so drastic that organization would
have been abandoned in all but a handful of local and industrial
strongholds—a return, in effect, to the grim tactics of the union's
first dozen years.

The Workers' Union fared particularly badly in these last
depressing years. Between the General Strike and the amalgamation, over a third of its remaining membership was lost; total
trade union membership fell by only an eighth over the same

[17] This last figure may have represented in part a paper loss; the TGWU appears
to have calculated membership more restrictively than the Workers' Union.

period. In general, losses comparable to those of the Workers' Union were suffered only by unions far more seriously involved in the General Strike. Thus the Railwaymen and the TGWU were severely affected; but by 1928 both were clearly recovering. Despite regional variations, the same was true generally of the miners. The NUGMW, which like the Workers' Union had a smaller proportion of its members on strike in 1926, fared no worse than trade unions generally. In its collapse—as in its growth—the performance of the Workers' Union was exceptional.

Membership composition was partly responsible for the union's chronic decline. It has often been noted that 'general workers' present special problems of trade union organization; general unions have typically a membership turnover well above average, and require a higher than average proportion of officers—and hence a greater expenditure per head on management—in order to retain, renew, and service their members. The Workers' Union—'a "general" union of most miscellaneous membership'[18]—displayed these characteristics most clearly in this period. The TGWU before 1929 approximated to an industrial union of dockers and road transport workers.[19] Accordingly, it enjoyed a considerable advantage in times of depression: membership was far more homogeneous than in the Workers' Union, and in many cases had developed a deep-rooted tradition of trade union solidarity; to a large extent it was geographically concentrated, simplifying the work of organization; and some sections of this membership were less affected by unemployment than workers generally. The industrial coverage of the NUGMW was more diverse; but it benefited from the fact that a large proportion of its membership was concentrated in municipal employment and public utilities.[20] This section escaped the worst effects of the depression, and was rarely involved in costly industrial disputes. The Workers' Union, by contrast, was in a weak position to face the ravages of the 1920s. Its largest group of members, in engineering, was severely battered by the early years of the depression, and no other

[18] G. D. H. Cole, *Introduction to Trade Unionism*, 1953, p. 88.

[19] In 1925 the four Trade Groups covering these workers held over 70 per cent of total membership.

[20] The proportion was estimated at just under a third in 1926, nearly half in 1937 (H. A. Clegg, *General Union*, 1954, pp. 31–2).

industry—certainly no 'sheltered' industry—provided a section large enough to stabilize membership during the decade. On the contrary, the union's final burst of expansion during the post-war boom provided it with a large group of members whose only common characteristic was that their occupations had previously been thought to offer little hope of trade union organization. The growth during and after the war had also given the union a geographical coverage more widespread than that of any of its rivals. It had proved that, in good times, the organization of industrially weak or geographically isolated workers could be an economic proposition, even if not a highly profitable enterprise. But in adverse conditions such a membership, it appeared, could be maintained only at a loss.

As at the start of the decade, however, a factor in the union's final decline was avoidable: a prolonged and bitter internal dispute. The issue involved was the level of expenses received by members of the Executive—who, as elected lay representatives, were liable to loss of wages while attending meetings and had always been compensated from the union's funds. Until 1919 the rules had specified the exact payment; but the revised rules of that year—possibly because of the experience of rising prices making any fixed sum soon inadequate—merely stated that the GEC should 'receive such remuneration . . . as may be approved by the members'. This slightly ambiguous provision was apparently interpreted by the Executive as a licence to fix its own payment; and a generous scale was agreed, providing £2 for each day spent on union business or in travelling to and from meetings. In the same period, the Executive also increased considerably its own volume of work; by 1925 some members were therefore drawing on average £7 a week in expenses—far more than the rank-and-file membership could hope to earn, and indeed well above the income of most full-time organizers.

In March 1925 Beard and Duncan pressed for a reduction in the amounts charged. It is unclear why they raised the question at this date, having concurred in the level of expenses during the years of extreme financial crisis; it seems likely that a generally strained relationship had developed between the Executive and the national officers, particularly Beard.[21] In any event the

[21] EC members later argued that Beard and Duncan raised the issue as part of a 'secret campaign' to replace an experienced body by more pliant

GEC refused to reduce their own income, and instead proposed economies at Central Office and in organizers' expenses.

After this rebuff, Beard discussed the issue with his fellow Divisional Organizers. These had their own grievances: a decade earlier they had been able to exercise virtual autonomy; but with the growth of national bargaining they had seen negotiating authority centralized, while the GEC had in their eyes usurped the position of full-time officials in taking seats on Joint Industrial Councils. Next, a conference was called of all organizers; and these in turn were incensed to learn of the income which Executive members had been receiving whilst they themselves had accepted heavy wage reductions. It was finally agreed that the whole question should be laid before the Rules Revision Committee—a body created by the rules of 1919, composed of Executive members and National Officers, Divisional Organizers, and lay representatives, which was to meet for the first time in June 1925. After considerable argument this body at length specified a scale of charges, which it instructed the GEC to apply immediately; but the Executive insisted— technically correctly—that the new provisions could not be binding until approved by a vote of union members. Violent controversy ensued; at one stage the Executive threatened Beard with expulsion from the union, and various methods of harassment were used against him; Beard himself considered resigning as President and standing for re-election on this issue, and later commenced legal proceedings against the GEC; even the forcible expulsion of Executive members from Central Office was seriously contemplated.

After a move towards compromise on both sides, the original issue was settled when in April 1926 the new rules took effect; but the conflict did not rest here. In the campaign to reduce expenses, Beard had throughout desired to avoid damaging publicity; but resistance from the GEC had forced him to specify detailed complaints to the organizing staff and to the Rules Revision Committee, composed in part of lay members. By 1926 active members in several districts were aware of the dispute; pressure began to develop both at rank-and-file level,

---

members. Most of them had served since before 1920, and were far more willing and able to take their own decisions than any previous Executive. But while this caused evident friction, the charge of conspiracy seems far-fetched.

and among some organizers, for the resignation of the Executive and a special conference of members to consider the issue. Beard, and most senior organizers, opposed this; the whole affair, they urged, had been satisfactorily settled by the new rules. But understandably, there were many who disagreed. The depression had led to drastic reductions in members' benefits, the dismissal of many officials, and lower wages for those who remained. But as the militant London United Districts' Committee argued, 'to our amazement we have found that the body that should have set an example has failed miserably. . . . The members of our Executive Committee have so arranged matters that they have been taking monies from the Union Funds in the way of fees and expenses which are out of all proportion to the work they do.'[22]

A compromise was achieved when the Triennial Conference planned for 1928 was brought forward to the summer of 1926. Much of its discussion centred on the Executive's misdemeanours and it was finally agreed, by a narrow majority on a card vote, that all GEC members concerned should resign and be ineligible for re-election. Once more internal conflict raged. The EC members took legal advice, announced that the Conference had no power to expel them, and remained in office. Beard appeared convinced that no further action could be taken; but inevitably, members who had pressed for the Executive's removal protested; some threatened to commence legal proceedings against the GEC. While this controversy was at its height, full details of the quarrel were published in the Communist *Sunday Worker*, and repeated in the whole national press; the Workers' Union even achieved 'the honour—doubtful as it may be—of being the first Union in this country to have its internal affairs broadcasted by the B.B.C.'.[23] This was a development which many officials had feared; but one beneficial result ensued. The publicity forced the Executive to yield somewhat to their critics; they agreed to submit to a referendum of members a resolution that they were 'morally bound . . . to resign and offer themselves for re-election'. The ballot was held in January 1927, and resulted in a majority of over four to one in favour of this course; the six EC members affected thereupon resigned, and only two were re-elected. Despite some criticism

[22] Circular, Mar. 1926.   [23] *Record*, Apr. 1927.

of the fact that the Triennial Conference decision had not been fully implemented, it appears that most members were now more than willing to let the whole issue drop.

However, the repercussions of the dispute were to continue. The EC member most sharply attacked for his expenses claims was Neil Maclean, the Scottish representative, who was also the M.P. for Govan. For two-day Executive meetings his charges had included three days' travelling time, even during weeks when he was already in London for Parliamentary business; in addition he had angered members by charging for sleeping compartments on his rail journeys from Glasgow. During 1927 Maclean issued a series of circulars in unsuccessful attempts, first to retain his Executive seat, and later to defeat Beard in the triennial election for President. In these he defended his own actions and made counter-charges against his critics. His scale of expenses had been fixed by the other Executive members, including Beard and Duncan, when he joined the GEC in 1920; though Beard and Duncan claimed to be concerned with the union's finances, their real aim was to consolidate their own power by securing the removal of an experienced Executive; the issue of expenses was thus merely a stratagem. Not only had they sanctioned these expenses for a period of five years; they had 'themselves been most extravagant with the money of the Union'. In 1919 Duncan, who was an honorary official of the Police and Prison Officers, was involved in a libel action on its behalf; though the Workers' Union was in no way involved, over £700 in damages and costs was paid from its funds. In 1920 Duncan twice stood as the union's official candidate in Parliamentary by-elections, and spent altogether £3,500—nearly twice the legal limit. In neither case did the Trustees—who included Beard and Duncan—question this use of the union's finances. These and other accusations were widely circulated round the union's branches, and their impact must have been heightened by the fact that Beard and Duncan made no direct denial. Instead, the new Executive expelled Maclean from the union, for a breach of rule in issuing unauthorized circulars. Widespread publicity occurred once more, for Maclean commenced legal proceedings to invalidate his expulsion. His action finally came to court over a year later, and was dismissed with costs.

Understandably, this long process of scandal and recrimination had a demoralizing effect on membership; by the conclusion of the affair it would have been easy to believe that the whole administration of the union was corrupt. Even when the dispute was in its early stages, one organizer reported that 'already . . . some big branches wouldn't take much effort to send the members off to other unions',[24] and throughout 1926 Beard's opposition to drastic action reflected his concern at the likely effects of adverse publicity. These fears were clearly justified; once the affair reached the national press it was reported that the effect on some sections of membership was disastrous. Later still, Beard could speak of 'an uncertainty that has crept into the minds of everybody': 'We have today a lot of people trying to save the Union and in order to prove their saving capacity they have to show that the Union is a damnation. . . . It never strikes their imagination . . . that when you declare the hopelessness of things in order to draw attention to your heroic doings, the mass of people don't stop to see your heroism but get out.'[25] With a disheartened rank and file, an inexperienced Executive, and a President and Secretary who disagreed on vital issues of policy, the union's final predicament was scarcely a happy one.

The changing composition of membership during the decade reflected the varying fortunes of different sections of British industry. Most notable was the declining importance within the union of engineering; in 1920 some 60 of the hundred largest branches were based principally on engineering, but during the decade the number fell to about 35.[26] Though this remained the largest single section of membership, it is doubtful whether it constituted much more than a quarter of the total by the date of the amalgamation. In other sections of heavy industry, such as metal and chemical production, it appears that losses of a similar magnitude were sustained. The decline in agriculture was even more severe: from over 100,000, numbers fell to a mere 5,000. By contrast, three main sections of membership appear to have fared relatively well. The first was in public em-

[24] Morley, Letter to Beard, 9 Feb. 1926.
[25] Letter to Shingfield, 15 June 1928.
[26] Even this number may be an exaggeration; some of these branches were mixed, and in many of these engineering may have lost its primary importance during the decade.

ployment, where workers were largely isolated from the effects of the depression. Most government workers organized by the union were employed at the naval dockyards of Portsmouth, Chatham, and Devonport; these branches increased in importance during the 1920s, as did the Whitehall membership. Municipal employees were more widely dispersed within the union's organization, but during the decade they came to form the largest section of membership in many branches. The second group comprised workers employed in the building industry and the manufacture of building materials; building was a relatively sheltered industry, and the production of materials was sustained in turn. While membership among builders' labourers was scattered and thus difficult to estimate, in a number of areas— e.g. the Kent brickfields, the Warwickshire cement works, the Derbyshire pipeyards or the Essex window-frame factories—the union clearly benefited from this fact. Finally, the production of consumer goods became an increasingly important source of membership. Food, drink, and clothing remained essentials even in times of economic slump, and a range of branches based on such industries—again, geographically scattered—survived the 1920s relatively unscathed.

THE UNION IN ENGINEERING

In a period when industry as a whole suffered from unprecedented depression, engineering was among the worst hit. Unemployment among all insured workers reached a peak in 1921 of 18 per cent; in engineering the proportion was 27 per cent; only in the second half of the decade did the unemployment rate in the industry fall to the same level as in the economy as a whole.

The impact on industrial relations matched the severity of the economic conditions. In March 1921 the Engineering Employers' Federation demanded wage reductions of almost 20 per cent. The unions now regretted their decision to end the arbitration agreement, for mass unemployment left them in no position to resist. Worse was soon to come. The industry's grievance procedure had previously operated on the basis that the *status quo* should be maintained pending negotiations; this practice was now challenged by the employers. At the end of 1921 the Federation attacked the Amalgamated Engineering

Union (the product of a recent merger between the ASE and several smaller societies) over its interpretation of the national overtime agreement; it demanded that the Union should admit the employers' right 'to exercise managerial functions in their establishments'—in other words, that they should be able to alter existing conditions *before* going through procedure. Soon the EEF was demanding a similar declaration from all unions in engineering. Protracted discussions failed to bring agreement, and a national lock-out was imposed: first, in April 1922, of AEU members; then, at the beginning of May, of all unions. After a month the unions gave way, and there was a return to work in June.[27] The employers were then quick to hammer home their victory. Within a month they were demanding a further wage reduction of 16s. 6d. The unions were in no mood to face a second lock-out, and the cuts were enforced with almost indecent haste.

Like the increases of previous years, the wage reductions involved for the most part flat-rate money sums. So the lowest-paid suffered proportionately worst. In little over a year most labourers lost more than 40 per cent of their wages, and real earnings were reduced to their pre-1914 level. Similar losses were inflicted on female workers.

The gradual economic improvement after 1923 only served to demonstrate the impotence to which the unions had been reduced. Early in 1924 a joint claim was submitted for a £1 wage increase, to restore the bulk of the earlier losses. Negotiations dragged on interminably, both sides refusing to budge from fixed positions (though it is doubtful whether any union leader seriously expected to obtain anything approaching the amount demanded). Finally—after more than three years—agreement was reached on a derisory increase of 2s., to apply to time-workers only.

Though all engineering unions were severely weakened by the depression, it was the general unions which were worst hit; their status was once again very much an inferior one. The

[27] For details see A. I. Marsh, *Industrial Relations in Engineering*, 1965. The national agreements of 1898 and 1907 provided that pending negotiations work should proceed 'under the current conditions'; the 1922 agreement changed this clause to 'under the conditions following the act of Management'. The new clause did not apply to general alterations in wages, hours, or officially agreed conditions.

NFGW, which had previously often submitted separate demands to the employers when those of the craft societies were thought unsatisfactory, now followed the decisions of the skilled unions. Indeed, the NFGW soon ceased to fulfil any positive function of importance, and in 1924 it was formerly dissolved, leaving the general unions even less able to take an independent line.

Loss of membership had the most drastic effect on the status of the Workers' Union. Even among the general unions the depression cost it its previous clear lead, and with the merger of the General Workers and the NAUL in 1924 it was forced to accept second place. As for the challenge it had once presented to the craft societies, this was now deprived of all credibility. Occasionally the union asserted that it had the right to represent every grade of skill, but this was now little more than a hollow verbal declaration. The true situation was shown in the course of the £1 wage claim: Workers' Union officials complained bitterly in private at the refusal of the skilled unions to discuss a smaller increase; this intransigence seemed merely to insure that engineering workers got nothing while workers in other trades were obtaining increases. But the union never publicly broke ranks by proposing a compromise. Such reticence would have been improbable in the years of the union's strength.

The collapse of membership was most notable in the union's former strongholds: over 90 per cent was lost in Birmingham and Coventry. One reason was the local incidence of unemployment, for the area was the first to feel the impact of depression. As early as September 1920 the *Ministry of Labour Gazette* reported much short time in local engineering shops; the situation deteriorated in subsequent months, and by December 'large numbers of workpeople were unemployed, and short time was general'. According to the same source, 'employment in the motor car industry was particularly bad'. In Coventry, particularly dependent on this industry, 41 of the 46 federated firms were operating a two- or three-day week, and had reduced their labour force between 10 and 75 per cent.[28] By February 1921, 22 per cent of engineering workers in the West Midlands were unemployed, while in the North (subsequently the most de-

[28] Coventry and District Engineering Employers' Association, Executive Committee *Minutes*, 6 Dec. 1920.

pressed area in British engineering) the figure was only 8 per
cent. By the summer, one in three was out of work. Until well
into 1922 the Midlands remained among the worst affected
regions.

The union may also have suffered, both here and in other
areas, from its previous history. Before 1914 the NAUL and the
Gasworkers (the latter to a lesser degree) were basically labourers' unions; they cultivated good relations with employers and
with the craft unions, and were well established in their areas of
organization. By contrast the Workers' Union—particularly in
the Midlands—recruited machine workers rather than labourers,
had to fight employers to gain recognition, and clashed repeat-
edly with the craft unions. Though the union's officials sought
industrial peace in the latter half of the decade, the attitude of
employers could not have altered radically; doubtless many saw
the depression as the occasion for a counter-attack. They possessed a particular incentive where the union based its organization on production workers; the NAUL and the NUGW in
their strongholds covered principally the less important sections
of the labour force. In some areas at least the employers did
launch such a wholesale attack. According to the Coventry
organizer of the AEU, 'many employers are seizing the chances
of the economic position and ruthlessly scrapping every agreement. . . . It is questionable if ever there was such a panic.'[29]
Less firmly entrenched than the AEU, and organizing largely in
areas with no strong tradition of trade unionism, the Workers'
Union was particularly vulnerable to such attacks.

With the general decline in membership, a number of sections
of the industry in which wages were outside the control of the
EEF became of increasing importance during the 1920s. At the
time of the amalgamation, twenty of the union's fifty largest
branches covered engineering. Five of the twenty were mixed
branches in which the importance of engineering had almost
certainly declined during the decade; of the remainder, four
(Swindon, Derby, Gorton, and Willesden) drew members from
railway shops, two (Prescot and Helsby) from electric cable
works, two (Woolwich and Enfield) from government factories,
and a further two (Braintree and Witham) from the non-
federated Crittall Manufacturing Company. These figures in-

[29] AEU *Monthly Journal and Report*, April and May 1921.

dicate a general tendency in the composition of the union's engineering membership. In cable works and railway shops, greater wage stability was achieved than in engineering generally; at government factories, Whitleyism brought a major improvement in industrial relations. Finally, Crittalls was a striking example of a non-federated firm at which the union's position was unusually favourable: conditions were better than at most other local factories, while a closed shop ensured a relatively stable membership. But for such islands of stability, the union's record in the 1920s would have been still worse.

THE UNION IN AGRICULTURE

In agriculture, the experience of the 1920s was even worse. The great expansion of organization had been launched under the umbrella of statutory wage control. But with the onset of depression the government reversed, almost overnight, its whole agricultural policy. In June 1921 (only six months after a new Agriculture Act had confirmed the arrangements introduced in 1917) it was announced that both price guarantees and wage-fixing machinery would be abolished. Despite bitter resistance to this betrayal, three months later the Agricultural Wages Board ceased to exist.

At once wages tumbled, with the two farm workers' organizations struggling desperately to co-ordinate a defensive strategy. In the summer of 1921 the lowest county minimum was 46s.; a year later the unions were fighting to maintain a general standard of 30s. By the end of 1922 a wage of 25s. was prevalent in many counties, and real incomes had fallen below the pre-war level. Early in 1923, Norfolk farmers proposed an even more drastic deterioration in conditions: a further cut of 2s. 6d. in wages, and a 4 hour increase in the working week. The National Union of Agricultural Workers had felt unable to resist the previous reductions, because of heavy unemployment among its members. But now it stood firm, and the resulting strike soon spread to Workers' Union members in neighbouring Suffolk. For a month the farm labourers held out, until the employers withdrew the bulk of their demands and a settlement was reached.

The dispute marked a turning point. As one of the Workers'

Union strikers commented, 'looking back now it doesn't appear to have been a great victory, but never again did farmers even mention an increase in hours'.[30] The collapse in farm prices was now coming to an end, and the workers' successful resistance brought a halt to the wholesale attack on their conditions. Ironically, when the unions by their own efforts had finally stabilized the situation, the Labour government of 1924 introduced a modified form of statutory wage machinery. Thereafter, small but valuable improvements were achieved, and by 1926 a minimum of 30s. was obtained in every county.

But as far as union organization was concerned, the damage was already done. Massive unemployment, the breakdown of collective bargaining, and the savage wage reductions brought complete demoralization to workers who were for the most part novices in trade unionism. While the NUAW lost three-quarters of its membership, the Workers' Union suffered even more disastrously: by 1924 it is doubtful if a fifth of its agricultural membership remained. The subsequent improvements in conditions brought no recovery. For two years the TUC financed a 'back-to-the-unions' campaign, but the results were minimal, and in the Workers' Union the general decline continued. By the end of the decade it was reported that numbers had fallen to a mere 5,000.

As in the early years of war, the Workers' Union thus suffered far worse than its rival, and the explanation appears to be the same. In the growth years, success had been based on an enthusiastic rank and file and numerous full-time organizers, spurred on by the knowledge that the union was on the offensive. Now, not only was the rank and file discouraged; the organizing staff was drastically depleted. About half the 50 officials dismissed after 1921 had been primarily concerned with agriculture; few of those who survived could continue to devote much attention to farm workers and their problems. The NUAW *had* to maintain its organization if it was to survive; but the Workers' Union could no longer afford to subsidize its rural organization, and the temptation was to cut its losses altogether. 'It is terribly uphill work and very expensive,' wrote one of the union's leaders; 'I must say it is hardly worth the candle for the time taken by our organizers and the expense incurred.'[31]

[30] T. Balaam, letter, 1 Jan. 1965.   [31] Giles, letter to Beard, 21 Mar. 1925.

Executive policy was that each official had to cover his own costs by income from his area.[32] Some concentrated all their efforts on the more responsive industrial membership and left the rural branches to stand or fall by their own devices; others were less favourably placed and were dismissed. Only in a few districts, where the agricultural population was fairly concentrated, was the maintenance of an organizer exclusively for farm workers still an economic proposition.

DISTRICT ORGANIZATION: THE CONTOURS OF DECLINE

The geographical structure of the union's organization changed little throughout the 1920s. One new division was created: the North Midlands, placed under the control of Joe Clark in 1921; this was a natural move towards decentralization in the large Birmingham division following the effective end of Beard's supervision. In 1922 two divisions lost their independent existence: South Wales, which came once more under the control of Matt Giles, and the East Midlands, which became part of Clark's area; both mergers were understandable, since the divisions had been only recently formed and were small even in 1920.

In the Midlands the loss of membership was somewhat greater than the proportion nationally, but within the region there were striking contrasts. The Birmingham division (reduced in size, and now confined principally to branches in Warwickshire, Staffordshire and Shropshire) lost 90 per cent of its membership during the decade, the worst performance in any area of the union's organization. Local membership was particularly concentrated in engineering, and—as has been seen—unemployment in the first years of the decade was worse here than in any other part of Britain. As a result, the metal and engineering branches of Birmingham, the Black Country and Coventry, with some 50,000 members in 1920, were reduced to about 4,000 by the date of the amalgamation. An organizational factor which may also have affected the area was Beard's triple role as President and Birmingham and London Divisional Organizer;

---

[32] The policy followed was in fact more stringent than this may suggest; any organizer whose wages and expenses came to more than a third of the income from his district faced special wage reductions and ultimately dismissal.

11—W.U.

only in 1925 was control formally transferred to a local official, George Geobey. By 1929 only six of the union's 100 largest branches were in the division, compared with eighteen in 1920. Only one was in Birmingham itself: Stirchley, composed mainly of production workers at Cadbury's chocolate factory; two—Wolverhampton and Walsall—were mixed branches in the Black Country; two more contained Warwickshire cement workers, and one, tile workers in Shropshire.

In the West Midlands, the union also fared relatively badly, for much of its 1920 membership had been in engineering and agriculture. Throughout the decade railway shopmen at Swindon formed easily the largest branch, and by 1929 provided almost a quarter of membership in the division. Melksham rubber workers also withstood the depression reasonably well.

In the North and East Midlands, however, the loss of membership was almost the lowest in the whole union, and by the end of the decade this new division had become the union's largest. It benefited from the concentration of membership in relatively sheltered industries: the Burton breweries and the Swadlincote pipe trade, artificial fibres in Derby, hosiery yarn spinning at Leicester, brickfields in the Peterborough district. In the Derby railway shops also a reasonable organization was maintained; but elsewhere engineering membership appears to have suffered as badly as in the union generally. For this reason the membership in Lincolnshire, more firmly concentrated in engineering than in the rest of the division, slumped badly. Other factors may also have contributed to the stability of local membership: Clark was easily the youngest of the divisional organizers, and perhaps better able than most to face the demoralizing conditions of the 1920s; while he himself attributed his success in part to his refusal to popularize the immediate benefit scheme.

In Yorkshire also, membership suffered less severely than in the union as a whole. This was particularly true of the first half of the decade; latterly, perhaps because of its membership in coal-mining, the performance was more disappointing. Within the division, the pattern of membership remained remarkably constant: the largest branches in 1929 were, almost without exception, those which had been dominant in 1920. The Calder Valley, with its varied sources of organization, remained the principal stronghold in the division. Throughout the decade the

Halifax branch itself continued as the largest branch in York-shire, and one of the largest in the whole union.

In the Lancashire division the general record was similar. In Manchester, engineering membership slumped badly, but branches of corporation workers and railway shopmen were less seriously affected: the former lost only a third of its membership with the onset of the depression, and succeeded in regaining its previous numbers later. The Salford district lacked such stabil-izing sections, and membership fell from 6,000 in 1920 to under 1,000 in 1924, declining still further in subsequent years. In the Rochdale district, however, membership withstood the depres-sion well; despite considerable unemployment in the woollen textile industry, a solid organization was maintained. The Preston district, based mainly on electrical and motor vehicle engineering, fared reasonably well; so did the Prescot and Helsby branches, based on the British Insulated and Helsby Cable Co. The best record of any district, however, was achieved in the Isle of Man where membership—some 3,000 in 1920—was still 2,000 in 1929; the all-embracing character of the union's organization, and the special nature of the island's labour force, both contributed to this stability.

In Southern England, as in the Midlands, membership suf-fered somewhat more than in the union as a whole, but again there were variations. The London division fared better than most; but the fortunes of different branches varied considerably, and no clear pattern emerges. Sections which withstood the depression years well were the civil service minor grades in the Whitehall branches, the Clerkenwell cloth finishers, the Willes-den branch of power station workers and railway shopmen, and pottery and rubber workers in Lambeth. The branch at the Enfield Lock Royal Small Arms Factory also retained a large membership, though only about a quarter of its 1920 level.

Membership in Kent suffered more seriously than in London, falling by about 85 per cent during the decade. Again, there, were local variations. Woolwich Arsenal—like Enfield Lock—had by 1920 already lost considerable membership as a result of post-war discharges, and there was a further fall of some 75 per cent during the 1920s. Nevertheless the branch remained, with one brief break, the union's largest. Among Admiralty em-ployees at Chatham—though discharges were less severe than in most naval dockyards—similar losses were experienced; but membership among local civilian workers—particularly tramwaymen and other municipal employees—was far more stable, remaining at 40 per cent of its 1920 level. The branches of East Kent brickworkers also fared better than average, retaining nearly a third of their peak membership. In central Kent, however, where considerable organization had been achieved among agricultural workers, there was almost total collapse.

The Home Counties formed the principal centre of the union's membership among farm workers, and also suffered severely: the rate of decline was above that of all other divisions except Birmingham and the West Midlands. The organizing staff was halved during the decade—the most drastic reduction in any major division—and most of those dismissed were rural organizers. Within the division, organization in the Eastern Counties was most stable. Farm workers here were thicker on the ground, and it was thus easier to prevent total collapse of organization; by 1929 about half the union's total agricultural membership was located in Essex, Suffolk, and Cambridgeshire. Several urban branches also helped maintain the organization in the area. In the north-west of the division, only the Witney branch of blanket workers—which retained half its 1920 membership— was of major importance by the end of the decade. In the Southern Home Counties, the branches of dockyard workers in Portsmouth and municipal workers in Eastbourne stood out as the most stable; by contrast the organization among farm workers, considerable in 1920, was almost wholly lost.

In Devon and Cornwall, the over-all level of membership followed closely the union's national fortunes. At Devonport, stability was greater; about 30 per cent of the 1920 membership —which admittedly was already depleted by discharges—was retained. In the St. Austell clay area, the other main centre of organization in the division, losses were far heavier—nearly 90 per cent. Surprisingly, smaller concentrations of clay workers elsewhere in Devon and Cornwall fared better; otherwise, loss of membership in the rest of the division was also considerable.

Bristol and South Wales, having failed to match the general expansion of the previous decade, suffered less than most areas in the years of depression. Ironically, though South Wales lost its status as a separate organizing division, the membership here was the more stable. Losses at the Dowlais steelworks were severe, but organization held together far better among the metal workers of Swansea and Llanelli, while nearly half the union's membership among Cardiff flour mill and building workers was retained. In the Bristol area, by contrast, the scattered nature of the membership led to greater losses. Organization in Bristol itself was relatively stable, and even increased towards the end of the decade with the opening of branches for skilled engineering workers in the city, and smelting workers at Avonmouth. But in the smaller towns of Somerset and Dorset there was almost total collapse.

Scotland followed the national pattern throughout the decade. In general, branches based on the engineering and metal trades slumped badly. Of the Glasgow membership, builders' labourers and grain millers proved the most resilient. Elsewhere, the Border Counties textile workers and the East Coast herring coopers provided the most stable sections.

Irish membership, which like that in South Wales had failed to display the general expansion of the previous decade, now proved more stable during the 1920s. The main losses were experienced outside Belfast, where only the textile branches maintained a significant organization. In Belfast itself, however, membership in 1929 was still half its 1920 level. Here too, textile workers were important, providing half the local membership by the end of the decade. A large building trade branch was also maintained, and the shipyard branch, despite heavy losses, remained sizeable.

Overseas membership also declined, though less sharply than in Britain. The attempt to obtain a mass membership in South Africa was abandoned early in the decade; soon the only branch surviving was at Simonstown naval base. One new branch, also for dockyard workers, was opened at Hong Kong. By the end of the decade, however, the total foreign membership was less than a thousand.

INTER-UNION RELATIONS

In the years of its growth the Workers' Union had been something of an outcast in the world of labour; in its decline it became more closely integrated into the movement's establishment.

As in engineering, so in industry generally the union's ambitions to challenge the entrenched positions of the craft societies lost their previous force; while the skilled unions themselves had begun to face changed realities and were moderating their traditional exclusiveness. In adversity, the accumulated hostilities of the past were soon dissipated.

A further reason for the union's acceptance may have been its obvious lack of any intention to dominate the councils of the movement. Its contribution to the proceedings of the TUC were less than memorable: in a typical year it would submit one motion of an uncontroversial character and provide half a dozen speeches of a similar nature. The same was true within the governing organs of Congress. The first attempt to gain representation on its Parliamentary Committee was made in 1919, when Duncan stood unsuccessfully; in the following year Beard obtained election. The formation of the new General Council in 1921 made his position secure; the general unions (excluding those based on docks and road transport) were allocated four seats, and the Workers' Union had an obvious claim to one of these. At the same time, a further two seats were assigned to representatives of women workers, and Julia Varley was one of those elected. Apart from a single defeat in 1925, she too retained her place thereafter. After nine years on the Council, Beard was elected its Chairman in 1929, acting as President of Congress in the following year. But this reflected, not any dramatic leadership role, but his more prosaic work in the Congress committee rooms.

In the political activities of the movement, the union's record was very similar. In the general election of 1918 the union sponsored its first candidates: Duncan and Morley, who were both defeated. This was a modest contribution, both by comparison with the union's original political pretensions, and with the actual efforts made by other major unions. This led to some internal criticism, and at every subsequent election six nominees were supported.[33] Duncan, after fighting two unsuccessful (but expensive) by-elections in the Wrekin in 1920, was returned for the mining constituency of Clay Cross by a large majority in

[33] This panel was elected by a ballot of membership. Competition for a place was always keen; and though many lay members took part, those elected were always full-time officials.

1922; one of the remaining five official candidates was also elected. More were successful in subsequent elections, until in 1929 the whole panel reached Parliament. Several other union members also secured election, though without official union backing. But none achieved glory as political champions of labour; indeed, Duncan is chiefly remembered as 'the best dressed man in the House of Commons'. Within the wider Labour Party, the union's impact was as unremarkable as within the TUC. It consistently supported the Party leadership on political questions; but like trade unions generally, it played little part in the determination of the Party's detailed policies. Indeed, its delegations were perhaps the least vocal of any major union during the war and the post-war years.

Why was the union's impact on the policies of the wider labour movement so limited that its very existence is now widely forgotten? First, the time factor was important. In the formative years of the Labour Party, the Workers' Union was an organization of little significance. When the union achieved a mass membership, it was Labour's main Parliamentary spokesmen, rather than the industrial leaders, who had become most prominent within the Party. Many of the leading Parliamentarians were also union officials, but their political role had become predominant; Duncan, on the other hand, was more concerned in industrial than in political work. The TUC, when the Workers' Union was eventually admitted in 1917, was largely dominated by the Miners' Federation and the craft societies. Only with the creation of the General Council was power more evenly distributed: and this coincided with the calamitous decline in Workers' Union membership.

Also important was the question of personalities. Beard and Duncan, in later years at least, seemed more at home in organizing or committee work than on the conference platform. Beard had been physically weakened after a serious illness in 1919; Duncan was in his sixties by the date of the amalgamation; both seemed to have lost their earlier dynamism in the aftermath of the union's misfortunes. The most colourful of the union's conference spokesmen was Neil Maclean; but even before his removal from Executive office he was distrusted by many of his union colleagues. More generally, internal divisions of opinion and conflicts of personality may have detracted from the union's ability to exert a vigorous influence on the movement. So while a new generation of more forceful leaders helped shape the destiny of British trade unionism, the Workers' Union retired into the background.

THE BREAKDOWN OF THE NAWU

At the turn of the decade the National Amalgamated Workers' Union was already established, and the General Workers had entered the discussion of a complete amalgamation. Detailed negotiations proceeded through 1920, and after considerable argument the joint sub-committee reached agreement on a number of points. The governing body of the new amalgamation would be a large General Council chosen on a district basis, with equal representation of lay members and full-time officials (as was the case in the NUGW). Between its meetings, executive authority would be exercised by a smaller committee, chosen initially by the four amalgamating unions (with one representative of the MEA and two each of the other unions). Finance would be centralized, but districts would possess considerable autonomy in the field of organization.

These proposals were circulated to the various unions in January 1921 for Executive consideration; and it was soon clear that major differences of opinion existed. The EC of the Workers' Union did not regard this as 'a satisfactory basis for an amalgamation scheme'; in particular it objected to the two-tier Executive structure, and demanded that full-time officials should have only a token representation. The NAUL also demanded a reduction in the powers of officials, and insisted that final authority should be vested in a conference of lay delegates. The NUGW had less to complain of—for the proposals were based almost exclusively on its own constitution—but it objected to the suggested basis of membership on the Executive Committee; by now easily the largest of the four unions, it insisted on proportional representation. In the succeeding months, many of these differences were resolved. The sub-committee agreed to the demand of the NUGW. The structure of the General Council and Executive was not otherwise changed, but as a sop to the NAUL—which had most to lose from proportional representation—its proposal for a sovereign conference was conceded, and it was also agreed that official posts should be subject to election (a question previously undecided). The Workers' Union, however, gained nothing in the process; indeed from its viewpoint all the changes were for the worse.

Understandably, the union's representatives were reluctant to concede these points, and considerable delay resulted—to the anger of the other participants. 'An Executive is bound to go slowly', Beard insisted, 'when it has heard open expressions of contempt in regard to Executive rule and also towards organisers. There are vital questions still to be settled. . . . Further, our members have a right to have proposals put before them that they can understand.'[34] Friction was apparently exacerbated when the NUGW sent circulars to branch secretaries of the Workers' Union complaining about the attitude of its Executive. At the beginning of 1922 the situation was made even worse when the NUGW pressed a series of new demands, including a major reduction in the number of Workers' Union officials, a promise of a conciliatory attitude towards craft unions, and a guarantee for the financial position of its own Parliamentary Candidates and M.P.s. At the same time, the Workers' Union demanded an audited account of the financial position of all four unions. Final breakdown came over arrangements for the ballot which was to authorize complete amalgamation. The majority proposal was that the interim Executive should draft a set of rules, which would then be submitted to a delegate conference: but the Workers' Union insisted that they should require instead the approval of a further ballot vote.[35] At a meeting on 7 March 1922, the other unions called on the Workers' Union to withdraw this amendment; it refused to do so, or to recommend the scheme as it stood to its members.[36] A

[34] Letter to Cox, 1 Nov. 1921.

[35] Though there was some ambiguity, it does not appear that the union demanded, 'an individual ballot of all the members on each rule (an impossible step)', as is suggested in *General Union* (p. 10), but only on the rule book as a whole. Nor would such a ballot have needed the 50 per cent vote required by the Trade Union (Amalgamation) Act of 1917, as Bell of the NAUL implied (Circular to NAUL members, 17 Aug. 1922). This procedure was indeed of a type to which the NAUL was committed only a few years previously.

[36] Quite reasonably, the refusal to endorse the scheme 'seemed to representatives of the other three Unions equal to saying that they did not believe in the scheme' (Bell, *ibid*). However, the union's E C later claimed that it would have given its endorsement had its demand for a second ballot been conceded.

resolution was then passed by the other unions 'that the representatives of the unions whose Executives approve the terms of
the scheme of amalgamation now proceed to the next steps of
amalgamation . . .'. 'As this resolution had the effect of excluding the Workers' Union from further participation in the
negotiations, the representatives of the Workers' Union had
no other course left to them but to leave the meeting.'[37]

With the union's exclusion from the negotiations, the NAWU
collapsed. Throughout the period of its existence, the Workers'
Union had paid £400,000 to the amalgamation; initially, this
had accounted for over a third of its total expenditure. But the
depression had seriously affected the NAWU; by June 1921 it
was in debt, and the Workers' Union was in no position to support it. On the contrary, at the end of 1921 it owed £35,000 to
the amalgamation, and in 1922 paid only £7,500 in contributions. Since the NAWU at its close was insolvent, its collapse
involved the union in no financial loss.

Though each side blamed the other for the breakdown in
amalgamation negotiations, it is difficult to assess whose responsibility was the greater. It has been suggested that the enthusiasm of the Workers' Union leaders declined when they realized
that they would only be junior partners in an amalgamation;[38]
this may have been true, but they continued to negotiate long
after this had become apparent. It would be surprising, too, if
the union's weakened financial position made it reluctant to
continue with amalgamation; on the contrary, as was seen in
1928, this was a strong incentive to accept amalgamation on
almost any terms. It seems more plausible that its financial
troubles made the Workers' Union seem a less attractive partner
to the NUGW, and encouraged the latter to drive the hardest
possible bargain. Beard's opinion that negotiations 'broke down
on fundamentals as much as on details'[39] was probably correct:
it appeared that the union's views on every contentious issue
were to be ignored, and that the result would be total absorption
rather than amalgamation on the basis of mutual compromise.
It is noteworthy that while delegates at the 1923 Triennial Conference called for further efforts to achieve amalgamation, none
criticized the attitude taken by the union's leaders in 1922.

[37] *Record*, Sept. 1922.
[38] Clegg, *General Union*, p. 10.   [39] Triennial Conference, Sept. 1923.

It was ironical that despite the energy with which it had pursued amalgamation for so many years, by 1924 the Workers' Union was the only important general union which had not merged with other major organizations. Even so, hope was never abandoned; the Triennial Conferences in 1923 and 1926 discussed the issue at length and declared in favour of renewed attempts. This commitment certainly contributed to the successful amalgamation of 1929. It is true that the union's desperate financial plight had a powerful influence on its leaders; but it would be a distortion to see the amalgamation with the Transport and General Workers' Union as a mere shot-gun marriage.

THE BALANCE TO THE FUTURE

The record of these disastrous years was an unhappy one; but it is important that the losses and defeats alone should not be overemphasized. To the end, the Workers' Union remained one of the largest of British trade unions; while its loss of membership did not compare unfavourably with that of many 'new unions' in the less severe trade depression of the 1890s. 'Despite all the difficulties in the path of the Workers' Union, we have still been one of the most useful organizations of workers in this country', wrote Duncan in his last *Annual Report*. It had continued to pay benefits—even if reduced—which many craft unions had been forced to suspend, thus providing 'a wonderful mainstay to our members in facing the difficult and adverse circumstances', at a time when the generosity of the state was severely limited. Industrially, many of the gains of previous years had been lost; but few members worked for real wages below the level at the start of the previous decade, while a shorter working week remained almost universal. Among groups of workers who, twenty years earlier, had been largely unorganized, the union's losses had been agonizing; nevertheless, at least a skeleton organization generally remained. This was to provide a basis firm enough for renewed achievement within the wider amalgamation.

6

AMALGAMATION

It has been seen that for most of its history the Workers' Union was an enthusiastic advocate of the principle of amalgamation, though its plans had come to grief in 1922. But by 1927 the union's financial straits had made amalgamation not merely a desirable objective but an urgent necessity if bankruptcy was to be avoided. Only two organizations could reasonably be approached. One was the General and Municipal Workers; but there was no reason to think that it would now offer terms more acceptable than those of five years previously, and its 'tired administration' was no attraction to the leaders of the Workers' Union to swallow their pride and make a new initiative.[1] The other alternative was the Transport and General Workers' Union, which had by contrast achieved a forceful reputation and was in terms of membership clearly the more successful.

Beard made the first informal approach to Ernest Bevin, the TGWU General Secretary, in September 1927; this was followed by exploratory talks between representatives of the two unions. Bevin explained the structure of his organization, in which seven Trade Groups operated with considerable autonomy over industrial policy; he suggested that during the transitional period of an amalgamation the Workers' Union could function as an additional Group. It was then agreed that each union should provide the other with full details of its rules and financial arrangements.

Here the first serious problem arose. Trade unions have developed varying scales of contributions and benefits to suit the requirements of their separate memberships, and the mutual desire for unity cannot always bring agreement on provisions which while actuarially viable do not sacrifice the interests of any large group of members. This problem had been avoided in the formation of the TGWU, for its rules allowed the members

---

[1] See H. A. Clegg, *General Union in a Changing Society*, 1964, pp. 134–6. There was a further objection to amalgamation with the NUGMW: it would almost certainly have demanded the dismissal of many of the Workers' Union organizers.

of the amalgamating unions to retain their existing financial arrangements, subject to a minimum contribution. Bevin suggested that a similar arrangement might be possible for the Workers' Union. But the union's contributions were lower than in other organizations—4*d.* weekly for adult males, compared with 6*d.* in the other two main general unions—while the range of benefits which had so long been its boast were often thought by outsiders to be unduly generous.[2]

Because of its heavy financial losses in the General Strike, the TGWU was in no position to take risks, and Bevin raised this point as the only serious obstacle to a merger. 'My Executive Council,' he wrote, 'cannot see how they could possibly guarantee the benefits of your organization and honourably meet their obligation thereto, on the basis of the contributions now being paid.'[3] The Workers' Union was in no position to bargain. Previously its Executive had rejected the proposal of some organizers that contributions should be raised, fearing that it would cause further losses of membership. The rules already allowed members to pay 6*d.* to the general fund and receive additional benefits; the union's leaders now agreed that members should be obliged to transfer to the higher scale after the amalgamation. Doubtless they appreciated that the onus of enforcing the increase would fall not on them but on the TGWU administration.

Once this point was settled, detailed negotiations proceeded smoothly, and in November 1928 a Scheme of Amalgamation was approved by both Executives. It was agreed that the name 'Transport and General Workers' Union' would be retained. For a transitional period of two years the Workers' Union would become a National Group within the TGWU, with two representatives on its Executive Council. Members (with a few specified exceptions—notably farm workers) would be obliged to pay the 6*d.* contribution by the end of the transitional period; they would be able to remain eligible for the Workers' Union

---

[2] Because of the compulsory out-of-work contribution, the minimum contribution for most members was in fact 5½*d.* In 1927, in order to retain the Ministry of Labour administration grant, an attempt was made to make 3*d.* the minimum payment to the out-of-work fund, and most members were thus forced to pay at least 7*d.* weekly. But, for this sum, Workers' Union members received a benefit which other unions had abandoned.

[3] Letter to Duncan, 31 Jan. 1928.

scale of benefits, or opt for those of the TGWU. The sick and out-of-work funds would remain for existing contributors only, but would have to be self-supporting, if necessary through a special levy on contributors.

Once agreement had been reached at Executive level, the remaining hurdle was the ballot of members. New legislation in 1917 had eased somewhat the statutory requirements, but they remained rigorous: at least half the members of each union had to cast their votes, and at least 55 per cent of these had to endorse the amalgamation proposals. The first stipulation was the crucial one; an Executive could normally expect a fair majority of votes in a ballot, but it was far more difficult to get a large proportion of members to vote at all. The two unions therefore made every effort to secure maximum participation. Copies of the amalgamation details were widely distributed among the membership. Throughout December and January, meetings were addressed by national speakers in all parts of the country, and many more were arranged by local officials; the aim was to ensure that all members understood the scheme, and that all doubts and misconceptions were removed. The ballot was possibly the most protracted in the history of trade unionism; voting papers were issued at the beginning of December, and it was decided that the date of completion should be in the following May. Within the Workers' Union no effort was spared to derive the maximum advantage from this six-month voting period. As the completed voting papers were returned by the branches to Central Office, each organizer was informed of the votes registered by the branches under his control and asked 'to take immediate steps to see that the outstanding votes are collected'. At weekly intervals this advice was repeated, and as the closing date approached officials were urged to rouse particular branches where voting had been low.

Actual opposition to the merger was never a serious problem. The only concerted criticism came from the Communist Party and Minority Movement. Their objections were threefold: the amalgamation would render unattainable their ideal of industrial unionism; it would deprive Workers' Union branches of various rights of independent action; and it would increase Bevin's personal influence within the Labour movement. But

Communist influence within the union had never been strong; and some Communists were even reported to favour the amalgamation. There was more general opposition to the scheme in isolated districts—notably Manchester—but this reflected a wider distrust of the union's leaders in the aftermath of the earlier internal conflicts. It would also seem that a few officials, apprehensive of their own status within the amalgamation, encouraged such resistance. But this caused little concern at union headquarters, where a certain amount of opposition may even have been welcomed as a means of increasing interest in the ballot. As Beard shrewdly noted, 'the votes for are pretty emphatic and it will be less harmful to have a number against than to find ourselves in the position of not having had sufficient votes'.[4]

The wisdom of this attitude was borne out by the actual result of the union's ballot: 59,801 in favour, 9,632 against. The total poll, as a proportion of membership at the end of 1928, was 55½ per cent; had the votes against not been cast, it is possible that the amalgamation could not have taken place. As it was, the votes of both unions satisfied the legal requirements, and were formally announced to a joint meeting of Executives at the end of May. On Saturday, 3 August 1929, both unions formally ceased to exist. On the following Monday the new Transport and General Workers' Union came into being.

THE PROCESS OF ABSORPTION

The effect of the amalgamation on the ordinary member was limited. In general, he remained in the same branch and was served by the same officials as before 1929. He could continue to pay the contributions and receive the benefits of the Workers' Union; and until 1931, even his membership card was the replica of that of his old union. The main change was the increase of the minimum contribution to 6d., and the institution of the TGWU system of 'quarterage'—a double weekly contribution four times a year. There was inevitably some discontent at these changes; initially, Bevin reported 'organized

---

[4] Letter to Cliff, 12 Jan. 1929.

opposition on the part of the members of the Yorkshire district of the Workers' Union Group'.[5] However, these financial changes had been agreed before the amalgamation; and since most Workers' Union members had previously been paying compulsory out-of-work contributions for a limited scale of benefits, the hardship was on the whole a small one. In general, this transition occurred smoothly.

In the branches also, there were few major adjustments. Most retained their previous identity, and even their record numbers were not immediately changed—causing some confusion in the transitional period. The branch officers were more immediately affected, particularly the secretaries: whereas they had previously sent all monies to Central Office, financial administration in the TGWU was based on the thirteen Areas,[6] and a transition was made during the first half of 1930. Later, the various officers suffered a reduction in their commissions: from $7\frac{1}{2}$ to 5 per cent for branch secretaries and collectors, while the smaller salary paid to chairmen for their nominal treasurership (a position which did not exist in the TGWU) was abolished. Though it may be assumed that this change caused some resentment, no serious disaffection was recorded.

At district level, the organization of the two unions was merged after the amalgamation. Since those Workers' Union District Committees still in existence were generally based on the union's principal strongholds, where the membership of the old TGWU had been comparatively small, many retained their identity and continued to function without major alteration in their composition. At Area level, the TGWU possessed a network of representative committees with important functions within the rules—a provision which had no parallel within the Workers' Union. Soon after the amalgamation the co-option of Workers' Union members to these committees was proposed, but was rejected by the GEC on the grounds that the consummation of the amalgamation was taking place centrally. Shortly

[5] Finance and Emergency Committee *Minutes*, 31 July 1930.
[6] The TGWU subsequently replaced the term 'Area' by the present title 'Region'.
[7] General Executive Council *Minutes*, 19 Nov. 1929 and 17 Feb. 1920. The change of policy probably followed protests by ex-Workers' Union branches and District Committees.

afterwards, however, with the process of financial decentral-
isation almost completed, this decision was reversed, and
temporary representation was arranged 'in an improvised form'.
From 1931, when the amalgamation became fully effective,
former Workers' Union members were able to obtain direct
election to their Area Committees.

Nationally, the Workers' Union Executive continued to
function as a Trade Group Committee until the dissolution of
the Workers' Union Group at the end of 1931, and the transfer
of its membership to the General Workers' Group and the new
Metal, Engineering, and Chemical Group. In accordance with
the TGWU constitution the Committee was allowed considerable autonomy on trade matters; it also continued to supervise
the special benefits of the Workers' Union, and in 1929 it chose
the union's quota of delegates to the TUC and Labour Party
conferences. The Committee selected two members to sit on the
General Executive Council of the amalgamated union (composed in part of directly elected Area representatives and in part
of Trade Group nominees); and from February 1930 it was represented in an advisory capacity on the Finance and Emergency
Committee (a sub-committee which carried out Executive
functions between the quarterly meetings of the GEC, now
known as the Finance and General Purposes Committee).

With the completion of the amalgamation, a number of for-
mer Workers' Union members were elected to the National
Committees of the Trade Groups to which they were assigned.
The first representative of the Metal, Engineering, and Chemi-
cal Group on the GEC was a former member of the Workers'
Union Executive, Fred Hobbs; he was soon joined by George
Morton, a member of the last Workers' Union GEC, representing
the General Workers' National Committee. Subsequently, many
ex-Workers' Union members attained seats on the Executive
Council. In addition, on of the Workers' Union Trustees, Fred
Beechey, was for many years elected to a similar position in the
TGWU.

From the viewpoint of the rank and file, it may be concluded,
there was little cause for complaint. The financial adjustments
were small, and the scope for participation in internal democratic processes was no less than before the amalgamation; but
there was an obvious gain through the backing of a strong

union in place of the ailing organization which the Workers' Union had become.[8]

The amalgamation had its greatest effect, however, upon the full-time officials. Under the Scheme of Amalgamation all Workers' Union organizers were taken onto the TGWU staff but there was no guarantee of continued employment. Of a hundred officials, seven were dismissed as redundant between 1931 and 1933, and four others were prematurely retired. In view of the terms of amalgamation it might seem that there was little reason for complaint; outside the TGWU, the Workers' Union would certainly have needed to reduce the size of its staff, and the cases of a number of those dismissed had been under discussion before 1929. However, it seems possible that some informal undertaking may have been given organizers that their positions would be secure.[9] Moreover, the dismissals which occurred resulted from the general decline of membership after the amalgamation rather than from any overstaffing which existed previously in the Workers' Union; yet almost without exception, redundancies affected ex-Workers' Union officials alone. There were individual complaints of harshness in the manner in which the dismissals were enforced,[10] but in general such charges were unjustified; many of those dismissed received lengthy paid leave in order to find new employment, others were offered full-time branch secretaryships in order to continue trade union work without causing a drain on the union's funds.

Numerically more important were the organizers who were retained. The first major problem which the amalgamation created was the division of labour between the officials of the two unions. A re-allocation of functions took place on a piece-meal basis, following discussions between Bevin and Executive

[8] The verdict of one of the most vocal critics of the amalgamation proposals, who was later to serve for many years on the Executive Council, was that 'I now think it turned out a good thing' (B. H. Coley, letter, 23 Nov. 1966).

[9] Allegedly, a similar undertaking was given to clerical staff, many of whom were however dismissed after the amalgamation.

[10] The angriest reaction was caused by the dismissal of the Coventry women's organizer, Alice Arnold. Though she had for years been a member of the Coventry Council and was soon to be elected its first woman Mayor, the TGWU insisted that she could retain her employment only if she moved to Birmingham. The TGWU leaders were accused of vindictiveness; certainly their attitude in this case contrasted with the more accommodating treatment of other officials who attained municipal honours.

representatives, and each of the various Area secretaries. One of the latter reported that ' the aim of the Amalgamated Union is to concentrate organization on the Areas; to this end divisional organization is being created within most of the Areas, with divisional officers responsible for the organization of all grades coming within the divisions, technical officers of the Areas being available for negotiations within the divisions as and when necessary.'[11] Under this procedure, many Workers' Union officials were assigned positions as district officers or divisional general trades organizers that involved few changes in coverage and nature of duties from their previous posts. Others became Area Trade Group officers, carrying out over a larger area the bargaining functions to which they were already accustomed. Only a minority were required to transfer to a wholly new district, or to cover sections of industry of which they lacked previous experience. Even fewer were appointed to the highest official positions within the amalgamated union. Sam Kyle of Belfast was the only organizer to become an Area Secretary, but the number to obtain national positions was greater: Jack Beard became National Officer of the Agricultural Section; Andrew Dalgleish, National Secretary of the Metal, Engineering and Chemical Trade Group; Clem Akroyd (at the time of the amalgamation the chief clerk in the Yorkshire division), National Secretary of the Administrative, Clerical, and Supervisory Group; and Julia Varley, Florence Hancock and Ellen McCullough (a member of the central office staff at the time of the amalgamation) successive Women's Officers.

That so few officials reached the most important posts within the amalgamated union was perhaps a consequence of the fact that the Workers' Union staff was an ageing one,[12] and that few major posts fell vacant during the 1930s. It might however be taken as evidence of unequal opportunity of promotion by comparison with former TGWU officials. There was some feeling that the Workers' Union leaders were badly treated: Duncan was asked to retire early, in order to facilitate the merging of the Workers' Union and General Workers' Groups; Beard's nomination for the TUC General Council ceased after 1934, despite an undertaking apparently given at the time of the amalgam-

[11] Area 4 Secretary's *Report*, 23 Jan. 1930.
[12] The average age at the date of the amalgamation was forty-nine.

ation. Some ex-Workers' Union organizers sensed that their TGWU colleagues 'acted superior', in the knowledge that its desperate financial condition had forced the union to amalgamate. The situation was particularly delicate for the Divisional Organizers, who were necessarily placed in positions subordinate to those they had previously held. In the Midlands, friction occurred which forced Bevin to rebuke the Area Secretary, and similar trouble occurred in Yorkshire. Any sense of inferiority with regard to status was reinforced by the fact that the pay of former Workers' Union officials remained for many years, as at the amalgamation, considerably below that of their ex-TGWU counterparts. At the same time they were required to make large contributions to the union's superannuation scheme (none had existed within the Workers' Union) in order to qualify for benefit. In addition, the Organizers' Fraternal (a body which had represented full-time officials in wage discussions with the Workers' Union Executive) was disbanded at the insistence of the TGWU leaders, though it might have proved valuable in helping settle problems of the transitional period.

It would be wrong, however, to suggest that there was general dissatisfaction among former Workers' Union officials. All valued the consolidation of trade union strength which the amalgamation achieved, and most found scope for organizing initiative at least as great as within the Workers' Union itself.

THE LEGACY TO THE TRANSPORT AND GENERAL WORKERS' UNION

The TGWU had taken over an ailing organization; but despite its deteriorating finances, the Workers' Union was not yet bankrupt. The final balance sheet showed debts amounting to £39,000; against this were recorded assets of £72,000. This figure was of dubious validity. It included branch funds totalling £18,000; since 1919 these had been by rule the property of the union nationally, but the Workers' Union Executive had never been able to obtain effective control of them, and the TGWU was no more successful. Bevin was naturally aggrieved, arguing that he had been misled about the union's financial position. It is questionable whether the union's loans and investments, listed at £15,000, could all have been realized at their face value. But somewhat surprisingly, the union's premises were considerably undervalued on the balance sheet, at just under £35,000. 'Highfield', the Central Office, alone fetched over £36,000 when it was sold in 1930; in the same year two other properties realized more than their balance sheet valuation. Assuming that the Workers' Union had not overvalued its other office buildings, its premises must in all have been worth about £50,000. It would then be reasonable to assume that there was a total balance of assets over liabilities of at least £20,000.

It might be argued that despite this capital gain, the TGWU absorbed an organization which was suffering a continuous deficit in terms of current expenditure. However, economy measures taken immediately before the amalgamation helped stem this loss, and thereafter the transfer of members to the higher scale of contributions brought further relief. Within a year, solvency had been restored: 'the loss which was accruing to the Workers' Union prior to the Amalgamation has been stayed, and a surplus is now being built up. Stronger and more efficient methods of management are having their effect. The greater co-ordination of the work of the officers throughout the country and the co-operation now being displayed, is resulting in an upward development.'[13] Thus in no way did the TGWU inherit a financial liability.

In the long run, the financial aspect of the amalgamation was in any case the least important. Far more significant was the contribution which the industrial coverage of the Workers' Union made to the very nature of the TGWU. The union before 1929 was basically an industrial union of dockers and road transport workers. Despite its title, its 'general' membership was comparatively weak; and while the rulebook specified various classes of occupations for which the union catered, the category of 'general workers' was not included. The amalgamation transformed this situation. The immediate contribution of the Workers' Union was a membership of some 100,000, more than doubling the size of the existing General Workers' Trade Group

[13] Bevin, Report to GEC, 18 Feb. 1930. Though the healthy financial position of the Workers' Union Group was not long maintained, the deterioration was due to worsening economic conditions which affected the membership of the whole union.

and greatly extending its industrial coverage. Perhaps even more important in the long run, it also brought the recognition of employers and representation on negotiating machinery even in firms and industries where actual membership was a mere fraction of its earlier strength. In such cases, its recruitment rights were often similarly respected by other unions. The TGWU thus acquired a standing in a range of industries which allowed ready facilities for expansion when conditions became more favourable for union organization.

The implications of this fact for the subsequent development of the TGWU may be judged from the contrasting fortunes of its various Trade Groups. The following table shows their membership in 1928 and in 1966:

	1928	1966
Docks	96,000	56,000
Waterways	8,000	16,000
Administrative, Clerical and Supervisory	5,000	62,000
Road Transport (Passenger)	79,000	181,000
Road Transport (Commercial)	37,000	219,000
Power Workers	20,000	41,000
General Workers	68,000	338,000
Engineering (established 1931)	—	269,000
Government (established 1943)	—	58,000
Municipal (established 1945)	—	44,000
Agricultural (established 1945)	—	13,000
Building (established 1953)	—	53,000
Chemical (established 1953)	—	61,000
Total	313,000	1,411,000

The present membership of the Docks, Waterways, and Road Transport Groups is derived almost entirely from the original TGWU; the membership of the Workers' Union in these sections, though not insignificant, was comparatively small. The Power Workers' Group is based on the Enginemen's Union, which merged with the TGWU in 1926. The Administrative, Clerical, and Supervisory Group drew the bulk of its members originally from the transport industries; the Workers' Union then brought a range of white-collar workers in engineering and other industries, and this extended coverage was clearly of great importance for what is now the most rapidly expanding Trade

Group. The Building Group owes more to the Workers' Union than to the old TGWU, but its membership derives principally from the amalgamation of two societies of builders' labourers in 1934.

In all other Groups, the influence of the Workers' Union has been clearly predominant. The General Workers' Group has lost six of its sections since the amalgamation through the formation of new Trade Groups, but it remains the union's largest—as it became with the inclusion of the Workers' Union membership. Before 1929, its most important basis was in flour-milling; but mechanization has brought a decline in employment and thus in membership in this industry. Today, its largest section is employed in textiles, and is derived wholly from the Workers' Union and from subsequent recruitment. Of the many other trades covered by the Group, in all but a handful the majority —and sometimes all—the membership stems from the amalgamation with the Workers' Union.

The Engineering Trade Group, formed as an immediate consequence of the amalgamation, is the union's second largest and one of the most rapidly expanding. While the original interest of the TGWU in engineering was small, this was of course the principal source of organization for the Workers' Union. The power and influence of the union in engineering today, particularly in the motor industry, is directly attributable to the amalgamation. In chemicals, the TGWU had membership from the outset, but this was localized and concentrated in the heavy section of the industry. The Workers' Union brought a national membership including important sections in drugs and fine chemicals and in oil refining: the amalgamation was thus a major influence on the present coverage of the Group. The union's membership in agriculture (except in Scotland) is wholly derived from the Workers' Union. So, with minor exceptions, is the Government Workers' Group. Among municipal employees, the TGWU possessed a membership before 1929; but here, too, the Workers' Union had the greater coverage.

While in 1929 the membership of Bevin's union was three times that of its partner in amalgamation, it would be a reasonable guess to attribute half the present TGWU membership to the organization originally established by the Workers' Union. This membership, moreover, represents both regionally and industrially the fastest growing sections of the union. But for the amalgamation, the TGWU today—despite its history of dynamic leadership—would surely be no more than a medium-sized organization of transport workers, its influence within the broader movement declining with the changes in industrial structure. The debt to the old Workers' Union is obvious: the TGWU today owes its position as Britain's largest union, and its prospects for future advancement, at least as much to the subject of this book as to the organization which absorbed it.

CONCLUSIONS

THE introduction to this book listed a number of theoretical problems which necessarily arise in any attempt to understand and interpret the history of an organization such as the Workers' Union. Questions of 'trade union sociology' have been raised and discussed in passing throughout the narrative of the previous chapters. It is now time to confront these problems directly, relating the experience of the Workers' Union to the body of theory which has been erected, particularly in recent years, by writers in Britain and other countries.

In the pages that follow, four broad main topics are discussed. First, the essential functions of trade unions and their objectives in the field of industrial relations. Second, the reasons for union membership and explanations of union growth. Third, the extent to which the activities and goals of trade unions are affected by their organizational characteristics. Fourth, the nature of union democracy and the practical limitations to its operation. A final section attempts to draw certain general conclusions from this analysis.

JOB REGULATION AND COLLECTIVE BARGAINING: THE FUNCTIONS OF TRADE UNIONS

The attempt to define trade unionism—which has preoccupied many writers on industrial relations and labour history—involves far more than considerations of semantics. Take the Webbs' classic statement:

a trade union, as we understand the term, is a continuous association of wage-earners for the purpose of improving the conditions of their employment.[1]

The Webbs are not of course identifying to the uninitiated some esoteric phenomenon; rather, they are offering a concise distillation of their extensive observation and analysis. The definition, it might be said, encapsulates a theory: that certain

[1] S. and B. Webb, *History of Trade Unionism*, 1894, p. 1. In their 1920 edition the definition is broadened, referring not to 'their employment' but to 'their working lives'.

purposes and a certain structure are essential to the proper functioning of trade unionism.

The theory which underlies the definition has been emphasized explicitly by Flanders, in a passage which echoes the Webbs.

As in other industrial countries, trade unions in Great Britain came into being, established themselves on firm foundations and extended their power and social influence mainly as agencies for collective bargaining. This is to say they succeeded as a form of organization which enabled employees . . . to regulate and thus improve their wages and working conditions. All the activities which the trade unions have undertaken and all the other purposes they have acquired must be regarded as a by-product and auxiliary to this their major activity and purpose, since success in it has been the condition of their survival and the basis of their growth. Any theory of trade unionism which disregards this fundamental fact is bound to go astray. . . .[2]

Flanders' argument contains a subtle yet significant shift from that of the Webbs. Their own definition identifies the essence of unionism in the concrete improvements won for workers by their organizations; collective bargaining is conceived as one of three methods for achieving this purpose (the others are termed 'mutual insurance' and 'legal enactment'). The term 'collective bargaining' was itself devised to emphasize the exclusively economic functions which the Webbs thought central to trade unionism—an analogy with the individual bargaining which they saw as the worker's lot in the absence of collective organizations.[3]

In Flanders' analysis the key word is *regulation*; and underlying this distinction is a major elaboration and critique of the Webbs' concept of collective bargaining. The trade union does not sell the labour of its members, so collective bargaining is not a substitute for the individual contract of employment. The union is not engaged in an economic exercise, a collective alternative to individual bargaining, so much as a political exercise, the participation in the regulation of conditions of employment. Collective bargaining derives from, and should be

[2] A. D. Flanders, *Trade Unions*, 1957 edn., p. 76. In subsequent editions this passage is slightly revised.
[3] *Industrial Democracy.*

compared with, not individual bargaining but unilateral regulation (by management or workers).[4] 'If words are given a consistent and unambiguous meaning, then collective bargaining is not collective bargaining.'[5]

Thus while the Webbs conceive union success in terms of ability to 'deliver the goods' to members, Flanders' basic criterion is the quality of the regulatory processes established jointly with employers (the end result may, of course, well be the same). The effects of union action thus 'extend beyond the securing of material gains to the establishment of *rights* in industry'.[6] A further distinction is that while the Webbs identify the bargaining function in terms of 'market relations', Flanders' approach encompasses in addition the whole area of 'managerial relations': one of the fundamental achievements of collective bargaining, he argues, is to 'regulate the exercise of managerial authority in deploying, organizing, and disciplining the labour force after it has been hired'.[7]

As is clear from the passage quoted at length above. Flanders relates union success and stability directly to the willingness and ability to perform this function. This is because 'one problem which has always confronted trade unions is how to convert temporary movement into permanent organization. . . . To evolve from loose groups that could be destroyed when the economic tide flowed against them, they had to acquire sanctions strong enough to sustain continuous membership.'[8] Job regulation alone could serve this purpose:

as labour history demonstrates again and again, wages or hours movements have no more than temporary appeal and their momentum may be spent as much by success as it is by failure. Permanent organization could not be built on this foundation. To secure a permanent membership trade unions have to render a constant service to their members. This is made possible by their participation in job regulation, and the deeper and more extensive that participation the greater the service they can offer.[9]

---

[4] These do not exhaust the forms of job regulation listed by Flanders; see *Industrial Relations: What is Wrong with the System?*, 1965, pp. 21–2.

[5] 'Collective Bargaining: A Theoretical Analysis', *British Journal of Industrial Relations*, 1968, p. 3.

[6] Ibid., p. 12.   [7] Ibid., p. 17.

[8] 'What are Trade Unions For?', *Socialist Commentary*, Dec. 1968.

[9] *British Journal of Industrial Relations*, 1968, p. 26.

Unquestionably, Flanders reveals a major inadequacy and confusion in the Webbs' theory of trade unionism, and provides a valuable analytical approach to contemporary industrial relations. Moreover, he offers an important insight into the historical process in which organizational needs have guided trade union policies and actions firmly in the direction of 're-sponsible' participation in the joint regulation of employment—a topic which is examined in a later section of this chapter. The instability associated with 'immature' bargaining relationships was well exemplified by the early history of the Workers' Union. But at the same time, the union's history shows that *some* stability was possible even when its success in establishing processes of job regulation was minimal.[10]

It has been seen, in discussing the first dozen years of the Workers' Union, that its power to exert control over the wages and conditions of its members was insignificant. Often, indeed, membership at the individual workplace was so small that such control was wholly inconceivable. Towards the end of the period, as organization was extended, bargaining relationships remained rudimentary. The common pattern was the formu-lation of a claim for some improvement, ignored by the em-ployer; a strike, often largely spontaneous in origin; followed either by defeat and the collapse of organization, or by manage-ment concessions and a stimulus to recruitment (though the new membership often fell away as the excitement of conflict faded). Official contact between union and employer then ceased, until the cycle was repeated. The establishment of a habit of regular negotiations in the absence of mobilization for struggle was wholly exceptional; diplomacy was normally the pursuit of war by other means.

If the union's influence over members' working conditions was at best partial, tenuous, and sporadic, other 'subsidiary' functions, as was argued earlier, were of prime importance. The union itself—in its reports to members and in its recruitment propaganda—paid major attention to its activities as an in-

[10] The paragraphs which follow should not be interpreted as an attack on Flanders' basic argument: it is part of his thesis that trade union participation in job regulation is only gradually, and often unintentionally, elaborated. On the other hand, there is certainly a difference of emphasis at a number of points. The discussion in this section has benefited from Professor Flanders' comments and criticism—though he is of course in no way responsible for my arguments.

surance agency for working men: to its extensive range of friendly benefits and its provision of legal assistance. Of those functions customarily seen as central to trade unionism there was far less regular mention.

The Workers' Union, then, in its early years fell short of the prescriptions of the Webbs, and certainly failed to meet those of Flanders. For this reason—among others—it remained a struggling and insignificant organization with an unstable membership. Yet at least the union was able to survive in this state for over a decade, and even, towards the close of the period, expand considerably in numbers.

More important, it may be questioned how extensively, even in the years of its greatest success, the union was able to establish regular processes of control over conditions in the workplace. Collective bargaining, it was suggested in an earlier chapter, was a somewhat grand title for the processes applying to most members in the post-war period when expansion was most rapid. The union's regulatory functions were defined by its leaders almost exclusively in terms of market rather than managerial relations. The central objective was, first to establish standard hours and wage rates, and standard conditions for overtime and piece-work; then to obtain periodic general improvements.[11] It would have been surprising if the emphasis had been otherwise, for it reflected the most urgent needs and most burning grievances of the members themselves. Yet inevitably, once the objective of the trade union standard was achieved there remained no basis for continuous union involvement within the factory. Most employers who conceded recognition of an organization such as the Workers' Union, involving the negotiation of even the narrowest range of conditions of employment, did so with extreme reluctance, as a dangerous dilution of managerial prerogatives. Understandably, few seem to have admitted the possibility of genuine *joint* regulation, as a continuous involvement in a relationship in part at least co-operative; the structure of 'employer conciliation' in engineering typified well

---

[11] This is not of course to contradict Flanders' emphasis on job regulation—for 'economic' and 'regulatory' functions are by no means mutually exclusive. But it is to argue that the *scope* of the union's regulation was confined within narrow economic limits. It must also be stressed (again, this is not to contradict Flanders) that in this period it was the results of collective bargaining which the union's officials emphasized, rather than the value of the regulatory process itself.

the attitude of most employers with whom the Workers' Union came in contact.[12] Nor did the union seek such a relationship; its officials, it has been stressed, were in this period organizers rather than negotiators, to be involved in discussions with individual employers only in occasional instances of crisis. Joint regulation of a sort, whether through the traditional channels of deputations of workmen or the newer system of shop-steward representation, was almost certainly of importance for the union's members in many workshops—adequate evidence of the scale and coverage of such domestic bargaining simply does not exist—but instances were rarely mentioned, even obliquely, in officials' reports. Such incipient controls over managerial relations were clearly not conceived as relevant to the objectives of the union and were wholly dissociated from its official machinery.[13]

After 1914 there was a significant change, charted in detail earlier in the book. Under war conditions, employers were increasingly ready to recognize the union less as a dangerous interloper than as a potential aid in resolving labour problems. Added legitimacy was given to the extension of joint regulation by the Whitley recommendations. The union's own aspirations were certainly raised. Beard showed surprising prescience in appreciating that changes in technology and the organization of work would create problems which could be tackled only through 'the full recognition of our Union to ensure the fullest operation of collective bargaining';[14] managerial relations, in other words, would have to be subjected to joint regulation. If Beard's objective here was untypical (presaging his conviction that management-union relations should constitute a partnership), it was quickly realized by officials generally that the embarrassment of unofficial outbreaks could be controlled only by a more intimate involvement in workplace discussions.

[12] There is perhaps a danger of reading too much into the term 'joint regulation'; but it is surely questionable how far agreement emerging from a relationship of open or latent conflict (as was certainly normal for the Workers' Union at this time) can properly be termed a joint process.

[13] This is of course true of much of the shop floor control which workers exercise even today. It is often ambiguously related to the trade union as such, deriving rather from the largely autonomous activities of work groups (which may at times form the basis for a 'union within a union'). Such control is intimately related to the 'custom and practice', in no way the product of trade unionism, which seems always to have been important within industry as a regulatory mechanism.

[14] *Record*, Nov. 1914.

Developments after 1914 in both the coverage and the nature of collective bargaining were thus considerable. Yet the transformation should not be exaggerated. The employers of many members in the munition trades remained throughout resistant to union intervention; they observed standard conditions not through voluntary compliance in joint regulation but under the compulsion of the law. Even where recognition as such was freely given, acceptance of the rights of representation at the point of production was often grudging and limited. Nor did the union itself—or any other—devise a strategy for sustained involvement in the area of managerial relations; such a strategy was the monopoly of the Guild Socialists with their commitment to 'encroaching control'. Duncan, it is true, welcomed the formation of Joint Industrial Councils (derided by those actually committed to workers' control) as 'the first milestone towards the workers taking and playing some part . . . in the actual management of the firms employing their labour'; but his main interest was in their potential effect on wages.[15] And indeed, the failure to realize the Whitley aspirations for union participation in management is in part at least attributable to the lack of any operational commitment to this objective among the unions themselves. The record of the union's use of engineering procedure underlines this point: 94 per cent of the cases which it took to Central Conference in this period involved questions of an exclusively economic nature.[16] It is evident that collective bargaining, as conceived by Flanders, was as yet still underdeveloped.

Moreover, even this degree of joint regulation was short-lived. The managerial functions dispute in engineering was merely an extreme example of the successful attempt of employers in a range of industries, not—as in the United States—to destroy trade unions utterly, but to eradicate their influence over the major part of managerial decision-making. In general, job control became for the Workers' Union once more almost wholly external to the workplace; and even on the basic issue of wages the control was of a most tenuous nature. Recognition

[15] *Record*, Oct. 1919.

[16] Out of 138 issues raised in the years 1915–20, 105 were concerned solely with wages, 22 with hours (including overtime and shift arrangements and premia), and 3 with holidays. The remaining 8 cases involved manning of machines and shop steward representation.

was in many industries now little more than a formality; less than a basis for exerting positive influence on conditions of employment, let alone a guarantee of existing *rights* of any significance, it was rather a record of *past* status and a charter for *future* representation under more favourable circumstances.[17] It was indeed in large measure because it retained only vestigial regulatory powers that the Workers' Union suffered such a severe loss of membership; even so, more than 100,000 workers remained loyal, in times of such adversity, to a union whose utility in terms of influence on working conditions was so obviously limited.

Several conclusions may be drawn from the experience of the Workers' Union. In general, it exemplifies the thesis that limited participation in job regulation is associated with unstable unionism; and that the elaboration of regulatory functions permits more stable organization and growth. But a number of reservations are also suggested. First, the union was able to sustain a stable core of organization even in the period when its ability to participate in job regulation was small or non-existent. Second, the objectives of Workers' Union officials themselves in the field of job regulation were narrow in focus: in general their conception of collective bargaining followed (at times consciously) that of the Webbs. Third, the concept of recognition, implicit in any discussion of collective bargaining, was itself ambiguous: it might imply merely that in a specific dispute an employer was prepared to meet union representatives and hammer out a settlement, or, as in engineering, that formal provisions for avoiding disputes were accepted; there was no necessary assumption that future relations between employer and union would be on anything but a sporadic, *ad hoc* basis. Thus a body such as the Workers' Union—with its lack of craft control, the (for the most part) restricted strength of organization of its members, and not least its own limited aspirations—engaged in a form of job regulation which differed little from the conception of the Webbs. The job of the union organizer,

---

[17] The Whitley system allowed the Workers' Union, more perhaps than any other organization, to retain bargaining rights where actual membership was all but destroyed by the depression. One notable example was the Bobbin and Shuttle Making J.I.C., on which the union was represented throughout the 1920s; after the amalgamation it was found that not one member remained in this industry.

according to Beard, was to sell 'supplies of labour by bulk'.[18] Of course the union did not, strictly speaking, 'sell' the labour; it held no proprietary rights over its members (any more than does the trade association which specifies a standard price for its members' products). But the aim was explicitly to eliminate individual bargaining over wages and the basic conditions of employment. Individual bargaining *was* commonly the predicament of the factory labourer before the Workers' Union began its organization; and it was the union's achievement to play a part in its elimination; even in the dark days of the 1920s, the principle of the union standard was largely preserved. But this, in the main, was also the limit of its achievement in the sphere of job regulation.

To generalize: it should be emphasized that many unions, in their formative years, exercised regulatory functions which were similarly restricted; significant influence over managerial relations, or participation in a genuine process of *joint* regulation, was not necessarily the norm. Many organizations that were contemporary with the Workers' Union did indeed already participate extensively in such processes; but special features of their situation normally required this. A craft structure, with traditional worker controls at the point of production, stimulated *managerial* pressure for joint regulation (as in printing). This factor clearly applied to most of Britain's oldest unions, but to few others. Payment by results often entailed (as in coal-mining) that collective bargaining necessarily took place within the individual workplace, and embraced all those factors which could affect the worker's productive capacity. The Workers' Union did indeed possess a sizable piece-working membership in engineering; but here the managerial strategy—exemplified in the principle of 'mutuality'—was to exclude the official trade union from piece-rate bargaining. Hence the development of shop steward organization largely detached from official union machinery. The structure and attitudes of employers could also (as on the railways) direct union attention to areas of domestic regulation, as a substitute for the levels of collective bargaining machinery typical of most organized industries. But it would be rash to suppose that an ever-widening involvement in job regulation was a *necessary* development for trade unionism as a whole

[18] Triennial Conference, 1916.

in this historical period. Whether the period was itself *inevitably* a transitional one, in which underdeveloped regulatory functions marked the 'immaturity' of the movement, is a question beyond the scope of this discussion.

UNION MEMBERSHIP AND UNION GROWTH

Theories of the essential nature of union functions are often closely related to theories of union growth. The link is explicit in the passage, already quoted, by Flanders: the involvement of unions in job regulation is 'the condition for their survival and the basis of their growth'. The discussion in the previous section therefore leads naturally to an examination of explanations of trends in union membership, and their relevance to the history of the Workers' Union.

Theories of union growth may be seen as attempts to resolve three separate problems. First, the reasons for the origin, and long-run secular expansion, of the trade union movement as such. Explanations typically relate workers' reliance on unionism to specific features of the social and economic organization of work in modern society. Thus Marx, addressing the International Working Men's Association in 1865, argued that

the periodical resistance on the part of the working men against a reduction of wages, and their periodical attempts at getting a rise of wages, are inseparable from the wages system, and dictated by the very fact of labour being assimilated to commodities.[19]

Later the Webbs emphasized that

in all cases in which trade unions arose, the great bulk of the workers had ceased to be independent producers, themselves controlling the processes and owning the materials and the product of their labour, and had passed into the condition of life-long wage-earners.[20]

Two American approaches may also be noted. Among the best known is that of Perlman, who attributes collective organization to job scarcity and the consequent necessity of workers to compete for employment.[21] Tannenbaum's analysis is also widely

[19] K. Marx, 'Value, Price, and Profit', in K. Marx and F. Engels, *Selected Works*, 1955 edn., vol. 1, p. 441.
[20] *History*, 1920 edn., pp. 25–6.
[21] S. Perlman, *Theory of the Labour Movement*, 1928.

known. He contrasts the normative cohesion of feudal society with the atomization and *anomie* of the 'economic man' created by industrialization. In his view, the development of trade unionism 'fulfilled a necessary and inevitable service in re-creating a "society" within which the worker could regain his dignity as a man and once again play the part of a moral person'.[22]

Despite variations in approach, these explanations of the rise of unionism share a common basic theme. The institution of wage labour, the divorce of ownership from production, the competition of workers for scarce employment, the breakdown of traditional social values with respect to work—all are facets of a single historical process: the emergence of a society in which productive work is relegated to a mere element in an economic exchange between employer and employed, and in which the accumulation of capital is the overriding social goal. As one writer has argued tersely: 'trade unions from the very beginning were devised to protect their members from the exigencies of capitalism.'[23]

The second problem is to account for specific upsurges of union organization, and more generally to explain the cyclical movements of growth and decline. Undoubtedly the most popular theory is that which attempts to relate union fortunes to the business cycle. An early exponent of this approach was the American historian Commons:

In . . . periods of rising prices, when the cost of living was outleaping the rise of wages, when business was prosperous and labor in demand, then aggressive strikes, trade unionism, class struggle, suddenly spread over the industrial sections of the country. At the other extreme, in the periods of falling prices, with their depression of business and distress by unemployment, labor, in its helplessness and failure of defensive strikes, has turned to politics, panaceas, or schemes of universal reform.[24]

A rival school of analysis contests this interpretation vigorously: 'the conventional monocausal explanation for fluctuations in

[22] F. Tannenbaum, *A Philosophy of Labor*, 1951, pp. 99–100. See also his earlier work *The Labor Movement: its Conservative Functions and Social Consequences*, 1921.

[23] V. L. Allen, 'Trade Unions in Contemporary Capitalism', *Socialist Register*, 1964, p. 158.

[24] J. R. Commons, *History of Labor in the United States*, 1918, vol. I, p. 11.

union membership, the business cycle, is without general validity. . . . A multicausal system (including the cycle) is necessary.'[25]

Such a multicausal model of growth, it is now increasingly accepted, must incorporate a range of technological, economic, political, and social factors: the structure of the labour force, the size of companies, market fluctuations, the trade cycle, government policies, public attitudes towards industrial relations. One important reason for the complexity of any adequate explanatory model is the difficulty of treating union growth, as such, as a unitary phenomenon: totally different factors may account for the initial eruption of organization, and its subsequent extension and consolidation.[26]

The third problem to which theories of union development can offer a solution is the historical sequence in which various industrial and occupational groups have unionized. (A related question is the variation in strength of organization between different groups at any given time.) This problem is less susceptible of systemic analysis than the previous question of *general* trends in union membership: the emergence of organization among a specific employee group at a specific time is often the consequence of a combination of factors which 'might have a different effect, or no effect at all, at a different period of history'.[27] However, two broad types of explanation may be distinguished. The first points to intrinsic characteristics of employee groups which relate to their ability to organize. The Webbs pioneered such an approach, in their discussion of British unionism's early development:

We do not contend that the divorce [between capital and labour] supplies, in itself, a complete explanation for the origin of Trade Unions. . . . The formation of independent associations to resist the will of employers requires the possession of a certain degree of personal independence and strength of character.[28]

---

[25] I. Bernstein, 'Growth of American Unions', *American Economic Review*, 1954, p. 317.

[26] See D. Bell, 'Union Growth and Structural Cycles: Discussion', *Proceedings of the Industrial Relations Research Association*, 1954.

[27] A. A. Blum, 'Why Unions Grow', *Labor History*, 1968, p. 48.

[28] *History*, pp. 43–4. The Webbs contrast the 'semi-servile workers' and 'unskilled labourers' typical of the working class in the industrial revolution with the high 'skill and Standard of Life' of the craftsmen.

Dunlop offers a not dissimilar interpretation: 'labor organization emerges among employees who have strategic market or technological positions'. Such strategic groups, he argues, serve as 'points of infection' for the spread of unionism.[29]

A second line of explanation (not incompatible with the first) appeals to factors external to the employee groups themselves. Relevant here are the technology, skill distribution, and organization of work in the industry concerned; its market situation and general profitability; organization and attitudes of employers; and the impact of any changes in these determinants. A further factor which may be considered as external to the actual employee group is the trade union itself. It is easy to forget that the union is an important *variable*—particularly since students in this field learn quickly to discount over-enthusiastic attention, by some early chroniclers of labour history, to the unique excellencies of the unions and union leaders they describe. More recently, however, several writers have indicated that organizing success can be meaningfully related to the policies, leadership structure, and institutional needs of the union concerned.[30]

The rise of the Workers' Union provides evidence of the validity of a number of these approaches. It has been shown that the union's explosive pre-war growth was associated with a range of external factors: full employment and rising prices; the technology of expanding manufacturing industries; and the nature of employer attitudes. At the same time, organization was in many cases based upon a nucleus of employees with a strategic position in the production process. But it is also clear that the structure and objectives of the Workers' Union itself were of key importance: its success was in part at least a consequence of its unusual readiness and ability, at the crucial moment, to bring organization to the workers. Similar factors help explain the less dramatic but nevertheless rapid growth

[29] In R. A. Lester and J. Shister (eds.), *Insights into Labor Issues*, 1948, p. 180. Another such analysis is offered by B. Stoffer, 'Theory of Trade Union Development: the Role of the "Autonomous Workman"', *Labor History*, 1960. For an important criticism of aspects of this type of approach, see H. A. Turner, *Trade Union Growth, Structure and Policy*, 1962.

[30] Good examples are M. Olson, *Logic of Collective Action*, 1965, pp. 82–7; J. Shister, 'Logic of Union Growth', *Annals of the American Academy of Political and Social Science*, 1963; Turner, *Trade Union Growth, Structure and Policy*.

during the remainder of the decade. Finally, the catastrophic losses of the 1920s were obviously related to the drastic alteration in external circumstances, and to the consequent inability of the union itself either to devote the necessary resources to the work of maintaining organization, or to provide attractive returns to members. And here too, the characteristics of these members themselves were important: for many, the features of their employment situation which had kept them until so recently unorganized now made their predicament particularly desperate; while the very novelty of their association with trade unionism accentuated their instability in adversity.[31]

All the explanations discussed so far share the common element of identifying *structural* determinants of union growth (and decline)—'given' objective factors which are seen as causally related to organization. This characteristic distinguishes them from what are commonly termed motivational theories of trade unionism—those which 'choose to emphasize the habits of mind of wage earners'.[32] Such a perspective is central to Perlman's analysis: his key explanatory factor in relating job scarcity to unionization is the 'psychology of the laboring man'.[33]

These two approaches are in many ways parallel to the distinctive traditions, in sociological theory, of Durkheim and Weber: the study of 'social facts' and the analysis of 'social action'. And as in sociological theory, the conflict between 'structuralists' and 'motivationists' is to some degree misplaced. Any adequate explanation of union growth has to take account both of the external environment, and of the characteristics of the members and the nature of their response to their objective situation; a theory which excludes any of these elements is inadequate. Exclusive emphasis on structural factors represents in part a reaction, on the one hand against the 'great man'

---

[31] It should perhaps be emphasized that the argument of this paragraph is that structural analysis is indispensable for an understanding of the history of the Workers' Union. The discussion which follows is thus in no way intended to suggest that 'motivational' analysis is a methodological alternative. Rather, the argument is that a combination of *both* approaches is essential for a full understanding of union growth.

[32] Dunlop, in Lester and Shister, *Insights into Labor Issues*, pp. 173–4.

[33] *Theory of the Labor Movement*, pp. 237 ff.

school of history, already mentioned, and on the other against the *a priori* psychologizing to which some motivationists have been prone. At times it also reflects an attempt to explain union growth at the broadest level of generality; it is here most legitimate to discount variations in the motivation of employee groups. Yet not wholly legitimate; even at this level, the motivational approach is a necessary supplement to the structural. To point to environmental determinants is to identify the causes of growth but not to explain them; in order to *understand* the social processes involved, it is essential to appreciate how a particular objective situation relates to the perceptions and the goals of the actors concerned. The writer who discovers an association between, say, union growth and the trade cycle, has still to explain why the relationship exists; to do this he must explain how the trade cycle affects both the ability *and the willingness* of the worker to respond to the appeal of the union (or even to take the initiative in unionization).

Nor is it possible to dismiss workers' attitudes as mere dependent variables. While workers' goals, ideas and beliefs are themselves the product of objective determinants, and thus related to structural factors, the relationship is neither simple nor mechanical. For example, 'job-consciousness' obviously develops as a consequence of the objective competition for jobs. But its development at any given time is not an inevitable consequence of job-scarcity, for consciousness of the objective situation may be partial or even 'false'. And even if job-scarcity is consciously recognized, it can be taken as an explanation of unionization only if workers are assumed to seek security of employment. Yet workers' objectives may vary markedly with time and place, even when broad environmental circumstances are comparable.

It is therefore necessary to go beyond the worker's objective situation and analyse his own perception of this situation, the goals which he holds, and the manner in which these interrelate. A plausible hypothesis is that trade unionists are likely to be more critical of managerial authority, less convinced of the scope for individual advancement, and hence more conscious of the propriety and the value of collective organization than non-unionists. There is some empirical evidence, in studies of manual workers, to support this.[34] More commonly, however, the point has been made in contrasting the relative strength of organization among manual workers on the one hand and non-manual on the other. As one study argues, white-collar employees

feel close to management, often part of it . . .; they dress and speak more like management officials than like production workers; and they tend to identify more strongly with the business enterprise that employs them.[35]

A British comparison of manual and white-collar employees of a single company has revealed similar divergences of attitude in desire for promotion, identification with management in a situation of crisis, and approval of individual bargaining.[36] It may of course be argued that such differences in ideas and beliefs reflect real contrasts in objective factors: the work situation, career structure, and social status of the employee groups; and that when white-collar workers do become organized, it is because these objective differences have been removed by the process of 'bureaucratization'.[37] Here again, it must be insisted that the relationship between workers' goals and beliefs and their occupational situation is not a mechanical one. Traditional attitudes often prove stubbornly persistent even when their original objective foundation has long since crumbled; hence the use in social analysis of the concept of 'cultural lag'. An approach which considers environmental factors *alone* cannot explain the subtle process of white-collar response to bureaucratization. In the same way, it will be seen below, an explanation of the organizing success of the Workers' Union must go

[34] A good example is the Government Social Survey's study, *Workplace Industrial Relations*, 1968; this shows union members more ready to criticize management and approve strike action than non-unionists. Unfortunately, no systematic comparison of such attitudes was made. It should perhaps be added that to demonstrate an association between union membership and a critical attitude to management is not in itself to establish such attitudes as a *cause* of unionism (unionism might cause the critical attitudes, or both might stem from some third factor). Nor is it suggested that union membership necessarily implies any *general* anti-management attitude; the phenomenon of 'dual loyalty' is well documented.

[35] J. Seidman, J. London, B. Karsh, and D. L. Tagliacozzo, *The Worker Views his Union*, 1958, p. 265.

[36] A. J. M. Sykes, 'Some Differences in the Attitudes of Clerical and Manual Workers', *Sociological Review*, 1965.

[37] See, for example, D. Lockwood, *The Blackcoated Worker*, 1958.

beyond a simple analysis of changes in the economic and technological structure of the labour force.

Workers' beliefs and objectives, then, are not a simple
function of structural factors. And while the differing attitudes
of unionists and non-unionists may to some extent reflect ration-
alization or habituation, it would be absurd not to recognize the
decision to join a trade union as in part a *consequence* of the
workers' ideas and beliefs. For while there is no *logical* connection
between beliefs and action, the connection does exist in practice;
most beliefs have normative implications. To recognize the
weakness of the isolated worker and the potential strength of
collective organization is typically to believe that workers *ought*
to join trade unions and to act accordingly.

Beliefs of this nature are customarily social in origin. This aspect has been emphasized by Bakke:

a worker's willingness to join a union varies directly with the degree
to which association with and participation in the union would
reinforce normal group attachments and interests, would involve
practices consistent with his normal ways, and would be consistent
with the codes, the philosophy, the faith he shares with the group.[38]

Social norms prescribing union membership are commonly supported by sanctions, whether in the form of the 'closed shop' or
of more diffuse moral pressures. Such sanctions need not be
experienced as coercive. The closed shop is normally associated
with strong rank-and-file commitment to trade unionism.
Often it exists in industries based on communities in which the
union is seen as an important element in working-class life, and
in which the worker is socialized to view membership as an
essential feature of his own work role. In such a situation, the
obligation to join a trade union is effectively 'internalized'.[39]

Normative pressures need not however be *towards* union
membership. White-collar culture frequently inculcates the
values of individual achievement and loyalty to management.
Similar norms prevail in geographical areas where trade union-

[38] E. Wight Bakke, 'Why Workers Join Unions', *Personnel*, 1945, p. 38.

[39] Significantly, the Government Social Survey found that only 15 per cent of
workers in a closed shop situation would leave their union if membership was not
obligatory. In an American study of a 'semi-closed shop' situation, two-thirds of
union members reported joining 'with conviction' (Seidman, London, and Karsh,
'Why Workers Join Unions', *Annals of the American Academy of Political and Social
Science*, 1951).

ism is weak or unknown—as has been shown, for example, in studies of textile villages in the southern United States. Blauner has summarized these as demonstrating that 'the high degree of loyalty to the company which characterizes the textile industry ... is based ... on the common backgrounds of workers and management within a homogeneous community'.[40] Community norms are strongly influenced by religious institutions which stress the values of loyalty and submission.[41] Within such a culture, workers themselves are likely to reject as alien any appeal to the values of class solidarity; the union organizer is defined as an agitator and the union member as an intolerable social deviant. Similar cultural forces, though normally in less extreme a form, were encountered by Workers' Union organizers in their ventures into virgin territory. Beard related the common view among farm labourers, that by joining a union they would be 'only paying money to create big salaries for agitators'.[42] Such views, not surprisingly, were normally encouraged by those with authority in rural areas.

The argument so far is that the decision to join a trade union is commonly associated with a situation in which union membership is culturally prescribed—or, less strongly, where it is customary. But the existence of such norms or customs commonly reflects a social tradition; it is, in effect, a legacy of the historical experience of a social group. This explains the marked stability of trade union structure: the strongest-organized of British industries (coal, transport, national and local government, public utilities, cotton, footwear, paper and printing, metals and engineering) are almost identical with those of half a century ago. It would appear that the tradition of union membership, once established, is normally self-perpetuating—even if the organization itself is temporarily broken under adverse circumstances. The relative ease with which the TGWU re-established organization in areas once covered by the Workers' Union is evidence of the enduring character of the latter's pioneering efforts.[43]

---

[40] R. Blauner, *Alienation and Freedom*, 1964, p. 75. This is not of course to deny the importance of economic and other structural influences in such areas.

[41] See L. Pope, *Millhands and Preachers*, 1942.

[42] 'The Early Struggles of the Union', *Record*, Nov. 1919.

[43] Turner has emphasized the far more general importance of such a tradition of organization in explaining the process of unionization (*Trade Union Growth, Structure and Policy*, pp. 107, 194).

Yet the norms and customs of specific employee groups are capable of change—and necessarily have their origin in the innovating action of earlier generations of workers. It is such changes which are of particular sociological interest. Perhaps the most dramatic example in British labour history of such a collective transformation in attitudes is the 'revolt of labour' before the First World War. Though this development has been discussed in an earlier chapter, it is illuminating to examine certain aspects in more detail. The rapid growth of membership —by 60 per cent in three years for all trade unions, and by over 400 per cent for the main general unions—represented the acceptance of the case for trade unionism by a vast section of previously unorganized workers.

It is important to emphasize the transformation that this involved. The rise of the general unions was not merely a repeat of the 'new unionism' of 1889–90—a renewal of organization among workers with previous experience of unionism. Significantly, Tillett's Dockers' Union was the least successful of the main general unions in this pre-war period. Rather, the period of the 'labour unrest' enabled the general unions to construct and maintain organization in a range of manufacturing industries which had been only marginally affected by the earlier upsurge. The general view of workers in these industries—which they themselves shared—was that they were mere 'labourers', incapable of supporting a union and deserving only labourers' wages. Yet such workers by virtue of their experience and aptitude possessed a latent scarcity value, and they often contained key sections with largely unrecognized strategic skills. Often they constituted a relatively stable and cohesive labour force; in some cases they had even previously engaged in (usually unsuccessful) collective action. In a period in which inflation caused falling real wages, and in which these industries for the most part were clearly profitable and expanding, the chances of such spontaneous outbreaks were increased; while employers were unusually liable to respond with concessions. For these reasons, collective action by hitherto unorganized workers could achieve unexpected success; and each such success by apparently unskilled labourers was a demonstration to other workers of their own potential. The cumulative effect of such actions on workers' consciousness was demonstrated in the

Black Country Strike: the original initiative of isolated sections became the chief topic of conversation for workers throughout the area, sparking off a chain reaction. Trade unionism had previously seemed out of the question; now it was the subject for serious discussion. Thus a collective breakthrough in consciousness was achieved.

Such a breakthrough is eased, as Dunlop has noted, by the fact that 'no working community is ever completely unorganized'.[44] Work groups, often exercising autonomous control over aspects of the production process, are to be found throughout industry; they are in no way confined to unionized establishments. At times they may engage in rudimentary bargaining, and even strike action. Such informal organization presents ready-made the ingredients for unionization; and indeed, Turner has argued that the original associations of cotton workers were 'simple formalizations of certain natural links between the workers'.[45] According to Dunlop, such formalization of natural relationships is commonly precipitated by 'some danger to the stability and security of the group'.[46]

Such 'informal coagulations' were almost certainly of great importance for the success of the Workers' Union. This was demonstrably the case at the giant BSA factory, the nucleus of its organization in Birmingham. It was by no means unusual for groups of workers, sustained by this latent strength of organization, to take the initiative in their own recruitment. One example can suffice: the Melksham rubber factory where non-union employees, dissatisfied with their wages and conditions, walked out on strike and sent 30 miles to Bristol for an organizer to enrol them. Perhaps it was more typical for the original stimulus to come from the union itself—it would be difficult to generalize either way; but even then, much of the detailed work of recruitment was of necessity left to lay activists on the shop floor, and they naturally made use of existing group attachments.[47]

Nevertheless, the reason for the workers' collective initiative

---

[44] Lester and Shister, *Insights into Labor Issues*, p. 177.

[45] *Trade Union Growth, Structure and Policy*, p. 86.

[46] Lester and Shister, *Insights into Labour Issues*, p. 178.

[47] An informative account of such recruiting tactics in a Midland factory is given in a series, published in the *Record*, in 1915, entitled 'Life in a Workshop'.

or their positive response to the union's advances, *at this time*, has still to be explained; and Dunlop's hypothesis will not fit the situation. Unionization in the immediate pre-war years was rarely triggered off by a dramatic threat to customary rights and conditions. The slow deterioration in real wages, possibly coupled with a gradual intensification of the pressure of work, cannot in itself explain the sudden explosion of union membership. The critical additional factor—the catalyst within an increasingly volatile situation—was the changing manner in which workers *perceived* their work situation, and the changing *aspirations* against which this reality was measured. This indeed was Morley's insight: having catalogued his members' concrete grievances, he went on:

add to these facts the increasing knowledge of the workers' and their intelligent and just demand for a 'place in the sun', and you have the essence of the cause of the Labour unrest.[48]

The analysis could scarcely be bettered.

What, then, explains the radical change in the workers' consciousness and aspirations? The mechanics of this process may perhaps be illuminated by 'reference group' theory.[49] A large social grouping, such as a factory labour force, is rarely a homogeneous mass; typically it contains 'deviant' members whose attitudes or behaviour differ from those of the majority. Often, those who fail to adhere to the norms of the group to which they belong are sustained in their deviance by identification with some external group whose standards are embraced. Thus the worker with a deferential respect for upper-class values, or who aspires to upward social mobility, may refuse to join his workmates' union because it is part of the working-class culture he rejects. Or the deviant non-unionist may derive his values from some minority religious sect.

In the same way, the reference group of the union member

[48] *Annual Report*, 1911. Compare Clay's remarks on the same subject: 'Add to these economic grounds a growing sense of an incompatibility between political democracy and economic inequality, and we have a sufficient explanation of the pre-war extension of trade unionism' (H. Clay, *Problem of Industrial Relations*, 1929, p. 144).

[49] The term 'reference group' is used here in its normative sense: the group from which an individual derives his standards of behaviour. For a useful discussion of the distinction between normative and comparative reference groups see W. G. Runciman, *Relative Deprivation and Social Justice*, 1966, pp. 11 ff.

among largely non-union workers may often differ from that of his fellows. Since he gains no immediate advantage in terms of job regulation, his unionism is likely to reflect beliefs not shared by those around him. Typically this has involved adherence to some form of socialist ideology, and perhaps membership of a specific organization. Admittedly, friendly benefits and ancillary services may constitute an instrumental attraction to membership (this, we have seen, was true of the Workers' Union); but this fails to explain the case of the union *activist* in a non-union situation. Certainly, in its early years the tiny branches of the Workers' Union were commonly sustained by the activism of members of the Independent Labour Party or Social-Democratic Federation. Such deviants (like Owen in the *Ragged Trousered Philanthropists*) may have been merely tolerated by fellow-workers who believed that trade unionism was not for the likes of them; but the pre-war unrest allowed a transformation in their role. As broader social forces threw old assumptions and relationships into disarray, they could now help articulate the workers' growing sense of grievance, take the lead in spontaneous collective action, and act as catalysts in a general explosion of consciousness. As an American study has indicated: 'the existence of such a core of workers with pro-union sympathies in an unorganized plant helps to explain the rapid success of the organizing drives of unions . . .'.[50]

Interestingly enough, this process did not merely affect such groups as mass-production workers whose potential strength is in retrospect obvious. After the Black Country Strike the Workers' Union was able to organize virtually the whole of the local file trade, comprising a multiplicity of back-street workshops in which a labour force of half a dozen was unusually large. Elsewhere the union achieved temporary success with such groups as bill-posters or domestic servants; while its achievements in agriculture were in many ways comparable. Such sections of workers in many cases were on any 'realistic' view unorganizable—so isolated or economically weak that effective unionism 'ought' to have been impossible. But simply because the breakthrough *had* been achieved among sections who had previously appeared equally hopeless, such workers now saw no reason why they too should not be successful (nor

[50] 'Why Workers Join Unions', *Annals*, 1951.

often did their employers). The importance of workers' beliefs, as a means of mediating the objective, environmental situation, could not be more strikingly demonstrated.[51]

GOAL DISPLACEMENT

The concept of goal displacement is one of the few aspects of what is optimistically known as 'organization theory'[52] to be of direct relevance to the study of trade unions. It is a characteristic of organizations that they are more or less deliberately created, and are created in order to achieve some specific purpose. But it has long been recognized that original goals are often supplemented and extended; procedures devised for the efficient attainment of these goals become sanctified as ends in themselves; institutional goals develop, reflecting the needs of the organization itself (or its leaders), which may conflict with its overt objectives.

This same process may be identified in the trade union context:

unions as social organizations have developed a certain 'functional autonomy', that is, their growth and integrity have become ends in themselves.[53]

Another author has elaborated this argument:

as an institution expands in strength and status, it outgrows its formal purpose. It experiences its own needs, develops its own ambitions, and faces its own problems. These become differentiated from the needs, ambitions, and problems of its rank and file. The trade union is no exception. It is the beginning of wisdom in the study of industrial relations to understand that the union, as an organization, is not identical with its members, as individuals.

[51] Shister (*Annals*, 1963) has treated such a 'demonstration effect' (or as he terms it, 'proximity influence') as an objective factor, an element in the 'work environment'. But this is to reify the process: it cannot be mechanically assumed that any one group will recognize the experience of another as a relevant guide to its own actions or aspirations. Compare here the discussion by Flanders and Fox of what they consider a cumulative 'disintegration in normative systems' in this pre-war period (A. Fox and A. Flanders, 'The Reform of Collective Bargaining: From Donovan to Durkheim', *British Journal of Industrial Relations*, 1969, p. 169).

[52] Optimistically, since none of its practitioners has yet produced any integrated body of theory of general application to all forms of organization.

[53] A. S. Tannenbaum and R. L. Kahn, *Participation in Union Locals*, 1958, p. 3.

'This becomes more true', he adds ominously, 'as the union becomes better established and more "responsible".'[54]

The Workers' Union provides a striking example of the process of goal displacement. The objectives of its founders were
explicit: to transcend the inadequacies of existing sectional
union organization; to mobilize the working class for militant
action, both industrial and political, in order to maintain and
improve conditions; and ultimately to transform the structure
of society itself. It is scarcely conceivable that any of the initial
enthusiasts would have made their efforts if they could have
foreseen the pathetic results in the union's early years. Yet once
an organization was established, its survival became an un-
questioned objective, even though the original goals were
clearly unattainable. Institutional needs in turn came to dominate policy; to ensure the union's survival and expansion its
nature was further transformed. Mistakenly or not, its founders
believed that extensive friendly benefits spelled death for vigorous trade unionism; they precluded a militant industrial
policy which was the most worthwhile service that a trade
union could offer. Yet the range and generosity of its friendly
benefits was soon to become the most vaunted function which
the Workers' Union performed. The prospects of growth de-
pended on the co-operation, or at least the toleration, of established unions; so the original ambitions to overturn craft
sectionalism were long forgotten. The bulk of the original social
and political objectives were even more irrevocably abandoned; or at best, they were preserved as ritual incantations for
ceremonial occasions.[55] Rarely can the process of goal displacement have been so rapid yet apparently so unrecognized by
those directly involved.

A further example of the same process may be found in the
industrial policies of the mature Workers' Union. Ross, in the
analysis already mentioned, distinguishes between 'worker-
oriented provisions' and 'union-oriented provisions' in collective
bargaining. The latter relate to institutional needs—recognition, the extension of bargaining rights, recruitment facilities,

[54] A. M. Ross, 'The Trade Union as a Wage-Fixing Institution', *American Economic Review*, 1947, reprinted in Ross, *Trade Union Wage Policy*, 1956, p. 23.
[55] Ironically, for a quarter of a century Mann's aspirations of 1898 remained enshrined as the Preface of the union's rule book.

the closed shop—and may be balanced in negotiations against concessions of immediate and direct benefit to union members.[56] The validity of this distinction might perhaps be contested: what is good for the union as an organization is good for its members. But this is true only in so far as union policies and actions serve to further their interests and aspirations (and it is somewhat presumptuous to argue that any but the members themselves are the proper judge of this). The possibility of conflict is implicit in the function of job regulation, discussed in the first section of this chapter. As one author has noted,

the control over jobs that unions demand arises primarily from their desire for strength and survival. . . . It is the union as an organization, not the worker directly, that needs the 'job control'.[57]

Another writer insists—with satisfaction—that such control over employment has given unions in America the power to disregard their members' wishes: it 'has played a major part in getting unions to accept multi-year contracts, no-strike clauses, and binding arbitration agreements'.[58] The obvious implication is that workers would not have accepted such terms voluntarily.

The history of the Workers' Union offers a striking example of the pervasive influence of institutional needs. Not merely were the detailed objectives of negotiations and the specific content of agreements coloured by the demands of 'union security'; the whole direction of industrial policy was affected. Closely associated with growth in size and influence was an increasingly evident conservatism. Such industrial conservatism was emphatically endorsed by Jack Beard as the union's President; his own career personifies the policy developments in the organization as a whole. As the local official of a tiny and struggling union, faced by the uncompromising hostility of most employers, a fighting policy seemed essential; and Beard's attitudes were appropriately militant, seemingly embracing the syndicalist conception of a general strike. The Black Country Strike marked the apparent triumph of such tactics. But thereafter, with

[56] Ross, *Trade Union Wage Policy*, pp. 23–4.
[57] Olson, *Logic of Collective Action*, pp. 64–5, 87.
[58] J. W. Garbarino, 'Managing Conflict in Industrial Relations: U.S. Experience and Current Issues in Britain', *British Journal of Industrial Relations*, 1969, p. 322.

recognition widely achieved among the major employers, Beard became adept at the more diplomatic conduct of negotiations, and his public utterances became correspondingly more restrained. The outbreak of war took the process further: Beard's commitment to the war effort brought him into an even closer relationship with leading industrialists, culminating in his involvement in the 'Alliance of Employers and Employed'; while his anger and contempt were reserved largely for unofficial rank-and-file activists who endangered production.

It would be naive to interpret this transformation in terms merely of individual fallibility. No doubt the 'socialising influences' which Allen has discussed[59] were important. Constant exposure in negotiations to employer arguments can imperceptibly create an attitude of understanding and sympathy towards the managerial viewpoint, while in the absence of continuous contact with the rank-and-file beliefs and experience the members' demands can simultaneously come to appear increasingly 'unreasonable'. Not surprisingly, one American author has argued that 'the more a union leader concentrates on collective bargaining, the more conservative he is likely to become'.[60] This same process was indeed apparent in nineteenth-century British trade unionism: the changed social circumstances of the full-time official 'begin insidiously, silently, unknown even to himself, to work a change in his views of life. . . . Not his morality but his intellect is corrupted.'[61]

But there is also a more fundamental explanation of this process: the reformist nature of trade unionism itself. It is rare indeed for trade union commitment to major social change to be an operational one, in the sense of influencing day-to-day industrial policies or serious long-term strategies. And typically, the exceptions to this rule represent unions apparently incapable of achieving any significant results *without* major social change. The complexion of the 'general unionism' of the 1830s or the 'new unionism' half a century later reflects the belief that

---

[59] V. L. Allen, *Militant Trade Unionism*, 1966, pp. 24 ff.

[60] F. H. Harbison, 'Collective Bargaining and American Capitalism', in A. Kornhauser, R. Dubin, and A. M. Ross, *Industrial Conflict*, 1954, p. 277.

[61] Webbs, *History*, p. 470. It should be unnecessary to add that such an evaluation is not intended to reflect on the personal motivation of that ill-used individual, the full-time official; for the sociologist he is as much the victim of situational constraints as is the rank-and-file member.

the poverty and degradation of the mass of unskilled labour could be remedied only by transforming the political and economic structure of society. The same assumption was firmly held by the founders of the Workers' Union: it pervades the public discussion at the time of the union's inception. But the situation which confronts any *established* trade union appears quite different. By definition, the union has achieved a status in society. Workers' relations with their employers *have* been altered, and their conditions *have* been improved (at least for those sections of the working class that the union has succeeded in organizing). For those involved, the changes which have been achieved may well bulk larger than those which have not; and the structure of existing social institutions can easily appear infinitely flexible. In any event, the ability to work for additional improvements through the procedures already established inevitably makes the achievement of further structural changes lose its urgency.[62]

This point (originally recognized by Lenin) has recently been elaborated by Hobsbawm:

under conditions of stable capitalism 'trade union consciousness' is quite compatible with the *de facto* (or even the formal) acceptance of capitalism, unless that system fails to allow for the *minimum* trade unionist demand of 'a fair day's work for a fair day's pay'.... Spontaneous labour movements therefore are likely to act as though capitalism were permanent, reducing their socialist aspirations, where they exist, to politically irrelevant appendices to their 'real' activities.[63]

It would be difficult to find a more explicit expression of this attitude than Beard's argument towards the end of the war: it was essential, he insisted, 'to work through existing conditions and continuously recreate them till a permanently just state of things shall apply to all members of society'.[64] 'Control of industry by the workers', he told the Triennial Conference in 1916,

means that we must shoulder responsibility, it is not a thing to talk

[62] This argument is not contradicted by the fact of union involvement in creating the Labour Party; this reflected the growing threats to unions' existing status rather than a desire for a new one.
[63] E. J. Hobsbawm, 'Trends in the British Labour Movement', *Labouring Men*, 1964, pp. 334–5.
[64] *Record*, June 1917.

about but something to do, something to grow by practice. . . . How shall it commence? In my view by partnership undertaking between Employers' Unions and Workmen's Unions.

Beard was particularly concerned that unions should avoid 'the serious charge of trying to prevent production', and was indeed a precocious advocate of 'productivity bargaining':

it is bad business on the part of Trade Unions to attempt to hinder the capacity of the machine or to unreasonably conserve their energy. The only intelligent way to face the position is to say to the employer: we are capable of so much production, but we claim to share the advantages which come from organization of our labour power and from the elimination of wasteful energy and processes. . . .[65]

'The one thing that the workers must aim at', Beard told the 1916 conference, 'is to allow the machine to be used to its fullest capacity.' To the delegates in 1919 he appealed: 'I beg of you to aim to make the world better by these methods of construction of character rather than by a diminution and waste of productive capacity.'

Whatever the validity of these views,[66] their adoption in this

[65] Ibid., Nov. 1914.

[66] In fact, the socialist critique of capitalism has always pointed to *structural* factors which lead inevitably to waste, inequality, alienation, and exploitation. Accordingly, while 'working within the system' may moderate the excesses of injustice it cannot hope to achieve 'a permanently just state of things'. In other words, 'pure and simple' trade unionism is necessarily anti-socialist. Beard's arguments on productivity not only represent a step backwards from his original socialist convictions; they betray a certain lack of realism. If unions accept an absolute commitment to maximum productivity, productivity bargaining is itself impossible, for there is nothing to bargain about; serious negotiation is possible only if unions are willing to *refuse* co-operation.

It is interesting that Beard viewed 'restriction of output' solely as a negative manifestation. Applying the capitalist norms of economic efficiency he insisted that such practices depraved the worker's character, creating habits of idleness and dishonesty which would persist to blight a socialist society. He totally ignored the positive aspect of at least some such practices as a means of counteracting the drudgery and inhumanity of modern industrial employment. The socialist recognizes them not simply as negative restrictions but as the autonomous enforcement by work groups of their own rules—a refusal to accept the managerial definition of their role as mere instruments of production, a collective assertion of their own power and individuality. 'Restrictive practices' may thus be seen as a promise of the potentiality of total worker self-management in a socialist society.

Beard's emphasis on productivity as a central objective for trade unions may be contrasted with the arguments of R. H. Tawney during the same period: 'to those

period as official union policy is explicable only by reference to institutional processes. The key influence was the institutional need for 'union security', as inevitably experienced by a general union. A trade union (if its activities are to be governed by a conscious and consistent policy) has a choice of two alternative strategies for the control of its members' conditions: bilateral or unilateral job regulation.[67] The first is based on collective bargaining and collective agreement; and the union which adopts this strategy must seek an amicable relationship with employers through a readiness to accept compromise settlements of its demands, caution in exploiting positions of temporary bargaining strength, and strict adherence to agreements reached. Unilateral regulation involves the autonomous enforcement of union conditions, irrespective of employer reaction, through the inherent strength of organization; if collective bargaining and agreement are also used, these are not a central element in union strategy. But such a policy is likely to succeed only when a union enjoys specific advantages in the nature of its membership.[68] This must possess sufficient cohesion and discipline to be relied on to act as each situation requires; must hold a position of strategic strength such that industrial action is likely to bring rapid success, or else must be able to finance by high contributions or periodic levies any sections involved in protracted

---

who clamour, as many now do, "Produce! Produce!" one simple question may be addressed: "Produce What?" . . . What can be more childish than to urge the necessity that productive power should be increased, if part of the productive power which exists already is misapplied?' (*The Acquisitive Society*, 1961 edn., p. 39.) Beard's advice (which is widely accepted within the trade union movement of today) betrays a dwarfed conception of the goal of 'control of industry by the workers'. He demands the participation of unions in discussing how much is produced and how it is distributed; but the *fundamental* issue of the social purpose of production—what is produced and why—is absent from the agenda.

[67] A third strategy might be added: political action to obtain legislative control over workers' conditions. But this has typically been the resort of unions too weak to attempt the first two strategies.

[68] Such militant strategy was (and is) advocated also for its potential results beyond the field of job regulation, as a practical rejection of the methods and values of capitalism: trade unionists who genuinely object to the existing system of ownership and control of industry cannot easily establish cordial relations with employers. Such considerations, though involving important issues, influenced few officials of the Workers' Union; and it is integral to the earlier argument that this lack of influence was inevitable.

strikes or lock-outs; and above all must have reasonable security from dismissal, even in times of economic depression, as a protection against counter-attack by employers.[69]

Few sections of general union membership have possessed these attributes. As it has been seen, it would be wholly wrong to depict them as mere unskilled labourers; nevertheless, they have normally possessed limited strategic strength and little tradition of disciplined industrial action, have been able to afford neither high contributions nor heavy levies, and have been especially vulnerable to the trade cycle. They have therefore been particularly impelled to rely on collective agreement for the regulation of working conditions, and particularly dependent on the goodwill of employers to sustain recognition. The first 'new unions' learned by bitter experience that moderation was essential for their survival; from a realistic assessment of their own strength the subsequent great general unions developed as markedly cautious bodies.[70] The Workers' Union clearly exemplified this tendency.

'Moderation', it should be emphasized, need not merely constitute a negative aspect of trade union policy: the abstention from aggressive militancy. It may also represent a positive contribution which facilitates the task of management. At the very least, the union performs certain 'latent functions' both for the firms with which it negotiates and for the society within which it operates. In the first place, the union can act as a safety-valve. While its very existence necessarily reflects the fundamental social conflict between those who own and control industry and those who sell their labour power (a conflict which involves not only economic issues of pay and conditions but also crucial 'political' issues of power and control), the union can also serve

[69] Historically, the effective use of unilateral job regulation as a national policy has been restricted to craft unions with a rigid control over labour supply. At times of severe trade depression, as in the 1920s, even such unions could achieve little unilaterally.

[70] The more recent history of the TGWU may appear to belie this analysis. But the practical basis of its more militant image derives primarily from three sections of membership—dockers, busmen, and car workers—which possess special advantages in strategic strength and solidarity. In this context it is significant that it was the Coventry motor and engineering workers who provided the Workers' Union with one of its most dramatic strike successes and the most militant of its district organizers.

to moderate the intensity of this conflict. Coser, in his general analysis of social conflict, has argued that

> social systems provide for specific institutions which serve to drain off hostile and aggressive sentiments. These safety-valve institutions help to maintain the system by preventing otherwise probable conflict or by reducing its disruptive effects.[71]

The trade union often functions as such an institution. One author has indeed gone so far as to suggest that 'the operation of collective bargaining as a drainage channel for worker dissatisfactions is so obvious as hardly to warrant further elaboration'.[72] 'The labor union', Wright Mills declared in a well-known passage, 'is a regulator of the workingman's industrial animosity. . . ; the labor leader is a manager of discontent.'[73] Certainly this role was consciously embraced by the leaders of the Workers' Union, as their public utterances amply demonstrate. Because of this safety-valve function, it is possible to argue that the massive expansion in trade union coverage from 1911 was an important element in the de-fusing of the quasi-revolutionary unrest of the pre-war 'revolt of labour'.

The trade union renders a further service for the society within which it operates when it functions, not as a vehicle of oppositional ideology, but as a means of reinforcing the dominant social values. Trade union leaders, themselves particularly exposed to the 'socializing influence' of those in positions of authority, can channel such influences downwards. Profitability, capital accumulation, technological development, economic expansion—such reified economic goals constitute the driving force of our society, with consequences which can be particularly damaging for the status and conditions of the industrial worker. Yet unions can assist in the 'socialization' of their members through persuasion that such goals are without qualification in the interests of their own members. A union which performs this function 'both creates the machinery and provides the rationale for endorsement of capitalism by . . . workers'.[74] From 1914 onwards the leaders of the Workers' Union

[71] L. A. Coser, *The Functions of Social Conflict*, 1956, p. 48.
[72] Harbison, in Kornhauser, Dubin, and Ross, *Industrial Conflict*, p. 276.
[73] C. Wright Mills, *New Men of Power*, 1948, pp. 3–4, 9.
[74] Harbison, op. cit., p. 278.

consistently adopted this course (as is clear from the passages previously cited from the pages of the *Record*).

For management, the 'responsible' trade union can perform a more specific function. The worker's role in contemporary industrial societies necessarily creates grievances which, as industrial sociologists have long recognized, may be expressed in either organized or unorganized form. Unorganized conflict (absenteeism, labour turnover, individual non-co-operation) creates serious managerial problems and is not readily susceptible to managerial influence. Only if conflict assumes an organized form is effective managerial control possible. As the Royal Commission on Trade Unions and Employers' Associations was advised in one of its Research Papers, 'co-operation . . . needs to be engineered'.[75]

Trade union representation is an essential element in such 'human engineering'. Union machinery is able to *process* the grievances. It filters out the trivial from those of general concern or particular urgency, channels them to the appropriate level of management, and formulates them in a manner which facilitates a solution. 'Responsible' leadership may even preserve the shop floor workers from the regrettable and disturbing belief 'that negotiations on wages and conditions of employment are battles to be fought rather than problems to be solved'.[76] But at the very least, organization will tend to render their behaviour more predictable and manageable. Thus in return for recognition and goodwill the union offers an institutional direction and control for workers' grievances, together with 'the regulation of such irregular tendencies as may occur among the rank and file'.[77]

The institutionalization of industrial conflict creates powerful pressures which tend to accentuate the process of goal displacement. Collective bargaining, it is argued, should be conceived and developed as a commercial relationship, while the union itself should be 'modelled on the methods of capitalist industry'.[78] Such a definition of trade union functions leads to the 'business

---

[75] A. Fox, *Industrial Sociology and Industrial Relations*, 1966, p. 14.
[76] L. Evans, Preface to A. Pugh, *Men of Steel*, 1951, p. xii.
[77] C. Wright Mills, 'The Structure of Power in American Society', *British Journal of Sociology*, 1958, p. 37.
[78] M. Shanks, *The Stagnant Society*, 1961, p. 98.

unionism' which has long been an important feature of American industrial relations.[79] The 'business union' sees its purpose solely in terms of the economic concessions which it can negotiate for its members. As a salesman of labour, it can scarcely refuse to accept the contractual obligations of the normal business agreement. Thus the 'peace obligation' is the obverse face of the activities of such a union. Though the union may have been originally created as a challenge to managerial control, it now accepts a carefully delimited niche as an appendage to the production process: a slot-machine, so to speak, from which management can purchase industrial peace and co-operation. In the extreme case the business union becomes part of the 'control system of management'[80]—a development to be discussed in the concluding section of this chapter.

British unions have in general been notably reluctant to commit themselves *explicitly* to the philosophy of business unionism. The Workers' Union was an important exception. Beard's public statements deliberately stressed the analogies between collective bargaining and business relationships. 'We should . . . go to the employers and whenever possible should offer business arrangements', he told the 1916 conference. A year later he insisted that 'the best procedure possible should be set up to ensure wide and frank discussion, and of a character that will produce businesslike relationships.'[81] On the question of the 'peace obligation' he was equally explicit: 'No agreement is possible unless it is based upon the honour of the parties entering into it; and whenever there are charges of a breach of faith, it is better a hundred times that the defaulter should be the employer than the trade union.'[82] As far as can be observed, the union's practice normally matched this precept. Thus the self-definition of its function evolved yet further from the original conception of the union's purpose.[83]

[79] As originally defined by R. F. Hoxie in his *Trade Unionism in the United States*, 1923, the 'functional type' of business unionism involved the exclusive concentration on collective bargaining, rather than participation in political or social activities or the provision of welfare services for members. In Britain it is common for the term to be used in a looser sense, and it is so employed in the present discussion.
[80] D. Bell, 'The Capitalism of the Proletariat', *The End of Ideology*, 1960, pp. 214–15.
[81] *Record*, June 1917.   [82] *Record*, Mar. 1919.
[83] It was typical of the development of British trade unionism that institutional pressures brought a transformation in Beard's previous militant attitudes. In the

DEMOCRACY AND PARTICIPATION

Implicit in any analysis of goal displacement is the appreciation that trade unions develop 'official' policies which can diverge from members' conceptions of their own interests. The danger is that the membership may become the object, rather than the prime beneficiary, of job regulation. The discussion in the previous section thus leads naturally to a consideration of problems of internal union government.

One theme pervades the voluminous literature on this topic: the conflict between the goals of efficient and effective administration on the one hand and membership control of union policy and its execution on the other. A related finding often emphasized is the fact of rank-and-file apathy: in most situations only a small minority of members participate in the official processes of union government. But the interpretation of this situation provokes fierce controversy. Because of the significance and the complexity of the issues involved, it is necessary to examine these in some detail.

Studies in this area frequently bear the title 'union democracy'. The appellation invites confusion, for writers in this context employ the term 'democracy' with a variety of meanings. The Webbs in their classic study wrote that 'in the Anglo-Saxon world of today we find that Trade Unions are democracies: that is to say, their internal constitutions are all based on the principle of 'government of the people for the people by the people'''.[84] Allen chose to emphasize a different aspect in his *Power in Trade Unions*: 'democracy is a system of government which enables individuals in a society to achieve freedom and provides the mechanism to safeguard that freedom'.[85] A more recent author has suggested that '"the status of the opposition" is the distinguishing characteristic of democracy', defining the concept as 'the survival of faction'.[86] Other authors have, perhaps wisely, been less explicit. Perhaps the best known of recent

---

United States, by contrast, militant officials have often proved unable to transcend their initial attitudes and policies and have themselves been removed. Cf. Wright Mills, *New Men of Power*, pp. 167-8.

[84] *Industrial Democracy*, pp. v–vi.

[85] V. L. Allen, *Power in Trade Unions*, 1954, pp. 5–6.

[86] R. Martin, 'Union Democracy: an Explanatory Framework', *Sociology*, 1968, p. 207.

works is *Union Democracy*, a study of the International Typographical Union in the United States; here the nearest to a definition is a reference to 'the absence of oligarchy, that is, democracy'.[87] Many other writers on this subject give even less indication of the sense in which the term is to be employed.

Confusion clearly stems from the imprecision of the concept of democracy in modern discourse. Two rival traditions of interpretation can be distinguished. The first, and older tradition, which may be termed 'active democracy', defines democracy in terms of direct participative decision-making by all citizens. Thus it is a necessary condition that there should be active and informed popular involvement in the formulation of policy. The rival tradition, which may be termed 'passive democracy', merely prescribes that the governed should consent to the policies and actions of their governors. Here it is a sufficient condition of democracy that there should be periodic opportunity for the citizens to pass judgement on their rulers. The latter tradition is enshrined in the contemporary Western conception of Parliamentary democracy, which interestingly enough encapsulates as its central feature what was originally an *anti*-democratic position: the view that the populace should be allowed no positive, continuous control over their rulers, and that the legislative body should therefore be composed of representatives, not delegates, fully autonomous in the period between elections.

The conflict between these two traditions colours much of the literature on union democracy. It forms the starting point of the Webbs' analysis. The early craft societies displayed a pure form of 'primitive democracy'. Government was by the members collectively 'in general meeting assembled', and this meeting 'strove itself to transact all the business, and grudgingly delegated any of its functions either to officers or to committees'.[88] While growth in membership and geographical coverage made the rigid adherence to such processes no longer possible, the ideals of active democracy continued to exert a profound influence on the machinery of union government. The Webbs argued that this influence was potentially disastrous. If the rank and file was able, through the mechanisms of the referendum

[87] S. M. Lipset, M. A. Trow, and J. S. Coleman, *Union Democracy*, 1956, p. 5.
[88] S. and B. Webb, *Industrial Democracy*, pp. 3, 8.

and initiative and the delegate meeting, to overrule the full-
time officials, a coherent and consistent policy would be possible.
But if it failed to do so, there would be no effective countervailing power to the union leadership. Continued commitment
to active democracy would thus lead 'straight either to in-
efficiency and disintegration, or to the uncontrolled dominance
of a personal dictator or an expert bureaucracy'.[89] The Webbs
saw the solution to this dilemma in the quasi-Parliamentary
representative institutions operating in the coal and cotton
unions. The representative would constitute the key figure in
union democracy: a lay member, sharing the experiences and
grievances of the rank and file, yet sufficiently independent from
rank-and-file pressures to appreciate the problems confronting
the full-time official and to make reasoned policy decisions. The
representative assembly would therefore have the twin functions
of determining policy, and electing an executive which would
exercise detailed control over the officials. Meanwhile, active
rank-and-file participation would remain possible in the
branch, which would retain considerable autonomy in the
administration of friendly benefits, and could also act as a
channel of communication between the representative and his
constituents.

A second seminal analysis took a far less optimistic view of
the prospects for union democracy. Michels, in his study *Political Parties*, diagnosed an 'iron law of oligarchy' in the functioning of all working-class organizations. The demands of efficiency
necessitate strong central institutions run by expert officials,
which in turn acquire a monopoly of decision-making power.
The leaders (both in labour political parties and in trade
unions) inevitably acquire a status and outlook distinct from
those of the rank and file, together with a strong desire to retain
their positions. The professional experience and political skills
which they develop constitute an overwhelming advantage in
internal elections. Oligarchic control is reinforced by the apathy
of the mass of members, who lack any basis for critical appraisal
of leadership policies and are willing to accept the right of the
incumbents to rule.[90]

[89] Ibid., p. 36.
[90] R. W. E. Michels, *Zur Soziologie des Parteiwesens in der modernen Demokratie*,
1911; 1st English edn. 1915.

Innumerable studies have since examined whether mass apathy and oligarchic rule in unions result inevitably from an 'iron law', or whether, as the Webbs believed, they can be avoided by appropriate institutional arrangements. Only one has provided an important counter-example to Michels: the description by Lipset and his associates of the International Typographical Union. This account is best known for its analysis of the organized two-party system which for half a century has allowed alternating control of the union's government. But the authors are equally impressed by the high degree of rank-and-file participation in union affairs: members appear able to acquire both the knowledge and the political skills and experience necessary to perform an active role in the decision-making process. Yet the active democratic character of the International Typographical Union is obviously associated with other characteristics which make the union unique. It is a long-established craft society with a homogeneous membership of highly skilled and literate male workers, traditionally linked together in a cohesive occupational community, deeply concerned with work-related questions, and able to exercise unusual local autonomy in industrial matters.

The contrast with most sections of trade unionism could scarcely be greater. Commonly, work is not a central life interest and hence the union itself has only a limited claim on the worker's loyalty and involvement.[91] In those unions with a heterogeneous membership the rank and file normally lacks the inclination and the ability to concern itself with questions in which it is not directly involved; while the leadership is likely deliberately to restrict rank-and-file involvement in policy discussions for fear that sectional pressures may cause disruption.[92] Where collective bargaining takes place at a level above the individual plant, the union's actions of primary concern to the lay member are remote from his control; union officials are in

[91] The status of work in relation to 'central life interests' has been discussed by R. Dubin, 'Industrial Workers' Worlds', *Social Problems*, 1956. The effect of attitude to work on union involvement is explored by S. M. Lipset, 'The Political Process in Trade Unions', in M. Berger, C. Page, and T. Abel, eds., *Freedom and Control in Modern Society*, 1954; W. Spinrad, 'Correlates of Trade Union Participation', *American Sociological Review*, 1960; J. H. Goldthorpe, D. Lockwood, F. Bechhofer, and J. Platt, *The Affluent Worker: Industrial Attitudes and Behaviour*, 1968.

[92] Cf. Turner, *Trade Union Growth, Structure and Policy*, pp. 290–1, 304–5.

any case almost universally reluctant to dilute their own authority where industrial policy is involved.[93] The union conference
(even when modelled upon the Webbs' prescriptions) is rarely
a satisfactory mechanism for rank-and-file initiative; coherent
policy is usually achieved only by means of the domination of
the 'platform' on major decisions. In particular, as Clegg has
argued, 'the authority of trade union conferences over industrial
issues is severely limited'; this is an inevitable consequence both
of the limitations of conference procedures and of the nature of
the bargaining process itself.[94]

Since the scope for positive rank-and-file influence on union
policy is normally so limited, the phenomenon of membership
apathy is scarcely surprising. The most detailed British study
of this phenomenon is Goldstein's description of a branch of the
Transport and General Workers' Union. Out of a thousand
members, only between twenty and thirty normally attended
branch meetings, while a core of half a dozen was responsible
for all the major decisions. The unrepresentative character of
the branch leadership served to undermine its own authority;
full-time officials could ignore branch decisions with impunity.
The consequence of mass apathy, Goldstein argues, was 'oligarchy parading in democracy's trappings'.[95] More recent
studies of membership participation in general bear out Goldstein's findings. For example, the Luton study by Goldthorpe
and his associates found that only 7 per cent of union members
regularly attended branch meetings; excluding craftsmen, the
figure was below 3 per cent. Significantly, however, over 80
per cent were active in union affairs at workshop level, where
there was a real opportunity for effective influence on policy.[96]
This is in line with Goldstein's earlier conclusion: 'the Shop
Steward is for most rank-and-file members their first and only
contact with the Union. To them the Shop Steward rather than
the Branch is the Union.'[97] This finding is echoed by a recent

[93] See in particular J. R. Coleman, 'Compulsive Pressures to Democracy in
Unionism', *American Journal of Sociology*, 1956.
[94] H. A. Clegg, *The System of Industrial Relations in Britain*, 1970, p. 82.
[95] J. Goldstein, *The Government of British Trade Unions*, 1952. It is unfortunate
that Goldstein's flagrantly misleading title, and his ill-informed treatment of
membership turnover statistics, mar what is in essence a useful study of branch
government.
[96] Op. cit., pp. 99, 103.
[97] *Government of British Trade Unions*, p. 241.

study of the British motor industry: 'the shop stewards' organization has become the real union.'[98]

The decay of the branch as an organ of membership involvement is thus understandable. The primary function assigned by the Webbs—the administration of union friendly benefits—has been rendered practically irrelevant with the advent of state welfare provisions. The Webbs' faith that this crumb of autonomy would support an active branch life was in any case somewhat naïve. Membership apathy was already recognized as a problem in the nineteenth century;[99] and at the best of times it is hardly to be expected that membership enthusiasm will be fired by the administration of sick benefits. The assumption that the branch could form a solid link between the member and his representative in the central councils of the union was therefore ill-founded. As a recent American study has demonstrated, rank-and-file involvement in the subordinate units of union government is closely associated with the importance of the routine functioning of such intermediate bodies in the eyes of the membership. 'A natural source of union vitality is the members' realization that they do indeed have a reason for being, i.e., for coming to meetings, for making decisions, and in fact, for making the union their union.'[1] This realization is necessarily dependent on the existence of real autonomy over areas of union function of major concern to the rank and file.[2]

Writers have varied considerably in their reaction to the fact of membership apathy. Some have seen the lack of membership involvement not merely as a problem but as a disease, arguing that the health of a democratic society is dependent on the vitality of its component institutions. Goldstein has gone further:

[98] H. A. Turner, G. Clack, and G. Roberts, *Labour Relations in the Motor Industry*, 1967, p. 222.

[99] It was indeed noted by the Webbs in their *History*, p. 465.

[1] A. H. Cook, *Union Democracy: Practice and Ideal*, 1963, p. 187.

[2] Many students of industrial relations have assumed that participation would be significantly increased by a change from geographical to workplace-based branches. But significantly, Goldstein's branch was workplaced-based; and the study conducted for the Donovan Commission by the Government Social Survey showed that differences in attendance rates between the two types of branch were marginal. This suggests that while *structural* adjustments can increase the opportunity for membership participation and achieve some positive results, the basic problem is one of motivation which can be resolved only by changes in the branch's *function*.

to prevent the workers from becoming once again a defenceless group facing a new elite in this society, and to prevent the Trade Union from becoming an arm of the state which might itself fall victim to the irresponsible though purposeful seekers of power, the democratic base of Trade Unions must be fortified.[3]

At the opposite pole is the view of Allen, that unions are voluntary organizations with specific economic functions which might be undermined if a fetish were made of democracy:

trade union organization is not based on theoretical concepts prior to it, that is on some concept of democracy, but on the ends it serves. . . . The end of trade union activity is to protect and improve the general living standards of its members and not to provide workers with an exercise in self-government.[4]

Allen's argument rests however (apart from its conception of union function in purely 'business' terms) on the assumption that trade unions *are* voluntary institutions—hence the virulence of his criticism of the closed shop. It ignores the fact that the closed shop, as the Webbs recognized, is a logical extension of union regulatory functions; and that nearly half the trade unionists in Britain (as subsequent research has revealed) are effectively covered by a closed shop. In any case, if the trade union is viewed as an institution which provides important services for the worker, it is no solution to the problem of union democracy to offer the disgruntled member the right to lapse into non-unionism.[5]

Allen assumes that union leaders must remain responsive to the rank and file through fear of loss of membership; another line of analysis sees the fear of unofficial industrial action as a key motivating factor: 'union members who feel that their leaders misrepresent them may resort to wildcat strikes.'[6] This

---

[3] *Government of British Trade Unions*, p. 273.

[4] *Power in Trade Unions*, p. 15.

[5] On this question the TUC insisted to the Donovan Commission that 'there is no evidence that trade unionists are less engaged in their organisation's activities than are the members of other voluntary organisations' (*Trade Unionism*, 1966, p. 145). The relevance of this argument depends, of course, on the assumption that the government of a trade union can reasonably be compared with that of a chess club or women's institute.

[6] C. P. Magrath, 'Democracy in Overalls', *Industrial and Labor Relations Review*, 1959, p. 523.

argument is implicit in Clegg's study of the General and Municipal Workers: while he considers rank-and-file control of industrial policy decisions unattainable, he suggests that the ability of 'groups of members, and particularly shop stewards' to resort to strike action gives them a powerful influence on policy.[7] While clearly important, this ability can scarcely form the basis for a general theory of union democracy. Many sections of organized workers are so ill-placed to take unofficial action that the possibility may be safely disregarded by their leaders. In other situations, union officers may attempt to insulate themselves from such pressures by applying sanctions against unofficial strikers: the NUGMW, as Clegg demonstrates, has often been diligent in this respect, and trade unions generally are currently offered regular advice to follow this example. While influential opinion has often proved critical of the closed shop, it is less vocal in defence of the unofficial strike as a safeguard of union democracy and individual liberty.

Turner's remarks may finally be noted in this context:

since a pressure towards compulsory membership, under one form or another, seems inherent in trade unionism, it follows that its internal democracy is important. . . . One of the most significant indices of a union's inner democracy is clearly the extent to which its members not merely are *able* to take a hand in what it does on their behalf, but in fact do so. . . . However, a large proportion of trade unionists will not wish an active participation in their organization's management. So that a second test of union democracy could well be the degree to which such 'passive' members are also able to identify their leadership's policy and actions with their own interest.[8]

The problem here is to discern any means by which this 'test' might be made operational.[9] As Blauner has noted in another context, 'under "normal" conditions there is a natural tendency for people to identify with, or at least to be somewhat positively oriented toward, those social arrangements in which they are

[7] *General Union*, pp. 337–8.
[8] *Trade Union Growth, Structure, and Policy*, p. 303.
[9] Turner does indeed suggest that 'one indication . . . would certainly be the willingness of individual members or groups to join or stay in one union *rather than another*'. But workers have little basis for evaluating a union's policies *before* they join; while the possibility of transfers afterwards is seriously restricted by the Bridlington rules of the TUC.

implicated'.[10] Repeated studies have shown the bulk of members expressing satisfaction with the policies and administration of their union—even in organizations which on almost any definition are notoriously undemocratic.[11] A responsive paternalism, or a benevolent dictatorship, is likely to evoke membership satisfaction; in the final analysis the distinction between such a situation and 'passive democracy', if one exists, is tenuous.

The same point applies to virtually all current discussion of the optimum machinery for democratic union government. Many writers are preoccupied by a model of Parliamentary democracy. Americans in particular are often anxious to assess union democracy by the criteria of the United States constitution, at times even insisting in the separation of powers and a Bill of Rights. Several, in the aftermath of Lipset, go further and require an institutionalized opposition. Yet such obsessive concern with the formal machinery of government is mocked by the fact of membership apathy. The customary model of union democracy concentrates on the mechanics of consent, omitting participation as a relevant (or at least as a major) factor; but this omission undermines the practical validity of the whole model. This is particularly true of models which emphasize the electoral process: the passive consent of the majority is compatible with a wide range of freedom in leadership policy, since institutionalized passivity between elections habituates the rank and file to a permanently passive role.[12]

The theory of passive democracy is in any case closely associated with a view of trade union function which emphasizes its economic aspect. An increasingly influential school of thought in contemporary industrial relations assigns primary importance to the role of the union in providing a means of worker participation in the rule-making processes of modern industry. From

[10] R. Blauner, 'Work Satisfaction and Industrial Trends in Modern Society', in W. Galenson and S. M. Lipset, *Labor and Trade Unionism*, 1960, p. 341.

[11] See, for example, D. Bell, 'The Racket-Ridden Longshoremen', *The End of Ideology*, pp. 204–6.

[12] The same is of course true of Parliamentary democracy generally. The lengthy period between elections in which democracy is effectively in cold storage creates political apathy which cannot be transformed overnight into political consciousness. The absence of a politically sophisticated and concerned electorate creates the need for the personalization and trivialization of contemporary politics.

this perspective, the existence of positive membership control of union policy and action is clearly essential. Hence membership participation cannot realistically be viewed merely as a subsidiary aspect of union democracy; its practical importance is as crucial as that of the formal machinery of government.[13]

The Workers' Union could scarcely be accused of excessive adherence to democratic processes. Indeed, it would be attractive to see its progress as a paradigm of the 'pessimistic' theory of union government: a 'model' democratic constitution giving way to bureaucratization and oligarchy, and culminating in a squalid display of scandal, recrimination, and intrigue within the leadership. Yet such an interpretation would do scant justice to the manner of the union's development—which, it might be argued, was in many ways a historical accident. (A 'historical accident', it must be stressed, should be interpreted as a major development which, while causally explicable, stems from a culmination of factors none of which, taken individually, appears of great moment.) Turner has noted, perceptively, that 'the character of organizations, like that of people, is very much a product of their ancestry and the circumstances of their early growth'.[14] This is particularly true of the growth of the Workers' Union.

The union's original constitution was based on machinery which promised broad scope for active democratic participation. Authority was largely decentralized, and the central executive was itself directly representative of the districts. Supreme power was vested in an annual delegate conference; and when this was recognized as wholly impracticable within a tiny and financially weak trade union, a change of rule introduced the even more 'primitive' device of referendum and initiative. But as has been seen, these procedures fell rapidly into disuse as the union struggled against dwindling membership and income.

[13] Even where trade union functions are more narrowly conceived, membership participation remains relevant; Tannenbaum and Kahn (*Participation in Union Locals*, pp. 178 ff.) found it was positively associated with solidarity and effectiveness in the local unions studied. A plausible interpretation is that active participation increases 'total control' within unions. These findings also support the previous argument that members are most likely to participate in branch activities where these have some significant function: 'the *potentiality of control* itself acts as an incentive to the members to participate' (ibid., p. 172; italics added).

[14] *Trade Union Growth, Structure, and Policy*, p. 14.

The character of government in the Workers' Union was shaped by these early years of adversity. Duncan and Morley guided the union through the most testing phase of its existence in the absence of any democratic institutions at national level; no formal mechanism remained through which central policy could be influenced from below. (Presumably the biennial re-election of the national officers continued to operate, as required by rule; but there is no evidence of any contest before Beard's successful challenge for the Presidency.) Even the resurrection of the national executive, once numbers and finances improved, altered little. The meetings of the executive were infrequent, its membership transient, its functions largely routine. It was thus ill-placed, and did not seek, to exercise real initiative in policy-making. This is not, of course, to suggest that the *content* of central policies was unsound, or contrary to members' interests or wishes; indeed, the autonomy of the union's national leaders, by comparison with those of other general workers' organiz-ations, was cited in an earlier chapter as a reason for the union's spectacular success in the immediate pre-war years. It is the *method* by which these policies were determined that is at issue; inexorably and doubtless unrecognized by those most intimately concerned, a tradition was established within the Workers' Union: the tradition of what Turner, in a memorable phrase, has termed 'popular bossdom'.[15]

This state of affairs was tolerable, initially, precisely because the crisis conditions of the union's early years admitted no alternative. Later, no doubt, the situation was allowed to per-sist because it had become customary, and because the actual nature of central decision-making (mainly the routine admin-istration of the finances according to the rules) made the lack of democratic control seem of small concern.

But two developments brought new significance to the issue of control (though their importance was only tardily recognized). The first was the union's phenomenal growth. One consequence was the increase in organizing staff: from a handful in 1910, to forty at the outbreak of war, and 160 by 1920. Thus at local level, in the areas of the union's major strength, its main representative was increasingly a full-time organizer rather than a lay official, directly responsible to the branch. A second

[15] Op. cit., pp. 290–1.

consequence was the rapid growth of a central bureaucracy: two dozen Central Office employees by 1914, 100 at the end of the decade. Inevitably, this had implications for the power of the national leaders: as *individuals*, the President and Secretary could exercise only the most rudimentary control over activities at the base; serviced by an extensive *organization*, their power was potentially enormous.

The other development was the evolution of centralized bargaining processes, necessarily stimulating further centralization and further bureaucratization within the union's own machinery.[16] The autonomy over trade matters of the branches and districts had, for the first time, to be severely circumscribed. Symbolizing this change, the resort to strike action was formally subject to unprecedented control from above. At the same time, with the proliferation of national negotiating bodies, the function of bargaining became increasingly professionalized. Conditions were ripe for a massive consolidation of previous divisions between the union official and the rank and file.

The union responded to these developments pragmatically, in accordance with its by now established forms of government. Organizers and central staff were merely appointed to their positions, nominally by the executive, in practice on the decision of the General Secretary and President. Responsibility for the new collective bargaining functions was added piecemeal to the existing jurisdiction of full-time officers and executive. Finally, the latter obtained a major extension of both formal authority and actual control.

There was however no official recognition of the need for compensating adjustments in the union's governmental structure, in order to retain a positive function for the rank and file; or even, more passively, to safeguard their interests in the face of the radically enhanced powers of their leaders. The one gesture in this direction was the resurrection of the delegate

---

[16] Turner, it is true, has attacked the prevalent view that centralized collective bargaining necessarily led to centralized union government (*Trade Union Growth, Structure, and Policy*, p. 217). But he bases his argument on the experience of the cotton unions—whose members were both geographically concentrated and occupationally homogeneous, and could thus readily determine a common industrial policy by the mechanism of the delegate meeting. Such a system was less obviously open to a national, multi-occupational organization.

conference; but this met only triennially, its role was only advisory, and its advice was systematically ignored. While the national
conference was a mere decoration, the district committees were
deprived of effective functions, and no intermediate regional or
industrial bodies were established in their stead to exercise
decision-making or even advisory authority. The sole formal
embodiment of democracy was the principle of government by
an elected executive and national officials. The key assumption
of the governmental structure of the mature Workers' Union
was thus a totally unreal one: that elections could function as
a major mechanism of democratic control in a situation of institutionalized rank-and-file passivity. The events of the union's
closing years were to demonstrate this only too vividly.

It might be questioned whether the accumulation of centralized, 'oligarchical' control was avoidable. Certainly it did not
occur without strong initial rank-and-file resistance. Beard's
principal rival in the 1915 Presidential election centred his
campaign on this issue: 'I stand for making the union more
democratic than it is at the present time.... The members
ought to have greater control over the affairs of the Society than
they have at present.' Delegates at the 1916 conference showed
overwhelming support for decentralization, in particular in debates on the key issue of the appointment and supervision of
organizers. These delegates who resisted the erosion of rank-and-
file control were, almost to a man, the lay activists whose selfless
dedication had been indispensable to the organizing success of
the previous years. Given the nature of the union's membership, the problems of directing a giant organization, the current
trends in collective bargaining, it is of course arguable that these
aspirations for sustained rank-and-file involvement in policy-
making were demands for the impossible. Such an argument
must of necessity be inconclusive: the delegates' aspirations
were disappointed, not because their proposals were tried and
failed, but because the accumulated 'style' of the union's leadership proved stronger than the pressures for democratization.

The development within the Workers' Union of a tradition
of popular bossdom was matched by its obverse: mass apathy.
It would seem that attendance at meetings was normally
extremely low; according to an early issue of the *Record*, this
was a problem which was 'troubling the minds of our branch

officials'.[17] Some branches at least met only erratically, largely because of the difficulty in obtaining attendance. (Even at this early date, however, it seems likely that apathy in official union processes was often accompanied by more active involvement in shop-floor union affairs.) Minority participation in elections was equally marked: even in years when the contest for national positions was unusually fierce, it was rare for 10 per cent of members to vote.

There were other aspects of the union's electoral processes which left much to be desired, particularly in its later years. As has been seen, from 1919 the Executive was assigned almost absolute powers, but its members—until the palace revolution of 1926—enjoyed virtual security of office. The elections of President and Secretary (at first biennial, from 1919 triennial) were in most years little more than a formality; the only exceptions were 1913, when the vast growth of Midland membership carried Beard to power, and 1927, when George Dallas was able to mount a serious challenge (he could count on left-wing backing, while Beard suffered from the bitter internal recriminations of the previous two years). This is in part explicable by the advantages enjoyed by the incumbents of office. But action was also taken to reinforce these built-in advantages. Thus Executive members deliberately shielded themselves from critical appraisal by their constituents, through their control of the publication of their deliberations and decisions. In elections, the low level of participation offered considerable scope for irregular pressure. District Committees often attempted to influence nominations and voting in branches in their area, despite provisions to the contrary in the rulebook. At times, full-time officials also intervened. One notable example was in 1922 when organizers in one Division, angered at the emergence of the GEC as an effectively full-time body, worked to secure the defeat of its 'lay' chairman at the end of his term of office. More general intervention could occur in Presidential elections, since the main rivals were usually themselves organizers with claims on the loyalty of their fellow officers. 'We will use our best endeavours . . . to influence the vote', one Divisional Organizer promised a candidate in 1927. 'Nothing should be left to chance by your

[17] Nov. 1914.

supporters', wrote another; 'you can depend on my assistance to the last inch'. Yet another asked: 'let me have a list showing how the . . . branches voted in order that I would know how best to get to work in the second ballot. . . . I will do all in my power in your favour and I am sure of the support of the other organizers. . . . If you don't win it won't be our fault.' The candidate in turn urged supporters 'to see that even the smallest branches vote. . . .There are still a number of branches that can be got to vote and this is up to the organizers.'

Such manipulation was facilitated by the voting procedure used in the Workers' Union after 1919: a *pro rata* system whereby each branch was assigned a block vote to be cast in proportion to the actual votes of members at a specially convened meeting. Interestingly enough, when the introduction of such a system was proposed at the 1916 conference it was heavily defeated. No EC member spoke in favour, and Beard himself declared: 'let them guard against the danger of putting ballot papers into any man's hand. . . . They must . . . induce every member to use his vote and be interested in using it. If some other man was going to do it for him the votes would be at the disposal of a few men in the different branches, and he did not know a worse thing for trade unionism or a democratic organization than that it should be at the disposal of a few men. . . .' The manner in which this proposal was subsequently adopted is itself an indication of the power within the union which was wielded by 'a few men'. Revision of the rule book required a referendum of members, and for a 'general revision' the EC was required to invite proposals for amendments from the branches. But the Executive itself, on dubious authority, assumed the right to screen and supplement these proposals; in 1915 it submitted to the vote of members only 'such amendments as seemed to fit in and would, if adopted, effect improvements in the rules'.[18] Rank-and-file anger was expressed at the conference in the following year, and the EC was instructed to organize a further revision 'in the light of the decisions of this conference'. Yet conference decisions had of course no binding effect; and the rules submitted to the members in 1919 in many cases (as in the definition of the voting system) directly contradicted the wishes of conference delegates.

[18] Duncan, Triennial Conference, June 1916.

Thus as the union's central government grew in importance, the actual institutions of control increasingly accorded to the oligarchic model. It was, indeed, only an *internal* conflict in the 1920s that shook the power of the established leadership. The reasons for this development are provided in the foregoing analysis. First, the union's early development which established a tradition of popular bossdom. Second, environmental factors which induced centralization and bureaucratization within trade unionism generally. Third, the failure to devise any effective machinery for rank-and-file *involvement* in the new areas of policy-making. But a final point must also be noted: the lack of any coherent recognition by union members and leaders of the social processes in which they were participating, and which shaped the Workers' Union in a manner so contrary to the intentions of its founders.

CONCLUSIONS

It is not unreasonable to suggest that the processes so far analysed are interrelated. In sketching their relationship an obvious point of departure is the role of the worker in capitalist society. Previously in this chapter it was noted that various aspects of this role—the lack of autonomy in the work process, the divorce of the worker from the product and from the means of production, the insecurity of employment, the status of work as an economic relationship deprived of fundamental human significance—have long been as associated, both at the institutional level with the rise of labour organizations, and at the individual level with the motivation of recruits to trade unionism. And once more it may be emphasized that it was a fundamental objective of the founders of the Workers' Union to achieve a transformation in the structure of this society and the worker's role within it.

But the nature of the worker's role has serious implications for the internal functioning of trade unionism. The union is affected, first, by the worker's attitude to his job:

labour is external to the worker, i.e., it does not belong to his essential being. . . . The worker therefore only feels himself outside his work, and in his work feels outside himself. . . . The worker's

15*

activity is not his spontaneous activity. It belongs to another; it is the loss of his self.[19]

Alienation in work naturally colours the worker's attitude to work-related institutions, and hence the trade unionist's relationship to his organization; as suggested in the previous section, where work is not a central life interest the member's involvement in union activities is correspondingly inhibited. This constitutes a *tendency* rather than an 'iron law'; it can be outweighed by other situational factors. For example, occupationally-based communities can support a sub-culture which invests work with significant positive meaning, and the union in turn then assumes major importance as a feature of working-class life (as for example in mining, the docks, and certain crafts). But there is evidence that such 'solidaristic' communities are increasingly atypical of the worker's social environment; and that an alienated, 'instrumental' orientation to work and the union is correspondingly prevalent.[20]

A second feature of the worker's role which necessarily affects him as a trade unionist is its *passive* character. A central characteristic of capitalism is its reification of abstract economic processes, and its parallel devaluation of human goals and sentiments. Thus labour is transformed into a commodity, and the worker into an impersonal adjunct to the means of production. This status is reinforced by the division of labour in social and economic life: the properly socialized worker adapts to the authority structure of capitalist industry and society, and in particular responds uncritically to the instructions issued to him; he 'is not paid to think'. In so far as the worker fulfils the requirements of his role, he is ill qualified for an active and informed involvement in his union. Small wonder that the shop-floor trade unionist at times behaves in a manner which to the union leader appears ill considered or irresponsible. As Beard discovered with considerable irritation,

the ordinary trade unionist dislikes anything that demands that he shall apply business methods to himself; he shirks discipline and order; he is prone to slipshod ways; he prefers mob-talk. It is a mere

---

[19] K. Marx, *Economic and Philosophic Manuscripts of 1844*, 1961 edn., pp. 72–3.
[20] This argument has been most fully developed by Goldthorpe and his associates in *The Affluent Worker*.

lazy, careless way, and attractive. It gives him freedom to grumble, and an opportunity to shelve responsibility onto others.[21]

But it can be argued that the policies adopted by the Workers' Union positively encouraged such characteristics in its membership. As has been seen, the basis of its appeals for recruitment was the extensive variety of friendly benefits which were offered. Deliberately, the union fostered an extremely narrow image of its own function: the provision of a limited range of economic services *within* the institutional framework of the existing society. No serious attempt was made to broaden the perspective of its membership and to cultivate a critical consciousness of this society. Instead the union reinforced the natural tendency for members to adopt an instrumental, 'penny-in-the-slot' attitude to their organization.

Moreover, the union's industrial strategy had an identical effect. 'Business unionism' strove to model collective bargaining on orthodox commercial principles, and thus required that the relationship between the member and his organization should replicate that between the worker and the commercial enterprise. Beard's objectives were quite explicit. The primary task of the union organizer, he told the 1916 conference, should be 'making calculations for the purpose of selling supplies of labour by bulk'. On the same principle, lay negotiators were warned not to raise 'emotional' issues in their discussions with employers (for example, arguing that the conditions of work and standard of life endured by members were an affront to human dignity); rather, it was necessary to submit demands 'on a pure business basis and talk matters over as though we were selling bicycles'.[22] It would seem that Beard's involvement with employers had taught him to view the workers on *their* terms, as a mere commodity, a passive object for others to haggle over. (Yet a union which treats its members as cattle can scarcely complain if they sometimes behave as such).

Thus the union's leaders were conscious of the problems resulting from membership apathy; but rather than pursue a policy designed to encourage greater rank-and-file responsibility and initiative in union activities, they embraced industrial objectives calculated to have the reverse effect. Beard's hopes

[21] *Record*, Oct. 1918.   [22] Local Conference, Coventry, Feb. 1915.

for the future character of industrial control were cited in an earlier section: a gradual sharing of responsibility through 'partnership undertaking between Employers' Unions and Workmen's Unions'. Such hopes in fact were largely disappointed: the 'Alliance of Employers and Employed' was a notably ineffectual organization, while the Mond-Turner talks in which Beard was involved a decade later proved similarly abortive.

But it seems likely that such a pursuit of 'partnership' (which must necessarily be operative principally at leadership level) invites two harmful consequences for trade unionism. First, it may lead straight to the situation recognized by the authors of the *Miners' Next Step*: 'this power of initiative, this sense of responsibility, the self-respect which comes from expressed manhood, is taken from the men, and consolidated in the leader. The sum of *their* initiative, *their* responsibility, *their* self-respect becomes his.'[23] For the union leader alone is reserved the active, conscious role in industrial relations: defining the objectives, conducting the negotiations, registering the settlement. Rank-and-file members, accordingly, are officially defined as passive, unthinking, dehumanized—'bicycles'. As a result, the inevitable contrast in terms of consciousness and activity between leaders and members is widened into an unbridgeable chasm. The social, and more crucially the ideological, isolation of officials from the rank and file is accentuated. And the formal machinery of the union at rank-and-file level is deprived of all significant function and hence of all attraction to active participation. Under the impact of these mutually reinforcing developments, union government increasingly approximates to a one-way process: downwards 'communication' of leadership decisions, downwards control to ensure their observance. It is surely no accident that the marked decline in internal democracy in the Workers' Union coincided with the development of formalized and centralized collective bargaining institutions.[24]

[23] Unofficial Reform Committee, *The Miners' Next Step*, 1912, pp. 13–14.

[24] Hoxie, in his discussion of the business union (*Trade Unionism in the United States*, p. 47), recognized this link between structure and functions half a century ago: 'in harmony with its business character it tends to emphasize discipline within the organization, and is prone to develop strong leadership and to become somewhat autocratic in government.' More recently, Lipset has argued that the 'insistent cry for union "responsibility" often leads to undemocratic unionism since it sometimes becomes a demand that unions coerce their members. There is a basic conflict between democratic unionism and "responsible" unionism. . . .

Damaging consequences may also ensue for the basic purpose of the union: where its policy is one of 'partnership' with members' employers, the whole foundation of union function may be undermined. For partnership may well foreshadow the process of 'incorporation' discerned by several students of American industrial relations.

Business-labor co-operation within the place of work means the partial integration of company and union bureaucracies. . . . For something gained, something must be given. The integration of union with plant means that the union takes over much of the company's personnel work, becoming the disciplining agent of the rank and file. . . . Responsibility is held for the contract signed with the company; to uphold this contract the union must often exert pressure upon workers. . . . To have no strikes is the responsibility of both company and union. They are disciplining agents for each other, and both discipline the malcontented elements among unionized employees.[25]

As Dubin has argued, this is one of the 'unanticipated consequences of collective bargaining favourable to management':

the union is really caught up in the policing system controlling working behavior. By its very acceptance of the standards of right and wrong incorporated in the union contract and the company work rules, the union becomes a co-agent with management in maintaining work discipline.[26]

'Responsible' trade unionism involves the acceptance of an obligation to control the rank and file; but this in turn implies the acceptance of the legitimacy of managerial authority in an economic system the inequity and inhumanity of which is the very *raison d'être* of trade unionism; it requires the union to exercise quasi-managerial discipline against members who rebel against an oppressive work relationship.

It should be apparent that where a union so degenerates, it may continue to provide periodic economic returns to its

The dictatorial mechanisms found in many unions are an adaptation to management's insistence that its yielding on union security issues must be followed by union responsibility' (S. M. Lipset, 'Political Process in Trade-Unions', in *Political Man*, 1959, p. 360).

[25] Wright Mills, *New Men of Power*, pp. 224–5.
[26] R. Dubin, *Working Union–Management Relations*, 1958, p. 246.

membership, and may sustain a certain humanization in working conditions, but at the cost of incorporation into the dominant structures of a society which condemns the worker to the role of a passive instrument of production. Certainly it must be concluded that the Workers' Union ended a captive of the society it was created to transform. If this verdict is harsh, it is equally applicable to many of the institutions of the labour movement of today. Yet it is only through consciousness of this captivity, and of the social processes responsible, that those who retain the ideals of the union's founders may hope to see them realized.

INDEX

Abel, T., 209 n.
Adamson, William M., 50, 81, 105, 112
Admiralty, 93 ff., 112, 151 f.
Agricultural Labourers' and Rural Workers' Union, National (from 1920: National Union of Agricultural Workers), 99,n., 102, 118, 130, 147 f.
Agricultural Wages Board, 100, 102 f., 147
Agricultural Workers, National Union of: see Agricultural Labourers
Agriculture, 27 f., 45 ff., 68, 70, 98 ff., 142, 147 ff., 171
Agriculture Act, 1920, 147
Akroyd, Clem E., 131 n., 167
Allen, V. L., 183 n., 198,n., 206,n., 212
Alliance of Employers and Employed, 82, 224
Amalgamation, 72 ff., 94, 101, 106, 123 ff., 156 ff., 160 ff.
  with Transport and General Workers' Union, xi, 129, 159, 160 ff.
Anglesey Workers' Union, 101, 106
Arnold, Alice, 166 n.
Askwith, G. R., 58, 59 n., 64

Bagley, Harry, 53
Bakke, E. W., 189,n.
Balaam, Tom, 148 n.
Banham, Will, 18 f.
Barlow, John, 36
Barrett, Harry L., 21
Beard, John, 9 n., 14 n., 27 ff., 42, 45, 49 ff., 65, 71 n., 81 f., 87, 89 n., 92, 101 f., 104 f., 109,n., 115 f., 118, 125 ff., 131, 134 ff., 138 ff., 148 n., 149, 154 f., 157 f., 160, 163, 167, 178, 181, 190, 218 ff., 222
  elected President, 37, 216, 219
  in Black Country Strike, 51 ff., 197
  attitude to craft unionism, 71 f., 120 ff.
  ideological position, 82, 197 ff., 205,n., 223 f.
Bechhofer, F., 209 n.
Beechey, Fred F., 165

Belfast, 30, 112, 126 n., 152
Belgian Metal Workers' Union, 88 n.
Bell, D., 184 n., 205 n., 214 n.
Bell, J. N., 126, 157 n.
Bellars, P., 52 n.
Berger, M., 209 n.
Bernstein, I., 184 n.
Bevin, Ernest, 160 ff., 166, 168, 169 n., 171
Birmingham, 28 f., 42, 49 ff., 71, 104 f., 109, 145, 149 f., 166 n., 192
Birmingham Small Arms Company, 29, 42, 49 f., 52, 192
Black Country Strike, 50 ff., 70, 76, 194, 197
Blauner, R., 190,n., 213, 214 n.
Blum, A. A., 184 n.
Booth, C., 17 n.
Box, Sidney, 46,n.
Braintree, 67 f., 146
British Workers' League, 82
Burton-on-Trent, 61, 105, 150
'Business unionism', 204 f., 223
Byrne, William A., 107

Cardiff, 63
Cauhlin, Joe, 25 f.
Central Munitions Labour Supply Committee, 81
Chambers, Tom, 8 f., 11, 12 f., 20
Chester, T. E., 78 n.
Citrine, W. M., 135 n.
Clack, G., 211 n.
Clark, Joe, 61, 105, 149 f.
Clay, H., 193 n.
Clegg, H. A., 1 n., 44 n., 76 n., 78 n., 137 n., 158 n., 160 n., 210,n., 213
Clynes, J. R., 127
Cole, G. D. H., 68 n., 69 n., 84 n., 119 n., 137 n.
Coleman, J. S., 207 n., 210 n.
Coley, B. H., 166 n.
Colston Shepherd, E., 94 n., 98 n.
Committee on Production, 85 f., 89 ff., 96 f., 119
Commons, J. R., 183,n.
Communist Party, 162